MUST WE GO TO WAR?

Books by KIRBY PAGE

NATIONAL DEFENSE

LIVING CREATIVELY

LIVING TRIUMPHANTLY

LIVING COURAGEOUSLY

MUST WE GO TO WAR?
  A Book for Men With a Sub-Title for Women

MUST WE GO TO WAR?

A BOOK FOR MEN
WITH A SUB-TITLE FOR WOMEN

MUST AMERICAN WOMEN SEND THEIR
MEN TO FIGHT IN EUROPE OR ASIA?

By

KIRBY PAGE

FARRAR & RINEHART, INC.
NEW YORK   TORONTO

CONTENTS

Foreword

Must the Wars in Spain and China Develop Into a World War?

WHEN DEEPLY outraged by ruthless aggression in Ethiopia, Spain, and China, our sympathy goes out to these cruelly victimized peoples, and many are inclined to think that resort to defensive war is the only effective answer to the might of imperialism. For this reason, many Americans are now convinced that the foreign policy of the United States should be shaped in such a way as to help victims win their wars against aggressors.

But such a conclusion is certain to fill the minds of thoughtful persons with grave apprehension. If powerful alliances of heavily armed aggressors can be resisted only by taking up arms on a vast scale, then our civilization is indeed endangered. If Italy, Germany, and Japan can be held back only by resort to world war, then mutual suicide will be the fate of many peoples.

In its present form, and under prevailing conditions, *war is not a lesser evil, but is rather a combination, accentuation and continuation of monstrous evils.*

Some other way must be found, and to this search the present volume is devoted. The causes of the prevailing world-wide crisis must be traced back to their sources. Why are the peoples of the earth apparently so helpless in the face of ruthless aggression on the part of Italy and Japan? Why has the indispensable League of Nations proved to be so impotent at the moment when it is mostly sorely needed?

The beginnings of an answer may be found in a realization of the degree to which the peoples of Great Britain, France, the United States and the other great powers have justified the system of empire and have struggled to harvest its fruits. A glance at a map of the earth shows the extent to which armed conquest has been carried by the imperialist powers. Japan and Italy are the despoilers upon whom the horror-stricken eyes of humanity are now fixed. But yesterday it was Belgium in the Congo, and Great Britain forcing a deadly drug upon China in the indefensible Opium War, and the United States torturing Filipinos with the water cure and shooting down two thousand Haitians. *Like David of old, the sated imperialist powers may well cry aloud that the sins of their youth have sapped the strength of their resistance to contemporary aggression.*

So long as the system of empire is upheld and endeavors made by Great Britain, France, and the United States to continue the full enjoyment of the fruits of conquest, there can be no restoration for Ethiopia, and no security for China. Never let the fact be forgotten that the governments of Great Britain and France entered into an agreement with Mussolini by which they consented to the handing over to Italy of a huge portion of Ethiopia. And acquaintance with the history of the Far East causes one to realize that when other imperialist powers condemn Japan's aggression against China, it is a case of kettle calling pot black.

Japan's lawless and barbarous bombing of Chinese cities demands unrestrained condemnation. But more than denunciation is required if China is to be freed from the scourge of Japanese occupation and if a world war is to be averted. The springs of Japanese imperialism and militarism must be explored.

The key to an understanding of the policies of Germany, Italy and Japan may be found in a realization that these aggressor nations are now being driven by need and blinded by illusions into territorial expansion, and are following courses of action not unlike the practices of other imperialist powers in earlier days. The evidence is convincing that if the peoples of Great Britain, France and the United States were now placed in positions parallel to those of Germany, Italy and Japan, they also would pursue aggressive and belligerent policies.

Another great war in Europe and Asia is not inevitable, but it can be avoided only by bringing about through pacific means economic and political changes which will diminish economic distress in Germany, Italy, and Japan, and which will relieve emotional strain in those lands. Continued efforts to stabilize the international status quo and to achieve collective security through threats of or resort to armed action against these aggressive powers are likely to precipitate a general war. Drastic change is a prerequisite to stabilization, and a primary objective of the peace movement should be the bringing about of the required transformation.

Citizens of the United States who are familiar with the expansionism of their own forefathers should find it easy to understand, even while severely condemning, Japan's policy of expansion. In the words of an eminent spokesman, Japan's case in relation to China may be stated as follows: "First. In the cause of humanity . . . It is no answer to say this is all in another country, belonging to another nation, and is therefore none of our business. It is especially our duty, for it is right at our door. Second. We owe it to our citizens in China to afford them that protection and indemnity for life and property which no government there can or will afford . . . Third. The right to intervene may be justified by the very serious injury to the commerce, trade and business of our people, and by the wanton destruction of property and devastation of the country. Fourth, and which is of the utmost importance. The present condition of affairs in China is a constant menace to our peace, and entails upon this Government an enormous expense. With such a conflict waged for years in a country so near us and with which our people have such trade and business relations; when the lives and liberty of our citizens are in constant danger and their property destroyed and themselves ruined; . . . —all these and others that I need not mention, with the resulting strained relations, are a constant menace to our peace, and compel us to keep a semiwar footing with a nation with which we are at peace."

It was President McKinley, not a Japanese prime minister, who wrote these words—in his message to Congress on April

11, 1898. The only changes I have made are the substitution of "China" for "Cuba" and of "country" for "island" in the original.

Great Britain, France and the United States have built great empires through conquest and nothing could be more futile or more dangerous than the attempt to continue the full enjoyment of the fruits of aggression, while at the same time demanding that latecomers abandon all thought of expansion and accept the present division of the world's resources. Aggressors of an earlier day must share economic privilege with aggressors of the present hour if a world war is to be averted. And no solution is to be found in the handing over of colonies to Germany, Italy and Japan, but rather in affording favorable access to markets and raw materials.

Appropriate agencies of international justice are required if controversies among nations are to be settled peacefully. To this end national sovereignty must be sufficiently abridged to make possible the effective functioning of international agencies of legislation, administration and adjudication. The League of Nations is an imperative necessity. But under prevailing conditions, it is folly to rely upon Article 10 and Article 16 of the Covenant. Three powerful countries have forsaken Geneva and will resort to war rather than accept a continuance of the international status quo. Article 19 of the Covenant offers a way of escape from war. Pacific change, however, cannot be brought about by present-day aggressors; the favored nations alone can carry through the required transformation. Failure to make these changes and continued reliance upon coercive sanctions will result in another great war. Collective security cannot be achieved so long as three heavily armed nations look upon present arrangements as insufferable.

The recent address by President Roosevelt in Chicago is open to the charge of hypocrisy. Without any acknowledgment of guilt on the part of this country and without evidence of contrition, he severely condemned the aggression of Japan. "The present reign of terror and international lawlessness began a few years ago." A few years ago! For a long century various

imperialist powers have invaded foreign lands and massacred resisting populations. "Without a declaration of war and without warning or justification of any kind, civilians, including women and children, are being ruthlessly murdered with bombs from the air." But surely precedents for these atrocities may be found in the example set by France in Syria and by Great Britain in various regions of Africa and Asia. "Without a declaration of war" the United States has on 100 occasions sent armed troops into a score of foreign countries, and in several instances has engaged in fierce battles with "natives" in these lands; these patriots usually being designated as "bandits." *
Strong words of denunciation were used in attacking the huge expenditures for armaments by aggressor nations; whereas with complacency the President referred to the much smaller proportion of national funds being devoted to this purpose by his own government. No emphasis was placed upon the fact that, in spite of unequalled natural geographical and historical security, the United States is spending a billion dollars this year on current preparedness for war. "It seems to be unfortunately true that the epidemic of world lawlessness is spreading." But which great nation refused to become a member of the League of Nations and the World Court? Which country, even after it had signed the Kellogg-Briand Pact, sent its armed troops into Nicaragua? And which one is now zealously guarding its national sovereignty? And if all nations continue to cling tenaciously to this sovereignty, how can international anarchy be ended? Denunciation of Japan is in order, but only in tones of penitence for mutual guilt. An ancient admonition is relevant: "Let him who is without sin cast the first stone."

Great responsibility rests upon our country to help bring about required changes in the international situation. But the American peace movement must not concentrate upon long range change to the exclusion of an emergency program of immediate action. *The neutrality policy of the United States should be designed to keep this country out of war, rather than*

---

* See details in M. Offutt, *The Protection of Citizens Abroad by the Armed Forces of the United States.*

to help some other nation win a war. The present law represents substantial progress in the right direction, but it needs to be revised in several vital respects. The economic practicability of staying out of war is easily demonstrated.† The most difficult task is that of preparing the minds and disciplining the emotions of the American people for the self-control which will be required if a general war breaks out. This objective is formidable, but not impossible of achievement.

It is of the utmost importance that citizens who desire to keep this country out of war should insist that the provisions of the neutrality law be put into operation whenever armed hostilities occur in any foreign land. The test is not whether a formal declaration of war has been made, but whether extensive and continued fighting with the weapons of war is taking place. At the moment of writing, a million Japanese and Chinese soldiers and sailors are engaged in mortal combat in various parts of China. Yet the President and the Secretary of State have failed to invoke the neutrality law, standing upon the technicality that war has not been declared. An aroused public opinion was responsible for the enactment of this law which was designed for precisely this kind of crisis, and a minimum program during this critical period should include the following steps:

1. Set in operation immediately the provisions of the neutrality law.

2. Remove all American armed forces from the Far East.

3. Officially declare that American citizens who remain in the war zone do so at their own risk, and that trade which is permitted under the neutrality law is at the risk of the trader.

4. Revise the neutrality law at the earliest opportunity so that its provisions will automatically come into force whenever extensive armed hostilities occur in any foreign land, irrespective of whether or not a formal declaration of war has been made.

The United States can keep out of war in Europe and Asia. And if this country refrains from waging war on foreign soil, there is only a remote possibility that its citizens will go to war

† See pp. 157-161.

at all, since there is no likelihood that the United States will be subjected to unprovoked armed invasion by a foreign foe.

Citizens of the United States can keep this country out of war and render incalculable service to the peoples of other lands if they will act upon the realization that *war, rather than being a lesser evil, is a combination, accentuation and continuation of monstrous evils.*

Therefore, vigorous and continuous emphasis must be placed upon the desirability of keeping out of war—every war of every kind. We should cooperate in an international endeavor to prevent war; and if this effort fails, we should seek to keep the United States out of war; but if this country plunges over the brink, we should as individuals refuse to approve or to engage in war. The United States can render its greatest contribution to the peoples of Europe and Asia in other ways than by taking up arms or by cooperating in the waging of war; and American patriots can serve their own country and the world more effectively by refusing to approve of or to engage in war than by ever becoming a cog in the war machine.

Wars come not only because of what nations do, but also because of what nations fail to do. Inaction as well as action may be provocative. Changes in prevailing international arrangements, and in national sentiments are imperative; failure to initiate drastic changes will precipitate war. In a country like the United States, the rank and file of citizens have responsibility and power to determine foreign policy. The issue of war and peace is in their hands. *Indifference and inactivity are equivalent to a vote for war.* The lives and destinies of all those we love depend upon what we do about war. If another great war comes, it will be a desperate conflict of entire population against entire population. The noblest creations of science will be prostituted to the work of devastation and annihilation, and the consequences will be appalling beyond imagination.

The prevention of war is therefore the most urgent task now before us, and no sensitive person will seek exemption or request a furlough at this crucial hour.

Chapter One

What Is War?

WAR IS a method. The objective sought may be worthy or ignoble; the spirit shown by soldiers may be courageous or cowardly; but war remains a method, a means, a way. It is not enough, therefore, to be convinced that the goal is high and holy, and to recognize that many combatants are brave and sacrificial. To be justified in waging war, an ethical individual must also hold the conviction that war is a proper and effective method of dealing with the crisis. Consequently, it is imperative that we understand clearly the essential elements of this method.

War is planned devastation and organized slaughter. War is planned devastation and organized slaughter in an endeavor to reach objectives and to preserve values. War is planned devastation and organized slaughter through utilization of the instruments and weapons made available by modern science. War is continued devastation and slaughter until the enemy yields or until a nation's own defeat is acknowledged.

Normal human beings recoil from atrocity, that is if they recognize atrocity as atrocity. All of us remember the repugnance with which we listened to tales of German atrocity in Belgium and France, stories of babes with their hands chopped off, women with their breasts mutilated, Canadians crucified on barn doors, and prisoners disembowelled. Even after proper discount is made for false propaganda, the evidence is indisputable that every invading army perpetrates atrocity, so much so that *war may correctly be defined as atrocity.* Reference to various standard dictionaries reveals the following definitions of atrocity: *"A deed of violence or savagery; great*

3

cruelty or reckless wickedness; extreme cruelty; enormous wickedness."

War is atrocity and war cannot be waged without atrocity. Consider three instruments of modern warfare: bombardment, air raid, and blockade. What happens when a huge projectile is accurately hurled ten miles or thirty miles through the air at a target in the form of a densely populated city? What are the consequences of raining high explosive and deadly poison upon the residents of a metropolitan community? What are the effects upon the victims of a blockade which shuts out food and other requirements of life? War is atrocity; war is a method of savage violence.

Indeed bombardment, air raid and blockade constitute the most revolting forms of atrocity because they are not deeds of violence committed under the momentary, blinding influence of fear or passion, but are deliberately premeditated processes of devastation, mutilation and slaughter of men, women and children without regard to guilt or responsibility. The use of poisoned arrows against enemies is regarded as savage atrocity; yet every great power is now preparing to rain poison upon the habitations of other lands. Verily, civilized patriots strain gnats and swallow camels! War is atrocity if the word atrocity has any meaning whatsoever.

The war method includes falsehood as an integral part. Truth is indeed a casualty in war. To deceive the enemy is a constant endeavor of belligerents. In wartime governments feel obliged to pump a steady stream of distortion and falsehood into the public mind at home. Now that it can be told, we have been informed in nauseating detail of the manner in which we were fed poisoned propaganda during the World War. Rigid censorship enables the public authorities to manipulate information and to create a desired impression. Recent development of movies and radio has increased enormously the power of the government under rigid wartime control to feed the people upon distortion and falsehood. The wholesale peddling of lies is an inherent part of war.

The war method substitutes the doctrine of necessity for

ethical ideals. With their backs against the wall, belligerent nations resort to every measure which they think necessary to victory. Moral compunctions are pushed to the side in favor of military necessity. That is right which contributes to victory; that is wrong which magnifies the threat of defeat. In the mouth of a Prussian, the philosophy of militarism is repulsive to Americans. To dethrone the doctrine that might makes right was a major objective in the war against Germany. Yet in waging that war the Government of the United States embraced the very doctrine it was seeking to destroy. No practice of war is more cruel and atrocious than the wholesale starvation of women and children. The United States not only helped to encircle Germany with a strangle-hold but continued to maintain that starvation blockade for more than seven months after the Armistice, on the ground that if the blockade were lifted Germany might refuse to accept the peace treaty. No sane American desired to prolong the process of starving German women and children; this atrocity was continued because it was considered necessary. No idea is more inextricably interwoven into war than the doctrine of military necessity.

The totalitarian nature of modern war renders invalid the distinction between combatants and non-combatants. Conscription of able-bodied men is universally practiced in wartime and in future conflicts the energies of practically the entire population will be drafted. The work of men, women and children in munitions plants, factories, mines, and fields is just as essential to winning a war as the fighting of soldiers at the front. Modern war has therefore become a desperate struggle of peoples against peoples, with the result that continued adherence to the doctrine of military necessity will lead to mutual suicide.

The war method prevents those who take it up from worshipping God as Father of all men including the enemy and prohibits the practice of brotherhood toward the people of enemy nations. A god of war is enthroned.

"God heard the embattled nations sing and shout
Gott Strafe England, and God save the King;
God this, God that, and God the other thing.
'Good God,' said God, 'I've got my work cut out.' " [1]

Atrocity supplants compassion and mercy. Mutual forebearance and mutual forgiveness are suppressed as treason. The overcoming of evil by doing good is looked upon as impracticable and dangerous to national welfare. The war method has no place in it for the spirit and practices of Jesus. "Late in 1917 Dr. Willard A. Paul, a member of the Association to Abolish War, proposed to print the Sermon on the Mount, without note or comment, for free distribution. The Secretary of the Association, Mr. Wilbur K. Thomas, was officially informed that such a procedure would be regarded by the Department of Justice as 'pro-German.' " [2]

Wise and good people differ in judgment as to whether or not war is ever justifiable. *But they ought not to differ in their descriptions of the inherent and ineradicable characteristics of the war method.* The premise is debatable that the perpetration of atrocities is sometimes a patriot's duty; that the poisoning of the public mind with distortion and falsehood designed to inflame passions is sometimes a patriot's duty; that the sidetracking of ethical ideals in favor of the practice of military necessity is sometimes a patriot's duty; that the banishment of a loving Father of all men and the bowing down before a god of war is sometimes a patriot's duty. But if these be obligations resting upon patriots, let them be proclaimed as such in plain unvarnished language.

Failure to talk plainly about war constitutes a major reason for its continuance. A deep fog of obscurity is thrown about war by the use of misleading and confusing terms. War is not high ideals. War is not noble objectives. War is not gallant heroism. War is not sacrificial devotion. War is method. War is atrocity. War is wholesale falsehood. War

---

[1] Quoted by H. M. Tomlinson, *Mars His Idiot*, p. 226.
[2] Leaflet issued by the Association to Abolish War.

is the practice of military necessity. War is an utter denial of the spirit and example of Jesus.

Dwell upon the importance of *correct use of words* in discussing the problem of war. Should a patriot, in an endeavor to defend his country and to preserve high values, be willing to go to war and fight bravely and sacrificially? More accurately: should a patriot, in an endeavor to defend his country and preserve high ideals, be willing to perpetrate atrocities upon women and children of other lands, accept the doctrine that the end justifies the means, follow the practice of military necessity, inflame passions through distortion and falsehood, bow down before a god of war, and forsake the way of Jesus?

Upholders of war as a necessary means of defense are inclined to place great emphasis upon the willingness of a soldier to die for his country. And this sacrificial devotion is indeed worthy of high praise. But a more accurate interpretation would stress the willingness of a soldier to kill for his country. Killing is his main business; dying may be an unavoidable last resort. The importance of correct usage is revealed by calling attention to contrasting impressions that are gained from a verse of Scripture as applicable to soldiers in wartime: "Greater love hath no man than this that he lay down his life for a friend." A more accurate portrayal of the situation would be this: "Greater love hath no man than this that he perpetrate atrocity upon his enemy."

No claim is being made herein that the characterization of war as atrocity would automatically bring it to an end. It is not enough to picture the horrible realities of war. But surely it is desirable, as we endeavor to reach a rational decision as to what we shall do about war, that we cease to think of it primarily in terms of high ideals and sacrificial devotion, and constantly envisage its necessary and inextricable method as that of perpetrating atrocities.

In an endeavor to intensify vividness of appreciation of the real nature of war, a series of descriptions and interpretations is presented.

I

"Proving Grounds, Aberdeen, Md., Oct. 3.—A huge gun
which shoots thirty miles in seacoast defense, new mortars
which will send poison gas or a smoke screen across a battle-
field, barking 75's which scatter shrapnel over enemy lines,
and airplanes dropping 1,100-pound bombs were among the
exhibits displayed here today for more than 9,000 members
of the Army Ordnance Association, Acting Secretary Wood-
ring and representatives of foreign embassies and legations in
Washington.

"The demonstration of these modernized implements of war
was climaxed late in the day when an armored tank ripped its
way across a rough field at more than sixty miles an hour, while
its crew of seven men incessantly fired five 30-calibre machine
guns and a 1.37-millimeter gun at a house built in the middle
of the field. . . . Women and children were not allowed inside
the reservation today because of the danger of exploding
shells."—*New York Times,* October 4, 1935.

II

"London, Oct. 18.—Visions of the next war were unfolded
before the empire's Prime Ministers today when the War
Office revealed its newest monsters of destruction at Aldershot.
A new giant tank, like a steel crab on wheels, rumbled across
shell-holes amid the swirl of dust, the roar of engines and the
crackle of guns.   Old-fashioned caterpillar tanks controlled
by wireless fought a battle before the Prime Ministers' eyes
like portents of a war which would be fought not by men but
by machines.   New machine gun devices were brought into
action to reveal new refinements of destructiveness. . . . The
most hair-raising of all the day's monsters was the tank which
moved like a crab.   It has been designed to solve every problem of a shell-torn battle area and wriggle over obstacles which
during the World War had put caterpillar tanks out of action.
When it came to gaping craters it simply lifted its wheels in

the air one at a time and crawled to the other side. Like the
claws of a nightmare the tanks' wheels stretched from shellhole to shellhole, each wheel with its own driving power and
each with its own grip on the surface. . . . There was neither
color nor glory in today's picture of war. Drab gray iron-
clads swarmed over the countryside, often hiding behind smoke
screens. Only occasionally a glimpse of infantry betrayed the
fact that men were engaged. . . . As a last surprise a 'dark
horse' tank made its appearance—a mammoth sixteen-ton con-
trivance, which will supersede the type now used by the British
Army. The capacities of this tank are still a jealously guarded
secret, but it won the race around the Aldershot drill ground
today with the greatest ease."—*New York Times,* October 19,
1930.

III

"The feverish pace at which world air armament is going on
reveals itself graphically in estimates given out yesterday by
Howard S. Welch, vice-president and general manager of the
Bendix Aviation Export Corporation, and former head of the
automotive-aeronautics trade division of the Department of
Commerce, on aircraft production for 1937. Mr. Welch's
figures show that 28,500 planes or nearly half the total number now in existence, will be built during the year and that
four-fifths of them will be for military purposes. . . . He pre-
dicts that 21,150 of the new planes will be procured by the
United States, Great Britain, Russia, France, Germany, Italy
and Japan."—*New York Herald Tribune,* February, 1937.

IV

"It is . . . probable that the critical battles of the future
will be fought over great cities, and the chief sufferers will
be the civilians—men, women and children. . . . In the late war
some 300 tons of bombs only were dropped upon this country
(England). Air forces of today could drop the same weight

in the first twenty-four hours of war, and could continue this scale of attack indefinitely. I need not dilate upon this terrible and repulsive picture!"—Sir Samuel Hoare, the *London Times,* October 17, 1925.

V

"There is the thermite bomb—a very interesting new bomb, with manifold possibilities. Thermite is a mixture of aluminum powder, iron oxide, magnesium, and, for ignition, a detonator or heat (fire or match, etc.). These ingredients, mixed in the proper proportions, are packed in small bombs, a good-sized bombing airplane carrying a hundred or more. These can then be dropped over the enemy territory, choosing the most crowded sections for greatest effect, but without needing a direct hit or definite target. Wherever these bombs land an inextinguishable fire is started. (In fact, the magnesium continues to explode even more violently as either water or a chemical extinguisher is thrown upon it.)

"If enough thermite bombs are dropped, a city can be quickly set on fire, burning unchecked in different sections at the same time, rendering the populace desperate, homeless, and terrified. Add some gas bombs at the same time (deadly phosgene would be advisable in this case, though mustard could be as effectively used), some high explosive to topple over the skyscrapers, and the picture of modern warfare for modern crowded cities is before your eyes."—Elvira K. Fradkin, *The Air Menace and The Answer,* Page 46.

VI

"Imaginative accounts of the next world war have described vast fleets of pilotless airplanes arriving above London, Paris, New York or San Francisco, and loosing tons of poison-gas and incendiary bombs that extinguish all life below. Last week the British Air Ministry proudly announced the successful development of a robot airplane, controlled by radio from the ground, and nicknamed the 'Queen Bee.' The 'Queen'

takes off by itself, rises to a height of 10,000 feet and cruises at 100 to 120 miles an hour. It is being employed to test anti-aircraft batteries using live ammunition, and can be made to dive, loop and roll to escape gunfire. At present its radio control is not effective for more than ten miles. British engineers, however, are working hard to overcome this handicap. If the range of control can be extended, the robot airplane is likely to revolutionize all warfare as completely as the naval torpedo, in the hands of German submarine crews, revolutionized sea warfare in the World War. If Western civilization is really bent on committing suicide, a neater, more effective instrument for its purpose could not be devised."
—*The New Republic*, July 10, 1935.

VII

"Mr. Elmer A. Sperry, the American gyroscopic engineer, is the inventor of an aerial projectile which, after being shot from a catapult, rises to a predetermined height and is then directed by wireless towards an object up to thirty-five miles distant, upon which it drops with a margin of error expressed by a fraction of a mile. Mr. Sperry avers that there is no technical obstacle to the trebling of this range. Such a projectile could be charged with sufficient explosive to destroy utterly a small town. . . . Group Capt. MacNeece, in the paper on air defense which has already been quoted, emphatically asserts that: 'No matter what are the defensive arrangements, there can never be a question of a guarantee of immunity from air attack. In future wars, one side or the other will have superiority in the air . . . but there will not be anything so definite as a supremacy of the air. . . . It follows that victory will come to the nation which in an air war in the future has not only the strongest striking force but which shows the greatest stoicism and ingenuity in meeting strange and devastating terrors."

"So, to your gas-proof dug-outs, O Israel, there to don your gas-mask which we hope, though without much confidence, will be proof against the gases of high penetrative power now being brewed for your discomfort.

"The wars of the future may be shorter than those of the past, but they will be wars of attrition, nevertheless. The difference will be that the collapse will be quicker to arrive and more utterly complete, and the industrial life of the vanquished nation will be so irreparably smashed and that of the victor in a condition so little less parlous that world trade will be disorganized far more completely than at the end of the first world war. . . . The loss of life from indirect causes may be expected to be at at least no lower scale than that set by hostilities in the next war. Interrupted food supplies and crippled industrial output mean malnutrition and, later, starvation, with pestilence in its train; and the nervous condition occasioned by incessant bombardment, unnatural life, loss of sleep and lack of food will lead to waves of madness, revolution, civil war and anarchy."—A. E. Blake, The Future of Air Warfare, *The Coast Artillery Journal,* June, 1930, Pp. 507, 510, 511.

VIII

"Linden, N. J., Jan. 26, (INS)—A new war engine of defense and offense has been devised. If the claims of its inventor and the opinions of certain high military leaders are upheld, it will revolutionize warfare as much as did the machine gun, the airplane, the submarine. It is a military tank which flies. It can be attached to a plane through a special device. It can be released or dropped (you can't hurt a tank) through the action of a lock lever. Another compound model has wings attached directly to the tank. . . .

"The world's foremost tank designer pictured the new military tactics of the next war as follows: Thousands of tanks, easily transported from one sector to another through flying power, would advance toward the enemy lines, replacing the old-fashioned waves of doughboys. Seventy-five feet apart, at a speed of from 60 to 90 miles an hour, they would sweep forward, communicating with each other through radio contact and receiving signals from the central command far behind the lines. A noiseless transmission system permits exchange of radio signals. These flying tanks would be armed with a one-pound cannon, a .30 to .50 calibre machine gun and probably a chemical gun"—*The Omaha Bee-News,* January 26, 1933.

IX

"Recent predictions of possible weapons outdo Jules Verne. Eminent military authorities vie with imaginative writers in forecasting what science yet has in store for the surprise and torture of the enemy. Thus Major Gen. J. F. C. Fuller of the British Army envisions the next period of warfare as the electrical phase, in which unmanned machines, both on the land and in the air, will be controlled by wireless power to fire their guns and drop their bombs and spray their chemicals automatically, unerringly—vast nerveless robots of duralumin and steel against which human flesh will be as grass before a prairie fire. Every resource of mechanical, electrical and chemical technique is being explored for its usefulness in holding, moving and hitting—above all, for its capacity to produce casualties. . . . During the World War the largest bombs dropped on London or Paris weighed 660 pounds, but today 2,000-pound bombs are a commonplace in ordnance circles, and aerial bombs weighing two tons have been experimented with."—George W. Gray, Unceasingly War Forges Deadlier Arms, *The New York Times Magazine,* December 10, 1933, p. 6.

X

"Poison gas bombs spread deadly vapors which penetrate every mask and bring almost instant death, inextinguishable phosphorus bombs burn through the flesh to the bone in a few minutes. There are hundreds of tanks, each one of them able to spit out thousands of fatal shots per minute; machine guns, light automatic guns, which, in the hands of millions of men, can scatter hundreds of millions of bullets per minute. And, above all, this horror in the sky, darkened with thousands of airplanes, from which destruction pours on the earth. But that is not the whole picture: behind the lines, towns and villages fall in flaming ruin beneath shell fire from guns and airplanes."—Marshal Foch, quoted by Fradkin, *op. cit.,* p. 39.

XI

"In the next war, the hazards in events shaped by forces now barely surmisable will present our statesmen, sailors, soldiers, and airmen, with a situation which will make Gabriel on the Last Day feel that his trumpet need make no announcement. Should the great industrial powers again cut their communications with each other, scatter explosives on the seas and poison and blast each other's principal cities, the peace which will fall after the firing of the last shot will be the silence of the void. Whoever needs reminding that another general war would fill the workshops and factories of the white races with cobwebs more enduring than our problem of unemployment must be a Rip Van Winkle not yet awake."—H. M. Tomlinson, *Mars His Idiot,* p. 41.

XII

"In the next war will our young men be burned to ashes by a 'death ray,' shocked to fragments by sound-wave oscillations, or annihilated by the 'death centrifuge?' Will there be rays to reach into the skies and destroy aircraft? Will there be flying submarines, flying tanks, aerial torpedoes, and stratosphere bombers? Will there be available an 'invisible smoke' to choke aircraft engines and send them gliding down to earth? Will the soldiers wear clothes made out of glass or perhaps carry along iron cages as protection against 'death rays'? And which of these methods are ready for use? Which are still in the experimental stage? These important questions are answered by two German emigres in an ominous volume. . . .

"Great efforts have been made to adapt various kinds of rays for use in war. In the mind of the public all have been

lumped together under the term 'death ray.' The scientific
principles involved, however, and the rays employed differ
widely; a dozen different rays may be used for a dozen different
purposes. . . .

"An exceedingly dangerous death machine is the aerial torpedo. This is also guided from a distance. . . . These torpedoes
may carry bombs and drop them at various intervals, or they
may be bombs themselves and descend, according to direction,
at strategic spots. Still another kind of ray sets off mines and
other explosives, on land or in the water. There are blinding
rays, so bright that soldiers will be blinded at least temporarily
as by an automobile headlight a thousand times intensified. . . .

"The 'death centrifuge' was invented by an American, sold
to the British, and is now being used by the Japanese. It is
nothing more than a modernization of David's sling. A large
number of mechanical arms revolve at a terrific rate while
steel pellets are fed to them. The fantastic number of 33,000
rounds per minute can be fired by this machine. While not
as accurate as a machine gun, it is a devastating killing machine at close quarters. Moreover, it has the advantage of
requiring neither powder nor copper. . . .

"Add poison gas, incendiary bombs, high-explosive bombs,
and the killing machines well known from the last war, and the
stage is set for slaughter."—H. C. Engelbrecht, New Ways of
Killing, *The Nation*, March 13, 1937, pp. 290, 291, 292.

XIII

"Whilst the effects of chemical warfare are to some extent
appreciated, largely owing to the use of poison gas in the Great
War, little attention has been paid to the use of bacteria as
an offensive weapon. That such a weapon will be used in
future wars is almost certain. There is little doubt that some
of the belligerents in the last conflict were at least considering
it. . . . It would appear that the most likely method of attack
would be by aerial dissemination. Bacteria which could be
used for this method of attack, and which fulfil the other

requirement of readily producing immunity by inoculation, are the plague bacillus which when inhaled produces plague pneumonia, a most fatal disease; the glanders bacillus which readily infects man, and two germs which do not occur normally in Europe but which produce deadly infections, one the bacillus of meliodosis in Malay, a disease resembling glanders but more deadly to man, the other the bacillus of tularaemia, a disease found in western U. S. A. . . . We must not overlook another factor, namely, the effects of bacteria after poison gas. It is well known that mustard gas weakens resistance to infection. . . .

"The attack on the civilian population of a country need not be confined to epidemics affecting man alone. The destruction of food supplies could be readily effected by bacteria and viruses (minute scarcely visible germs). Foot and mouth disease, which is characterised by extreme infectivity, could be readily introduced by glass bombs and would effectually upset the cattle-stock, louping ill would play a similar role in relation to sheep, whilst swine fever has already proved the bane of the British pig-breeder. Diseases affecting the crops produced by insect carriers dropped by aeroplanes could be readily introduced with results which would not only disable the infected country from the viewpoint of war, but also ruin it economically for many generations to come.

"Would scientists consent to use their knowledge to such fiendish ends? Doubtless the majority would not consider the possibility. On the other hand, human nature is such that there will always be found individuals who, under the misguided banner of nationalism or patriotism, can be persuaded to prostitute their knowledge to the destruction of their fellow-men."—*The New Statesman and Nation,* May 27, 1933, pp. 678, 679.

XIV

"Who in Europe does not know that one more war in the West and the civilization of the ages will fall with as great a shock as that of Rome?"—Right Honorable Stanley Baldwin.

Chapter Two

Why Do Nations Fight?

A N EMINENT historian concludes a revealing portrayal of the origins of the World War with the observation that in the fateful hours of decision every belligerent governmen did "what might have been expected." [1]

If their respective situations had been reversed, Austrians would have acted as Serbians did act, Russians would have taken steps similar to those taken by Germany, and Bulgarians would have responded in the same way that the French did respond. Every army in the field slaughtered the enemy for doing what its own members would have done under parallel circumstances.

I

The peril and the tragedy of the present international crisis are found in the fact that once more the French are preparing to wage war against Germany for doing what Frenchmen would do if their positions were reversed; while the British are storing up high explosives for use against Italians for doing what Englishmen would do under the same circumstances. This is not to say that the French and the British would adopt every repressive measure now in force in Germany and Italy. But the evidence is convincing that they would respond in a highly bellicose manner.

Let us first consider the probable attitudes and actions of patriotic Germans if they had stood in French shoes from 1914 onward. In the World War the French were certain that

---

[1] G. P. Gooch, *Recent Revelations of European Diplomacy,* 1928 edition, p. 206. See also Sidney B. Fay, *The Origins of the World War.*

they were fighting in self-defense against an aggressive Germany. Twice within the memory of that generation French soil had been ravaged by invasion from across the Rhine. When victory came in 1918 after ghastly losses in blood and treasure, the French determined to put an end forever to Prussian aggression by breaking Germany's power to invade. Granted these premises, would Germans have done less? Would any nation have acted in a substantially different fashion?

The French policy of national defense at Versailles and subsequently may be stated simply: make France safe by keeping Germany weak and by making France strong. Prevent Germany from attacking by making it impossible for her to win. Therefore the French, with generous cooperation from other Allied powers, crammed into the Treaty of Versailles numerous provisions designed to weaken Germany's military, economic and political power. "The Treaty of Versailles of June 28, 1919, humbled Germany to the dust and imposed upon her terms so severe as to render her impotent in European international politics for many years. The Reich lost all its overseas colonies, Alsace-Lorraine, the Saar Valley, Eupen and Malmedy, the Polish corridor, part of Upper Silesia, and a portion of Schleswig. German investments and property abroad were seized. Germany's coal production was reduced by one-third, and her iron supplies by three-fourths. The German merchant marine was confiscated by the Allies. The German battle fleet was surrendered. The German army was limited to 100,000 men and was forbidden to possess tanks, heavy artillery, or airplanes. The new German navy was restricted to six battleships of not more than 10,000 tons, six light cruisers, twelve destroyers, and no submarines. The left bank of the Rhine and a fifty-kilometer zone on the right bank were demilitarized. The left bank and the bridge-heads were subjected to military occupation for fifteen years. A Reparation Commission was appointed to fix Germany's financial obligations to idemnify the victors for civilian damages, pensions, and the Belgian war debt, on the theory that the war was a result of 'the aggression of Germany and her allies.'[2] The Kaiser was arraigned 'for a supreme offense against international morality and the sanctity of treaties,' and provision was made for bringing him to trial, along with other German 'war criminals.' Thanks to the collapse of Russia and the attitude of President Wilson, the terms of the secret inter-Allied treaties of 1915-1917 for the division of the spoils were not literally executed. But Germany was nevertheless crushed to earth and not permitted to join the League of Nations, which Wilson insisted on including in the peace settlement."[3] Equally resolute efforts were put forth to increase France's might by unequalled fortifications, massive armed preparedness, and a series of military alliances. To all appearances, Germany was reduced comparatively to the rank of a third-rate power.

What would Frenchmen have done if they had stood in German shoes during those years? Remember that during the World War the Germans also were certain that they were fighting in self-defense against encirclement and strangulation. With unexcelled zeal and courage they fought against terrific odds. Their staggering casualties were in vain. They lost the war and were compelled to endure the crushing burdens considered necessary to France's safety. Hatred was intensified by the conviction that Germany was promised peace on a basis of Wilson's Fourteen Points and then betrayed. Concerning the Treaty of Versailles, a British statesman has written: ". . . seldom in the history of man has such vindictiveness cloaked itself in such unctuous sophistry . . . nineteen out of President Wilson's twenty-three 'Terms of Peace' were flagrantly violated in the Treaty of Versailles as finally drafted."[4] Failure to pay the impossible indemnity was answered by French invasion of the Ruhr. Inflation and economic depression produced indescrib-

[2] Article 231 of the Treaty of Versailles.
[3] Frederick L. Schuman, *International Politics,* pp. 445, 446.
[4] Harold Nicolson, *Peacemaking 1919,* pp. 187, 13.

able misery and an appalling sense of hopelessness.[5]   Under
these circumstances, what would patriotic Frenchmen have
done?   What would any despairing people have done?

The Germans turned to Hitler as their only hope of deliverance from oppression and tyranny.   He symbolized their hatred
and their determination to secure revenge.   "The Treaty of
Versailles," writes H. M. Tomlinson, "was but a bridge of
tinder over hell.   The men who framed it were told that at
the time.   It was made by statesmen whose views differed in
no essential from those now preparing for another war.   Berlin and Vienna are two of the lovely consequences of the peace
treaties.   Hitler's   fame   and   power   derive   from   France.
Poincaré and Clemenceau prompted Germany to an escape from
helotry into fatuous happiness with notions which make the
peoples on her frontiers anxious now as to what ecstatic dance
her illusion of glory will next lead her.   We can provide places
for unfortunates who know they are the reincarnation of the
Virgin Mary or Napoleon; but when a nation goes that way the
matter is more perplexing.   It was the logic of French realists
that re-created the German menace it imagined it was nullify-
ing." [6]   Any other nation would in such an hour turn to its
Hitler.   And the situation which he confronted caused Hitler
to become more and more bellicose.   Re-armament and spectacular displays of daring became absolutely necessary to the
success of his program.

The effect of all this on the French has been merely to
deepen their conviction that they are threatened by German
aggression and to intensify their determination to maintain
armed superiority over their hereditary enemy.   And the more
zealously the French adhere to their policy of national defense,
the more certain the Germans become that only through armed
might can they avoid strangulation.   If this collision results
in another great war, one side will be fighting again *aggression,*
while the other side will be fighting against *oppression.*

---

[5] See pp. 129-134.
[6] H. M. Tomlinson, *Mars His Idiot,* p. 31.

II

Consider also the respective cases of Italy and Great Britain. The evidence is convincing that if situations were reversed their respective foreign policies would conform in substance to the prevailing policies of these two nations.

Are the Italians an inherently belligerent people, whereas the inhabitants of the British Isles are essentially a peaceable people? In his relations with other countries, what is Mussolini the dictator now doing that stands in sharp contrast to the practices of successive prime ministers of democratic Britain? Fascist Italy is now avowedly bent upon conquest. She thinks she needs more territory and says that she must have it. She desires to dominate certain regions of the earth, including North Africa, southeastern Europe, and the waters of the Adriatic and the Mediterranean. She covets the glory and prestige that belong to conquering nations. To achieve these ends Mussolini is imperialising the minds of the Italians and building up Italian arms.

But surely we cannot forget that conquest, domination, imperialisation and navalism have long been practiced by Great Britain. A map of the earth presents convincing testimony. Her far flung possessions may have been acquired conscientiously in "a fit of absence of mind," but the results of her actions bear striking resemblance to armed conquest. And Britons can look Italians in the face without a sense of inferiority when British navalism is compared with Italian militarism. During the period when Britain was rounding out her empire, she insisted not only on a navy equal to that of any other country but demanded a two-power fleet equal in fighting strength to the combined fleets of any two other nations. And pride of empire has long been a dominant characteristic not only of prime ministers but also of the rank and file of British people. The popularity of Kipling the imperialist "increased so rapidly that by the end of the century it could be fairly said that no other writer of his time had so profoundly swayed the British mind. . . . More than any other writer he reflected the

diverse ideas that went under the general term of imperialism." [7]

"Why are we Imperialists?" inquired a writer in an outstanding British publication in 1899. "We are Imperialists in
response to the compelling influences of our destiny. . . . We
are the heirs of the ages, with all the great prerogatives and
solemn obligations which attach to this high privilege. We
are, and shall be, Imperialists because we cannot help it." [8]

In 1900 Gilbert Murray wrote: "In every nation of Europe
from England and France to Russia and Turkey, in almost
every nation in the world from the Americans to the Chinese
and the Finns, the same whisper from below the threshold
sounds incessantly in men's ears. 'We are the pick and flower
of nations; the only nation that is really generous and brave
and just. We are above all things qualified for governing
others; we know how to keep them exactly at their place without weakness and without cruelty. . . . The excellence of our
rule abroad is proved in black and white by the books of our
explorers, our missionaries, our administrators and our soldiers,
who all agree that our yoke is a pure blessing to those who
bear it.' " [9]

If the English and the Scotch and the Irish now stood in
Italian shoes, would they be less belligerent than the Italians
are at this moment? Certain words from a famous address
delivered by Field-Marshal Lord Roberts at Manchester on
October 25, 1912, are relevant at this point. Substitute Italy
for Germany and the frankness of this grizzled old warrior becomes still more revealing: " 'Germany strikes when Germany's hour has struck.' That is the time-honored policy of
her Foreign Office. . . . And, gentlemen, it is an excellent
policy. It is, or should be, the policy of every nation prepared to play a great part in history. . . . Germany advances. . . . Contrasted with our own apathy or puerile and

---

[7] William L. Langer, *The Diplomacy of Imperialism,* Vol. 1, p. 83.
[8] Quoted by Langer, *op. cit.,* Vol. 1, p. 93.
[9] Gilbert Murray: "National Ideals: Conscious and Unconscious" (*International Journal of Ethics,* XI, 1900, pp. 1-22), p. 21.

spasmodic efforts, how impressive is this magnificent and un-
resting energy! It has the mark of true greatness; it extorts
admiration even from those against whom it is directed. . . .
For how was this Empire of Britain founded? War founded
this Empire—war and conquest! When we, therefore, masters by war of one-third of the habitable globe, when we pro-
pose to Germany to disarm, to curtail her navy or diminish her
army, Germany naturally refuses. . . . Who amongst us, knowing the past of this nation . . . can accuse Germany or regard
the utterance of one of her greatest Chancellors a year and a
half ago, or of General Bernhardi three months ago, with any
feelings except those of respect?" [10]

Compare the following gem of militarism with the most
extreme utterance of Mussolini and decide which deserves
loudest applause from imperialists: "War is in the nature of
things, and history warns us that it is not good for a nation
to be too long at peace . . . the means of improvement must
be the same as in the past, namely, war, relentless war of
extermination of inferior individuals and nations. . . . History
proves up to the hilt that nations languish and perish under
peace-conditions, and it has only been by war that a people has
continued to thrive and exist. . . . Peace is a disintegrating
force, whereas war consolidates a people. War is no doubt a
dreadful ordeal, but it clears the air, and refines the race as
fire purifies the gold and silver in the furnace. . . . Furthermore, in defense of our warlike virtues, I would point out that
for some wise but inscrutable reason it has pleased the Almighty
to constitute all life in this world on a war and not on a peace
basis, and is it wise of the creature to dispute the wisdom of
the Creator?" These words were written by Lieut.-General Sir
Reginald G. Hart, later promoted to the rank of General, and
published as a 14-page article in a leading British periodical,
The Nineteenth Century, August, 1911, under the title, "A
Vindication of War."

At the end of the nineteenth century Lord Wolseley, com-

---

[10] Lord Roberts, *Message to the Nation,* pp. 5-9.

mander in chief of the British forces, wrote rapturously of the soldier's life: "All other pleasures pale before the intense, the maddening delight of leading men into the midst of an enemy, or to the assault of some well-defended place. That rapturous enjoyment takes man out of himself to the forgetfulness of all earthly considerations. . . . A sound, healthy, military spirit gives strength to a people. It is the guardian of the honour and interest of a nation, the safeguard of its freedom and liberties, the purifier of its civilisation, its defence against enemies from without, and degeneracy from within." [11]

III

Now compare or contrast the records of Japan and the United States. The prospect of armed hostilities between the United States and, for example, Japan, would be substantially diminished if citizens of the former country could be brought to realize that numerous parallels to the latter's aggressive policies are presented in the record of the territorial and economic expansion of the United States. A sound interpretation of the motives back of American pioneers' lust for new territory creates understanding and sympathy for the Japanese people, while producing deeper apprehension concerning the perpetuation of the belligerent policies which have characterized both nations.

The various arguments used by Japanese officials in defense of their policy in Manchuria and other parts of China can be matched almost phrase by phrase with citations from American expansionists. Failure to recognize this fact causes many American patriots to impute to Japan a special brand of military aggressiveness and to insist therefore that the strength of their own armed forces must be increased. One of the most ominous aspects of the present world situation is produced by the failure of most Anglo-Saxons to realize that numerous

[11] Lord Wolseley: "Is a Soldier's Life Worth Living?" (*Fortnightly Review*, May 1889, pp. 597-610) ; "War and Preparations for War" (*United Service Magazine*, March, 1897).

present-day policies of Japan, Italy, and Germany are perilous precisely because they are faithful reproductions of practices long followed by Great Britain and the United States. War results from a clash of the self-righteousness of the surfeited with the self-assertion of the frustrated.

Many volumes would be required to tell the story of American expansion in detail, but the essential facts are easily available. The very titles of several chapters in the Beards' history[12] are revealing: Agricultural Imperialism, Westward to the Pacific, Rounding Out the Continent, The Politics of Acquisition, Imperial America, America in the Balance of Power. A huge mass of evidence is presented by Albert K. Weinberg, under the title *Manifest Destiny: A Study of Nationalist Expansionism in American History.*[13] A comparison of typical utterances of American expansionists with recent statements by Japanese officials reveals an impressive similarity of attitudes.

(1) *The absolute necessity of expansion* has been stressed by spokesmen for the United States and for Japan. "When you know this historical background and understand this overflowing vitality of our race you will see the impossibility of compelling us to stay still within the confines of our little island home. We are destined to grow and expand overseas. . . . The path of expansion lies, then, naturally in the direction of Manchuria. . . . And I cannot help believing that, if you were in our place, you would be doing exactly what we are doing today."[14] In this fashion writes Baron Wakatsuki, a former Prime Minister of Japan. "This great pressure of a people moving always to new frontiers, in search of new lands, new power, the full freedom of a virgin world, has ruled our course and formed our policies like a Fate." These words were not written by a citizen of Japan but by Woodrow Wilson.[15] "Can

---

12 Charles A. and Mary R. Beard, *The Rise of American Civilization.*
13 Published by The Johns Hopkins Press.
14 *Foreign Affairs,* July 1935, pp. 584, 585.
15 *Atlantic Monthly,* Vol. XC, 1902, p. 726, quoted by Weinberg, *op. cit.,* p. 1.

you say to the tide that it ought not to flow, or the rain to fall?
I reply, *it must!* And so it is with well-constituted, and therefore, progressive and expansive nations.   They cannot help
advancing; it is the condition of their existence," [16] exclaimed
Attorney-General Cushing.   In an after-dinner speech Albert J.
Beveridge, later to become United States Senator, said: "Fate
has written our policy for us; the trade of the world must and
shall be ours. . . . If this means the Stars and Stripes over an
Isthmian canal . . . over Hawaii . . . over Cuba and the southern
seas . . . then let us meet that meaning with a mighty joy and
make that meaning good, no matter what barbarism and all
our foes may do or say . . . the stars in their courses will fight
for us and countless centuries will applaud." [17]

(2) *Self-defense is the justification offered* by spokesmen of
Japan and of the United States for the militant moves of their
respective nations.   "We have done nothing that was not justified by the strict need of protection for our nationals from the
persecution of the Chinese soldiers and our actions have been
entirely defensive and passive," declared Admiral Osumi, Japanese Minister of the Navy.[18]   "Japan is grieved to be called a
violator of the Peace Pact," wrote Dr. Inazo Nitobe, formerly
Under Secretary General of the League of Nations.   "She
maintains that she has acted within its provisions.   She resorted
to unpacific means not 'as an instrument of national policy,'
but as an instrument of self-defense. . . . Japan must be prepared for the worst.   She stands alone—a small country, face
to face with China, Russia and America, three of the giants of
the earth.   Japan stands alone for her right to live—not for conquest, as is so often alleged, but for the preservation of that
life with which God has endowed her." [19]   An outstanding
journalist declared that "the fear is genuine and general among

[16] Weinberg, *op. cit.*, p. 203.
[17] *Beveridge and the Progressive Era*, by Claude G. Bowers, pp. 68, 69.
[18] *New York Times*, February 5, 1932.
[19] *Japan and the Peace Pact*, pp. 7, 9.

the Japanese that America is pursuing a policy calculated to condemn them to suffocation and stagnation." [20]

Self-defense has likewise been the justification advanced in defending American expansionism. "The law of self-preservation overrules the laws of obligation to others," declared Thomas Jefferson.[21] Senator Gouverneur Morris expressed the conviction that "no nation has a right to give to another a dangerous neighbor without her consent." [22] The *New York Herald* once advocated, in the name of self-preservation, the seizure of Cuba, Mexico and Central America, confident that "this would be to them a boon which they would gladly accept, whereas, if we look unconcernedly on while a few European intriguers endeavor to establish among them a European protectorate and Spanish despotism, we shall only consent to their being immersed in more savage civil wars than they have yet witnessed, and become finally involved ourselves in a general war with the European alliance." [23] President Coolidge affirmed that "we are not making war on Nicaragua any more than a policeman on the street is making war on passersby." [24] In defining defense, Admiral Mahan at one time wrote: ". . . defense means not merely defense of our territory, but defense of our just national interests, whatever they be and wherever they are . . . the best defense of one's own interests is power to injure those of the enemy." [25]

(3) *The preservation of peace and the advancement of civilization* are motives which saturate the utterances of Japanese and American spokesmen alike. "It is Japan who is giving Manchuria precious principles of self-development, progress and spirituality," declared Yosuke Matsuoka, chief representative of Japan at the League of Nations during the Manchurian crisis. "This melting-pot of Asia . . . one day

---

[20] K. K. Kawakami, *Harper's Monthly Magazine,* March, 1927, p. 449.
[21] Weinberg, *op. cit.,* p. 403.
[22] *Ibid,* p. 31.
[23] *Ibid,* pp. 389, 390.
[24] *Ibid,* p. 441.
[25] Beard, *The Idea of National Interest,* pp. 339, 340.

may be able to save the whole of China. . . . China as she is today is the greatest danger to humanity in this century. . . . We hope that Manchuria will be a beacon to Asia. . . . We must be strong for the sake of our ideals." [26]   In discussing "The Foreign Policy of Japan," Tsunejiro Niyaoka wrote: ". . . Japan, as the only organized strong Power in Eastern Asia has an obligation to discharge which she cannot escape. . . . Therefore quitting the League and embarking on a course of her own became an absolute necessity for Japan if she were to play her role as the bulwark of peace in Eastern Asia." [27] Secretary Hay rejoiced that "no man, no party can fight with any chance of final success against a cosmic tendency . . . against the spirit of the age" in a nation "whose object and purposes are the welfare of humanity." [28]   In speaking of Mexico, Senator Reverdy Johnson declared "that we were constituted missionaries by Heaven, even by fire and by sword and by slaughter, to carry the light of civilization into that benighted land." [29]   Tyler Dennett refers to that "blissful and exalted assumption that any race ought to regard conquest by the American people as a superlative blessing." [30]

"As the period of American expansion recedes in time and takes on perspective," writes Dr. Albert Weinberg, "it stands revealed as an amazing phase of our national development. The mere physical extent of the territory acquired is impressive enough, but the really astonishing thing is the range of ideas and moral doctrines that have been advanced in justification of this extension of the national domain at the expense of another—and usually weaker—peoples. . . . A résumé of the interpretations of self-defense in the history of American expansionism resembles almost a progressive madness, and certainly has all the multiplicity and variety of a crazy quilt." [31]

---

[26] *New York Times*, January 8, 1933.
[27] *International Conciliation*, February, 1935, pp. 35, 36.
[28] Weinberg, *op. cit.*, p. 272.
[29] *Ibid*, p. 175.
[30] *Ibid*, p. 300.
[31] *Ibid*, p. 406.

Advocates of peace would do well to pray with Burns:

> O, wad some Power the giftie gi'e us
> To see oursel's as ithers see us!
> It wad frae mony a blunder free us,
> An' foolish notion.

The imminent threat of another great war is produced not by the special brand of aggression dominant in Germany, Italy and Japan, but by the fact that these nations are *now* bent upon conquest, whereas other great powers did their conquering in an earlier period and insist upon retaining the fruits of their aggression.

Professor Langer concludes a monumental survey of imperialism during the period 1890-1902 with these words: "One cannot study this period without marvelling at the exuberance and optimism which went hand in hand with recklessness and confidence in the conduct of foreign affairs. It was taken for granted that the world was marked out by Providence for exploitation by the European white man and that the principle of every man for himself and the devil take the hindmost was natural law. In the writings of the statesmen and in the writings of journalists there is very little trace of deeper understanding. The rise of Japan, the Adua disaster, the Boxer rising, none of these epoch-making events really opened the eyes of Europe. Even Lord Salisbury could see in the world nothing but a few virile nations and a large number of dying nations. The basic problem of international relations was who should cut up the victims." [32]

IV

A simple *parable of three robbers* readily comes to mind. The first thief went out early and by ten o'clock was back home with his haul. The second robber returned successfully at midnight. The third thief overslept and did not start his

---

[32] Langer, *op. cit.*, Vol. II, p. 797.

rounds until two o'clock. The first house he visited had already been robbed by the ten o'clock robber and the second one had been ransacked by the midnight robber. Whereupon in great indignation he went to the place at which the earlier thieves lived. But at one o'clock the latter had been converted and with a mighty oath had sworn that they would never steal again. They greeted the latecomer with a sermon on the sin of stealing and admonished him to mend his ways. The two o'clock robber was impressed and signed a statement that he would steal no more. But when he noticed the swag in possession of the earlier robbers, he demanded his share of the loot. The parable ends at the moment when the fighting among the robbers was about to begin.

V

War grows naturally and luxuriantly in the soil of a competitive society. Mankind will remain constantly on the verge of armed hostilities so long as it retains the forms of social organization now called nationalism and capitalism. Competitive actions on the part of vast social units are nearing the point of suicide because they are aggravated by the ideas and sentiments of nationalism.

Long familiarity with economic competition as a basis of social organization has blinded this generation to its real significance. Americans especially have been blinded because they have operated the competitive system under the favorable pioneer conditions of a huge undeveloped continent stored with vast riches. The dominant ideas and sentiments of this generation were handed down from fathers who lived on the edge of a forest. So long as the frontier could be pushed westward and productive land remained cheap and accessible, the advantages of economic competition were more conspicuous than its dangers. When production was carried on in small shops and establishments, the results of competition were less disastrous because the loser could more easily make a new beginning.

In the United States these favorable conditions have passed, but the ideas and sentiments which emerged from this soil remain dominant. That an individual has a right to all the money he can obtain by legal means is assumed without question by most Americans. Stockholders are gripped by an insatiable desire for higher and higher dividends. Speculation is looked upon as a legitimate way of acquiring a fortune and to an alarming extent fraud is practiced. The struggle for gain is characterized by ruthlessness. Competitors are driven to the wall and dog eat dog is the rule. Many corporations avail themselves of every legal means and some unlawful methods of combatting labor unions. Workers sometimes retaliate with violence for violence. Industry and commerce have become a gigantic battlefield.

Individuals who approve of economic competition as a method of producing and distributing goods within their own country are not likely to comprehend the true nature of the prevailing international crisis. Accustomed as they are to the ruthlessness of economic rivalry in their own land, and practiced as they are in defending self-interest and competition, most Americans are unable to realize the gravity of the world-wide struggle for economic and political domination or to adopt effective measures for the prevention of another great war.

Economic competition as a basis of social organization is deadly enough within a given country and if permitted to mature produces civil war, but when allowed to operate on a world scale it becomes utterly devastating. When self-interest is enlarged to national interest, when commercial competition becomes national rivalry, and when industrial ruthlessness takes the form of national armament and armed action, the consequences are catastrophic. Mutual suicide will be the fate of this generation if effective measures are not quickly adopted to diminish the intensity of economic competition among the nations. The units of combat are now gigantic beyond comprehension. The network of economic relationships among the various peoples of the earth is complex and fragile. The weapons and practices of modern war plough through this fabric of industry and commerce as thunderbolts of desolation and death.

VI

Economic competition among the peoples of various lands is rendered more threatening because it is aggravated and inflamed by the doctrines and sentiments of nationalism. Perspective is distorted. Emphasis is placed upon unlikeness to other nationalities. The virtues and achievements of one's own country are exaggerated, and its vices and failures are minimized; whereas in portraying other countries this practice is reversed. The resultant motions of superiority and inferiority tend to produce suspicion and fear and enmity. This mood sharpens the provocativeness of competition for economic advantage.

The doctrines of nationalism increase the destructiveness of economic competition. So familiar are we with the ideas and sentiments of nationalism that we are often insensitive to their significance. Consider the dogma of *national interest*. Everywhere it is taken for granted that national policies should be determined with a view to obtaining maximum advantage in all dealings with other peoples. Tariff schedules, for illustration, are set at the level at which greatest gain is supposed to be obtained by America, or at least by a dominant group in this country. The number of immigrants admitted is likewise determined by a judgment concerning the best interests of the United States. Rarely does Congress pay much attention to the consequences of our policies upon the citizens of other lands. "That's not our funeral; we have troubles enough of our own" expresses the prevailing popular sentiment.

Nowhere is the doctrine of *national sovereignty* clung to more tenaciously than in the United States. The right to do as we please in our relations with other countries is an inarticulate or a blatant assumption of many Americans. The idea of a superstate is viewed with abhorrence by most of our fellow citizens. Thus we have refused to become members of the

World Court and the League of Nations. But even a moment's sober reflection makes it clear that peace cannot be maintained among sovereign units every member of which is seeking its own gain in a ruthless struggle for control of the earth's economic resources. The sheer complexity of world relationships and the utter dependence of various peoples upon each other demand a sufficient abridgment of national sovereignty to make possible the creation and utilization of appropriate agencies of international justice. A major trend of history must be continued. The substitution of due process of law for arbitrary decision has ever been a condition precedent to the maintenance of peace. So long as tribes lived in a state of inter-tribal anarchy under the reign of respective patriarchs, inter-tribal war prevailed. Sovereign cities, sovereign baronies, sovereign states fought each other until sovereignty was abridged and cities, baronies, and states submitted to the reign of law. And only the blindest of the blind can fail to see that the prevailing anarchy among nations produced by insistence upon sovereignty is a primary cause of war.

Reliance upon *national armaments* magnifies the dangers produced by national interest and national sovereignty. The adequacy of an armed body is relative to the size of a potential enemy. Thus a race of armaments is unavoidable if peoples seek safety through armed strength. Modern armies and navies are highly expensive and huge appropriations must be obtained by governments if they are to maintain the pace required in a furious race. Citizens will not pay these bills unless they are kept in fear of consequences if their country falls behind in the race of armaments. Therefore advocates of armed preparedness feel obliged to spread suspicion and fear of other governments, and every country has its yellow press which fans the flames of international hostility. Jingoism is an invariable accompaniment of a race of armaments and in various lands citizens are terrified and infuriated by the fumes of poisonous propaganda. In this soil war flourishes luxuriantly.

National patriotism in its prevailing form is a dynamic cause of war. The idea that citizens are obliged to support their government in all controversies with other governments, even to the extent of waging war, and irrespective of whether their government is right or wrong, contributes powerfully to the outbreak of war. With the assurance that their policies will be supported, governments become more reckless and provocative in their dealings with other nations. Moreover, in the popular mind patriotism becomes synonymous with willingness to support armed preparedness and to wage war if called upon by the government. It is not accidental that "patriotic" societies almost invariably are committed to a policy of reliance upon armaments for security and that pacifism is considered disloyalty and treason. The true significance of the contemporary brand of patriotism may be grasped quickly if Americans will look squarely at its consequences in Germany, Italy and Japan. Surely it is obvious that the peace of the world is rendered more insecure by the willingness of the peoples of these lands to follow blindly wherever their rulers lead them. Yet the evidence is convincing that if respective situations were reversed, patriotic Americans would act in substantially the same way that patriots of Germany, Italy and Japan are now acting.

In subsequent chapters I shall attempt to outline a constructive program of positive war prevention. I expect to return to the parable of the three robbers and consider ways and means of dealing with their dilemma.[33] At this point, however, it seems imperative that the utmost emphasis be placed upon the fact that war is not caused by the special brand of aggression or militarism found in certain countries, but is *produced primarily by the ruthless competitive struggle for control of the earth's resources, a conflict made more devastating by the doctrines and sentiments of nationalism.* Differences in policy are due primarily to differences in situation. The time factor also is important. Perhaps the difference in policy is the difference between ten o'clock, twelve o'clock and two o'clock.

[33] See pp. 29, 30, 38 ff.

VII

Certain popular myths concerning war need to be exploded, beginning with the notion that war is made inevitable by man's fighting instinct. The explanation of the origins of international war is not to be found in man's biological equipment. However powerful may be the innate tendency toward pugnacity, it is not the chief source of war. This same fallacious argument was used for centuries in defense of dueling. It was popularly supposed that the abolition of dueling was impossible because of the presence and power of fighting instinct within gentlemen. In commenting upon the famous combat between Alexander Hamilton and Aaron Burr, a writer of that day said: "The duel is the demand of insulted feelings, the reparation of injured honor, the only recourse of violated character against malevolent and unworthy insinuations and aspersions. . . . In every view of the subject we are struck with the utter impracticability of forming legal prohibitions of the practice of the duel." In the year 1829 a British social reformer, after years of fruitless endeavor to persuade his countrymen to abandon the practice of dueling, confessed that "we found it was too generally considered that a practice sanctioned by time and precedent, which has withstood the raillery of the satirist, the terror of penal laws, and the admonition of the pulpit, nay, the fear of a future state, could never be abolished." Yet it is no longer customary for gentlemen to fight duels, although human nature is substantially the same as it was centuries ago.

Moreover, many types of war have already been abolished. Cities no longer go to war with other cities, as was the case with Athens and Sparta. States or provinces within nations in our day do not take up arms against each other, although in the past civil wars were frequent occurrences. It was not human nature itself that made civil war unavoidable in those days, because such wars have since been abolished without awaiting the transformation of human nature.

To realize the utter absurdity of the myth that war cannot

be abolished because of the fighting instinct within man, one has only to consider the requirements which must be fulfilled before a modern nation can wage war successfully. Citizens must first be aroused to frenzy of passion by a campaign of falsehood against the enemy. Then governments must idealize the motives and actions of their respective nations, proclaiming themselves to be angels of light in holy conflict with the fiends of darkness. But this combination is not sufficient. Conscription must be resorted to in order to secure the soldiers required for victory. Even after men have been drafted to the front, multitudes of them would not remain there except for fear that they would be shot as deserters. Instead of manifesting enthusiastic eagerness to wage war, as a result of the dominance of the fighting instinct, most men loathe the idea of killing their fellows. Yet advocates of armed preparedness continue to propagate the dangerous myth that war is unavoidable so long as man's biological equipment remains unchanged.

The "mad-dog" theory of war likewise must be dethroned. It would be a fatal mistake to assume that Hitler and Mussolini are the most ominous threats to world peace and that our primary task is to overthrow these dictators. Far more are they products than causes. Looking for a scapegoat is a favorite pastime. Let us not forget the extent to which the Allied world went in portraying the Kaiser as a monster. Few historians now maintain that the Kaiser and the Potsdam gang were chiefly responsible for the outbreak of the World War. In a review of the *Grosse Politik,* Professor Sidney B. Fay wrote: "While it is true that Germany, no less than all the other Great Powers, did some things which contributed to produce a situation which ultimately resulted in the World War, it is altogether false to say that she deliberately plotted to bring it about or was solely responsible for it. On the contrary, she worked more effectively than any other Great Power, except England, to avert it, not only in the last days of July, 1914, but also in the years immediately preceding." [34] Personally I abhor many

---

[34] Sidney B. Fay, quoted by Harry Elmer Barnes, *World Politics in Modern Civilization,* p. 315.

of the policies of Hitler and those of Mussolini, and with all my being I am opposed to their ruthless dictatorships. But I do not believe for an instant that Hitler is uniquely or primarily responsible for the tragic situation now prevailing in Europe. The French policy of security with its attempt to destroy Germany's power is directly responsible for the enthronement of Hitler. To unseat Hitler and leave the basic problem unsolved would prove to be as futile as was the driving of the Kaiser into exile.

Recognition of these essential facts does not, of course, remove the present threat to the peace of the world presented by fascism and militarism in these belligerent countries. Just because the German people have been subjected to extremes of provocation, they have now reacted in the most violent manner. Present-day German nationalism has been fashioned out of misery and hatred, and at this moment constitutes a terrifying threat to other countries. The utterly irresponsible character of fascist dictatorship, coupled with extreme recklessness in dealing with other powers, fills one with apprehension about the peace of the world. Elsewhere I have written at length about the evils of fascism and have recorded my abhorrence of it and all its works.[35] But to attribute the present desperate plight of the nations to fascism is to confuse cause and effect.

VIII

Whatsoever a civilization sows that will it also reap. Over a long period the fertile seeds of economic competition and national rivalries have been scattered freely over the earth. Whether this generation can avoid reaping an abundant harvest of desolation cannot now be predicted with assurance. But one fact stands out like Himalaya: another world war will surely come unless speedy steps are taken to diminish the ruthlessness of economic competition and to reduce the intensity of national passions.

---

[35] *Living Courageously,* pp. 32-46.

Chapter Three

What Must Be Done If War Is To Be Averted?

FOUR POSSIBILITIES are open to the robber nations.[1] First, the ten o'clock and twelve o'clock thieves may attempt through armed power to hold on to their loot. Second, they may divide the booty with the latecomer. Third, they may share the advantages which have accrued to them as a result of aggression. Fourth, they may bring to an end the looting system.

I

In considering the first alternative, we should keep constantly in mind the fact that *the governments of Germany, Italy and Japan will resort to war rather than continue the status quo.* They regard their present positions as intolerable and desperate, so much so that even war is looked upon as a lesser evil. For economic and emotional reasons they are demanding that drastic changes be made in the prevailing international arrangements. Efforts on the part of the more fortunate nations to freeze the status quo under the guise of achieving security will be resisted to the point of a general war by these handicapped powers.

"National Socialist Germany seeks ethnic unity, but in the mood of the modern machine period it also seeks economic security," writes Frank H. Simonds. "In the pathway of German unity, however, stands a military coalition of European states fearful of their own safety, while across her road to prosperity stretch the economic barriers constructed by states which are materially more fortunate and anxious to reserve for

[1] See pp. 29, 30.

themselves the exclusive exploitation of their own natural resources. And against both obstacles the German people are today in revolt. . . . Today those who are the masters of German destinies are not merely training a new generation to the use of arms but are also converting its mind to a gospel of violence because the present material circumstances of the Reich seem insufficient to sustain nearly seventy millions of people and the single alternative seems the choice between another war and a continued decline to economic want and political weakness. On its banners German Youth has embroidered the motto, 'We were born to die that Germany may live.' " [2]

Reasons why the Italians will not accept present arrangements are set forth by the same writer: "It is the example, and not the precept of the British and the Americans which the Italians accept. And with that example they do not quarrel in principle. They think that Italy was excessively badly treated at the Paris Peace Conference, particularly because, unlike Great Britain, France, Japan, and Belgium, she was denied a mandate. But they believe that the cause of her misfortunes was primarily the ineptitude of the Liberal regime which they have abolished. They also believe Italy can never expect better treatment save as Italian strength commands greater consideration. Internationally the strong nation takes what it needs and keeps what it has; that is the Fascist philosophy in a nutshell. And because it expects that Italy will one day be as strong in body as it now is in spirit, Fascism raises no protest to what other nations have done in the past, but only to what they now say about their deeds." [3]

Japan's case is vividly summarized by Nathaniel Peffer: "The basic premise of Japan's philosophy of action is that force is the sole determinant in the relation of nations, more particularly in the Far East. As an interpretation of the last hundred years the premise is unchallengeable, especially in the Far East. Japan can document it from its own experiences and from its

[2] Frank H. Simonds and Brooks Emeny, *The Price of Peace,* pp. 84, 85.
[3] *Ibid,* pp. 144, 145.

observations of China, the Philippines, Java, Malaya and India.
Japan re-entered the world at an abnormal time, a time of in-
ordinate rapacity, though veneered with cant: prime ministers
led congregations in prayer on Sunday, and on Monday sanctioned the rape of provinces and the plundering of helpless
races. Nowhere was the law of grab observed with more con-
secrated fidelity and complete success than in the Far East. In
Africa the international looting was only more brazen. . . .
From 1853 until before 1914 the Japanese watched the Powers
vying with each other in the plundering of China. What they
could not see in the Near East or Africa they could read about.
The connection of ideas they made was unfortunate but logical.
They deduced that no restraints were suffered by the strong in
dealing with the weak. Those took who could. Applying the
deduction, they have based their course in China on the assumption that China would be conquered in any case. It was only
a question which nation would be the conqueror. It is under-
standable that they elected themselves. . . . If Japan is to
realize its ambition it must do so in the next few years. The
time will never be more favorable. Now China is at its weak-
est and is least able to resist. Now the West, too, is at its weak-
est and is least able to oppose. Both conditions are indispensable to Japan's success and they must be present at the same
time. Their coincidence may never recur." [4]

The cumulative evidence leaves no room for doubt that these
three powerful nations will not much longer accept prevailing
conditions. "War is demonstrably the supreme evil for those
peoples which have by past conflict already acquired the essentials of tolerable national life, namely security, prosperity, and
unity. But it is also the sole means by which the peoples lacking these things can acquire them. Thus while the former are
now prepared to throw down the ladder by which they climbed,
the latter will cling to that ladder until a better stairway appears
. . . confronted by such inequalities which to them inevitably
seem unjust and therefore intolerable, peoples will unhesitat-
ingly choose violence rather than submission. That, after all,

---

[4] Nathaniel Peffer, *Must We Fight in Asia?* pp. 89-91.

is the unvarying lesson of history. It is also the contemporary
problem of world peace in a nutshell." [5]

II

No solution is to be found in a division of the loot. Handing
over to the latecomers territories seized in earlier days would
be in most cases impossible. India cannot now be turned over
to Hitler or Mussolini or the Japanese military caste. Several
of the most important British colonies have become independent
dominions. Texas cannot be returned to Mexico and the Philippines cannot be ceded to Japan. Nothing short of fantastic
is the suggestion that the Ukraine and other Russian lands be
awarded to Germany, or that Eastern Siberia be made a Japanese province.

Even though the ten o'clock and twelve o'clock robbers are
just as guilty as the two o'clock thief, the hands of the clock
cannot be turned back. Most of the stolen territory cannot
be restored to former owners and most of it cannot now be
transferred to new landlords.

The colonies taken away from Germany at the end of
the war might be returned to her as mandated territory.
Great Britain and France might make concessions of certain
African lands to Italy and Germany. A number of islands in
the Pacific might be turned over to Japan. But the taking of
these steps *would make little economic difference to the handicapped powers.* Consider four aspects of the problem: raw
materials, markets, fields of investment, outlets for surplus
population.

Germany, Italy and Japan desperately need raw materials
that are not available within their present territories, but these
necessary resources are not to be found in significant quantities
in lands that might now come peaceably into their possession.
If all Germany's former colonies were regained, no substantial
economic relief would be provided. The percentage of the
world's total production of raw materials coming from man-

[5] Simonds *op. cit.,* pp. 42, 43.

dated territories, including Germany's former colonies, is revealed in the following table, the figures being an average of 1930 and 1933: [6]

	Percentage of world's total supply produced in mandated territories.
Lead	1.74
Cotton	.12
Wool	.28
Natural Phosphate	4.25
Raw Silk	.31
Hemp	.20
Cotton Seed	.14
Sesamum	.71
Copra	8.23
Ground Nuts	.85
Palm Oil	5.40
Olive Oil	4.27

Emphasis should be given to the omissions from the above table. Entirely missing are coal, iron ore, petroleum, copper, zinc, tin, bauxite, rubber, sulphur, wood pulp, potash, nickel, manganese, chromite, tungsten, molybdenum, antimony, mercury, asbestos, flax, jute, linseed, hemp seed, and soya beans.

These mandated territories likewise offer comparatively little opportunity for exports of goods and capital from Germany, Italy and Japan. Standards of living are low and purchasing power slight. In the twenty years preceding the World War, Germany's trade with all her colonies amounted to 972 million marks, a negligible proportion of her total trade—in fact only four marks of each thousand marks of total trade.[7] During this period her expenses in the colonies were 1,002 million marks more than local receipts in the colonies. Between 1894 and 1932 Italian exports to and imports from all her colonies were 5,561 million lire. This was less than one lira in each 100 of Italy's total foreign trade in the same period. But during these years Italy spent on her colonies 6,856 million lire. "In 20 years Italy spent 1,300 million lire more on keeping control of her colonies than the total value of all her trade with them

---

[6] John C. de Wilde, *Raw Materials in World Politics*, pp. 166, 167, published by the Foreign Policy Association, 8 West 40th Street, New York City.

[7] Grover Clark, *A Place in the Sun*, p. 134.

in 40 years." [8] The costs of conquering Ethiopia and of its administration far exceed any gains to be derived from Italian control of that country. Mr. Grover Clark has estimated that in the case of Japan, profits from colonial trade approximated one-fifth of the total cost of the colonies to Japanese tax-payers.[9]

These colonies furthermore offer no substantial outlet for surplus population. In 1914 there were in German colonies in Africa and the South Seas only 19,696 Germans. In all Italian colonies, with the exception of the nearby Aegean Islands, in 1931 there were 55,843 foreigners, including Italians.[10] "Out of every hundred persons leaving Europe in the last 50 years to settle elsewhere, less than two went to Africa. . . . Most of the European territory in Africa was taken during this same 50 years. The struggle for that territory was extremely costly, and the jealousies and antagonisms aroused by it helped greatly to bring on the World War. Yet out of it all, the European Powers got territory to which less than 1.5 per cent of the permanent emigrants from Europe went. And those who did go were about seventeen ten-thousandths of the increase in Europe's population in the past 50 years." [11]

Equally revealing is the record of Japanese colonization. After a generation of expensive colonizing education and effort on the part of the government, there were in Manchuria in 1930 only 238,579 Japanese, or less than one-fourth of the annual increase of the Chinese population in Manchuria at that time. After 40 years of colonization, in all the world outside Japan Proper there are less than one and a half million Japanese, or less than two-years' increase in Japan's population.[12]

In the light of these relevant facts, it is disturbing to hear German, Italian and Japanese leaders still propagating hoary myths. A notable illustration is furnished by an article in

---

[8] *Ibid*, p. 134.
[9] *Ibid*, p. 138.
[10] *Ibid*, pp. 87, 88.
[11] *Ibid*, pp. 94, 98.
[12] *Ibid*, pp. 109, 114.

Foreign Affairs [13] by Dr. Schacht, German Finance Minister:
". . . for Germany the colonial question is not today, any
more than it was before, a question of Imperialism or Militarism. To this day it is still essentially a question of her economic existence . . . if her colonies were returned to her she
would proceed to develop them with far greater intensity. A
large part of the food supplies and raw materials which we now
lack could be furnished by them. . . . Germany must produce
her raw materials on territory under her own management.
. . . The German colonial problem is not a problem of imperialism. It is not a mere problem of prestige. It is simply
and solely a problem of economic existence. Precisely for that
reason the future of European peace depends upon it."

If Germany's economic existence depends upon the resources
of her former colonies, her people are indeed doomed. It is a
tragic illusion to believe that the acquisition of available territory by any possible means offers a way out for Germany,
Italy and Japan. Indeed salvation through colonies has long
been demonstrated to be a treacherous mirage even for the ten
o'clock and the twelve o'clock robbers.

At the conclusion of an exhaustive study of imperialism, Professor Parker T. Moon wrote: "Against the gain set the cost.
Many colonies are operated at a deficit, so far as the government's finances are concerned, and the deficit is paid by the tax-
payer of the mother-country. Most colonies are acquired at a
considerable cost, whether in the form of a purchase price or
in the form of military and naval expenditures. As one of the
chief purposes of armaments, especially of naval armaments,
has been to defend colonies against seizure, and to maintain the
diplomatic prestige and influence which make colonial acquisitions possible, part of the armaments expenditures of the last
half-century must be entered in the debit column of imperialism.
Add to that the cost of occasional wars, such as the Russo-
Japanese War, and of countless native insurrections, and the
charges become so heavy as to cast some doubt on the net value
of imperialism, measured in dollars and cents, to the taxpaying

[13] January, 1937.

public in general. In the case of Italy and of pre-war Germany, the net result of colonial ventures in Africa cannot be calculated as anything other than a loss. We can push the analysis farther if we recognize that the cost of imperialism falls on the government treasury, hence on the taxpaying public in general, whereas the direct gain from colonial markets is enjoyed by the corporations, firms, and individuals who do business with the colonies." [14]

The writer of another analysis of imperialism says: "Those in authority and pulling the wires behind the scenes succeeded in convincing their people that they should shoulder the tremendous costs of the preparations and the wars growing directly and indirectly out of the drive for colonies. How great those costs have been, no one ever will know: the costs in human suffering, in accumulated bitterness and hatred, in direct money expenditures in preparations for and during wars, and in property destroyed and trade ruined. A good share of the mad piling of armaments on armaments which ended in the appalling catastrophe of the World War, and of the War itself, must be charged against any benefits the powers received from the colonies which they took in the three decades preceding the War. The people whose lands were seized paid part of the price of this expansion, but the common people of the West paid more, in blood and money." [15]

III

The sharing of economic advantages offers the only way out. While the early robbers cannot in most cases restore the loot, and while an attempted division of the spoils presents no solution, they can share their superior economic advantages with Germany, Italy, Japan and other handicapped countries.

The extreme contrast in relative positions with regard to essential raw materials is revealed in the attached tables. Of the twelve most important strategic raw materials—coal, iron ore, petroleum, copper, lead, zinc, tin, bauxite, rubber, cotton, wool,

[14] Parker Thomas Moon, *Imperialism and World Politics*, pp. 532, 533.
[15] Clark, *op. cit.*, p. 16.

raw silk—Italy produces none or only a negligible quantity of
nine, while Germany and Japan each fail to produce seven of
these twelve essentials.   Careful study of the accompanying
data will reveal more clearly the real nature of the prevailing
international crisis.

SUMMARY OF RELATIVE POSITIONS
Production of 36 Raw Materials and Percentage of Total
World Production[16]

	Number of Commodities of which Specified Nation Produced 5% and Over of Total World Production	Number of Commodities of which Specified Nation Produced 1% to 4.99%	Number of Commodities of which Specified Nation Produced Less Than 1%
British Empire..	24	3	9
United States...	21	4	11
Soviet Russia...	12	5	19
French Empire..	9	9	18
Japan..........	5	7	24
Italy..........	5	3	28
Germany.......	4	3	29

Even more impressive is the result revealed by an examination of the world's production of the eight most important
minerals and of four other strategic raw materials: *coal, iron
ore, petroleum, copper, lead, zinc, tin, bauxite, rubber, cotton,
wool, raw silk.*   The number of these twelve essential raw materials produced by various countries and the percentage of total
world production are as follows:

	5% and Over	1% to 4.99%	Less than 1%
British Empire..	10	1	1
United States...	9	0	3
Soviet Russia...	3	1	8
French Empire..	2	5	5
Japan..........	2	3	7
Italy..........	1	2	9
Germany.......	2	3	7

The extremely favorable position of the United States is revealed in the following summary prepared by Professor
Staley: [17]

---

[16] de Wilde, *op. cit.,* pp. 166, 167.
[17] Eugene Staley, *Raw Materials in Peace and War,* pp. 14, 15.

"It will be seen from the table that in the period 1925-1929, which is used because it was then that world consumption and production of raw materials reached their highest levels, the United States consumed over 60 per cent of the world output of

asbestos, molybdenum, petroleum, platinum, silk, sulphur, rubber, and vanadium;

over 40 per cent of the world output of

aluminum, coal, copper, chromite, camphor, iron, nickel, mica, sisal, and tin;

and over 20 per cent of the world output of

antimony, bauxite, coffee, cotton, jute, manila hemp, lead, manganese, mercury, phosphates, sugar, tungsten, and zinc.

It was the largest consumer in the world of every important metal; of asbestos, coal, mica, petroleum, phosphates, and sulphur; of coffee, raw sugar, camphor, copra, cotton, manila hemp, rubber, raw silk, sisal, tobacco, wool, and probably wheat. It was the second largest consumer of nitrates and the third of tea.

"During the same period, the United States produced over 80 per cent of the world output of sulphur and molybdenum; over 60 per cent of the world output of petroleum; over 40 per cent of the world output of cotton, copper, coal, and zinc; and over 20 per cent of the world output of aluminum, bauxite, iron, lead, mica, phosphates, tobacco, and vanadium.

"The United States during the same period was the world's largest producer of aluminum, copper, iron ore, lead, molybdenum, zinc, coal, mica, petroleum, phosphates, sulphur, cotton, and tobacco, and was practically tied for first place in the production of wheat.[18] It was the second largest producer of bauxite and magnesite, and practically tied for second place in the production of wool.[19] It was the third largest producer of mercury, tungsten, vanadium and nitrates."

---

[18] It has since become definitely second to the Soviet Union.

[19] It has since definitely taken second place. Australia is first, the Soviet Union third.

PRODUCTION OF 36 RAW MATERIALS AND PERCENTAGE OF TOTAL WORLD PRODUCTION*

Column 1 shows number of raw materials of which specified country produces 5% and over of the total world production;
Column 2 represents 1% to 4.99% of total world production;
Column 3 represents no production whatever or less than 1%.

	GERMANY			ITALY			JAPAN		
	Col.1	Col.2	Col.3	Col.1	Col.2	Col.3	Col.1	Col.2	Col.3
Coal	x					x		x	
Iron Ore		x				x		x	
Petroleum			x			x			x
Copper		x				x	x		
Lead		x			x				x
Zinc	x				x				x
Tin			x			x		x	
Bauxite			x	x					x
Rubber			x			x			x
Cotton			x			x			x
Wool			x			x			x
Sulphur			x	x					x
Wood Pulp	x					x		x	
Potash	x					x			x
Nat. Phosphate			x			x			x
Nickel			x			x			x
Manganese			x			x		x	
Chromite			x			x		x	
Tungsten			x			x			x
Molybdenum			x			x			x
Antimony			x		x				x
Mercury			x	x					x
Asbestos			x			x			x
Flax			x			x			x
Raw Silk			x			x	x		
Hemp			x	x			x		
Jute			x			x			x
Cotton Seed			x			x			x
Linseed			x			x			x
Hemp Seed			x			x	x		
Sesamum			x			x		x	
Soya Beans			x			x	x		
Copra			x			x			x
Ground Nuts			x			x			x
Palm Oil			x			x			x
Olive Oil			x	x					x
Totals	4	3	29	5	3	28	5	7	24

*Prepared by the author from statistical data presented by John C. de Wilde, *Raw Materials in World Politics*, pp. 166, 167. Published by the Foreign Policy Association, New York City.

PRODUCTION OF 36 RAW MATERIALS PRODUCED AND PERCENTAGE OF TOTAL WORLD PRODUCTION*

Column 1 shows number of raw materials of which specified country produces 5% and over of the total world production;
Column 2 represents 1% to 4.99% of total world production;
Column 3 represents no production whatever or less than 1%.

	BRITISH EMPIRE			UNITED STATES			SOVIET RUSSIA			FRENCH EMPIRE		
	Column			Column			Column			Column		
	1	2	3	1	2	3	1	2	3	1	2	3
Coal	x			x			x				x	
Iron Ore	x			x			x			x		
Petroleum		x		x					x			x
Copper	x			x					x			x
Lead	x			x					x		x	
Zinc	x			x					x		x	
Tin	x					x			x			x
Bauxite	x			x					x	x		
Rubber	x					x			x		x	
Cotton	x			x					x			x
Wool	x			x			x				x	
Sulphur			x	x					x			x
Wood Pulp	x			x				x				x
Potash			x	x					x	x		
Nat. Phosphate	x			x			x			x		
Nickel	x					x			x	x		
Manganese	x				x		x					x
Chromite	x					x	x			x		
Tungsten	x			x					x			x
Molybdenum		x		x					x		x	
Antimony			x		x				x		x	
Mercury			x	x				x				x
Asbestos	x				x		x					x
Flax			x			x	x				x	
Raw Silk			x			x		x				x
Hemp			x	x			x					x
Jute	x					x			x			x
Cotton Seed	x			x			x					x
Linseed	x			x			x					x
Hemp Seed			x			x	x					x
Sesamum	x					x		x				x
Soya Beans			x		x			x				x
Copra	x			x					x		x	
Ground Nuts	x			x					x	x		
Palm Oil	x					x			x	x		
Olive Oil		x				x			x	x		
Totals	24	3	9	21	4	11	12	5	19	9	9	18

*Prepared by the author from statistical data presented by John C. de Wilde, *Raw Materials in World Politics*, pp. 166, 167. Published by the Foreign Policy Association, New York City.

Production of Essential Commodities by the Favored and the Handicapped Nations

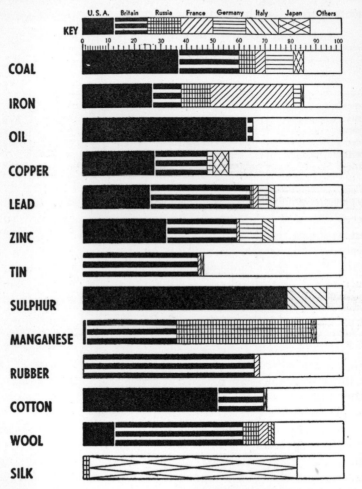

Prepared by the author from statistical data in de Wilde, *op. cit.*, pp. 166, 167.

Germany, Italy and Japan are highly industrialized countries and therefore cannot sustain their dense populations unless they are able to secure the required raw materials.   Truly life-and-death is the struggle for these essentials.   Comparative national incomes are shown in the following table: [20]

NATIONAL INCOME OF SELECTED COUNTRIES, 1928

Country	Income in Respective Currencies (in Millions)	Income in Millions of Dollars	Income in Yen	
			Aggregate in Millions	Per Capita in Yen
Japan.............	11,852 yen	5,501	11,034	178
Italy..............	110,038 lire	5,788	11,611	283
France............	249,745 francs	9,790	19,639	477
Germany..........	68,505 reichsmarks	16,345	32,788	516
United Kingdom...	3,500 pounds	17,032	34,166	748
United States......	88,992 dollars	88,992	178,520	1,488

Gift, conquest and purchase are the three means by which necessities may be obtained. The first alternative must be ruled out as impracticable and undesirable. Attempted conquest under prevailing conditions will lead to war, probably to a world war. Purchase of indispensable raw materials is therefore the only peaceable method of meeting the needs of these handicapped nations. In no other way can a general war be prevented.

How can Germany, Italy and Japan buy the raw materials not to be found within their own borders and yet which are absolutely essential to the operation of their basic industries? This is the crucial question of international relations to which all other inquiries are subordinate. A satisfactory answer offers the best possibility of averting another world war.

Other nations can buy raw materials in the United States and Great Britain, for illustration, if they are able to obtain the required quantities of dollars and of pounds sterling. American producers are eager to sell to buyers of all nationalities, but they will not accept payment in marks, lire, and yen. In fact there is a serious overproduction of raw materials un-

[20] Harold G. Moulton, *Japan,* p. 614.

der prevailing conditions.[21]   The real problem therefore is to
obtain the necessary foreign exchange.   Gold may be used as a
medium of purchase, but Germany, Italy and Japan lack gold
for this purpose.   Five primary means are available: the sale
of their own goods in the United States and other foreign
countries; receipt of foreign currencies for shipping services
rendered, etc.; receipt of dollars and other foreign currencies
from tourists who come to their lands; remittances from German, Italian and Japanese residents of the United States and
other foreign lands; and the obtaining of loans and credits.

The first of these alternatives is far the most important.   The
solution of the economic problem of handicapped countries
depends upon favorable access to the rich purchasing markets
of the earth.   If Germany, Italy and Japan could sell their
commodities on profitable terms in the United States, Great
Britain and other foreign lands they would obtain dollars and
pounds with which to purchase food and necessary raw materials.   Through selling and buying the standard of living
of their peoples would be raised and provocative economic
tensions diminished.

*High tariff walls around the richest markets constitute a far
more serious obstruction than the lack of additional colonies.*
If the Italians had more favorable access to the buyers of the
United States, they would reap greater gains than can possibly
be obtained through the conquest of Ethiopia.   Lowering of
tariff barriers by the United States and by other great powers
would relieve economic distress in Germany and Japan more
than can possibly be brought about by attempted conquest of the
Ukraine and the subjugation of North China.   International
trade is the life blood of nations that are seriously deficient in
essential raw materials.   And high tariffs have the fatal effects
of hardened arteries.

It is thus apparent that Germany, Italy and Japan are victims
of an international situation over which they have feeble control.   By peaceable methods they are not able to bring about

---

[21] See *Overproduction of Raw Materials,* published by The Foreign Policy
Association, New York City.

the essential changes in international economic policies. *Only the favored powers can make the necessary changes by pacific means.* If therefore the United States, Great Britain, France and Soviet Russia fail to make the required adjustments, there is every reason to be apprehensive that Germany, Italy and Japan will resort to war.

Positive and prompt action is called for. Drifting is likely to end in a plunge over the precipice of catastrophe. Lowering tariffs would not necessarily avert war. Other war-making factors will be considered in subsequent paragraphs. But the evidence is clear that apart from the reduction of tariff barriers by the dominant powers there can be no economic salvation for the peoples of the less favored countries.

That the lowering of American tariffs would be beneficial to the nations which desperately need access to our market is apparent. *But what would be the effects upon the United States?* The answer is that various groups in this country would be affected in different ways. This obvious fact is frequently ignored in discussions of the tariff. Many American newspapers concentrate their attention on a single group, with the result that the picture they present is utterly distorted. That some American producers and workers would, at least temporarily, lose profits and jobs if large quantities of foreign goods are bought by their fellow citizens is obvious. For generations therefore high tariffs have been defended as a necessary means of defending American producers and workers.

The extent to which American industries would be adversely affected by foregn competition is often grossly exaggerated. The Foreign Policy Association recently made an exhaustive study of Japan's competition with the United States.[22] From this authoritative document the following quotation is taken: "The importance of Japan in United States trade is not generally recognized. In recent years Japan has usually ranked third among foreign countries as a market for American goods, being exceeded only by the United Kingdom and Canada. As

---

[22] *Japan's Trade Boom: Does It Menace the United States?* by T. A. Bisson.

a source of American imports, on the other hand, Japan has ranked second, exceeded only by Canada. . . . In recent years the United States has ranked first as a supplier of imports to Japan, and until 1934 was Japan's largest export market. In that year China, including Manchuria and Kwantung, took first place in Japan's export trade, with the United States second. . . . Most of the commodities imported from Japan free of duty are materials used by American industry or agriculture. Many of them are not produced in the United States, while the remainder are almost entirely supplementary to rather than competitive with domestic production. . . . A comparatively small section of Japanese imports—only 8.2 per cent of the total value of imports from Japan in 1934—has offered substantial competition to the American manufacturers."

UNITED STATES IMPORTS FROM JAPAN IN 1934

(of items valued at $12,000 or more, classified according to competitiveness with American products)

Classification	Value	Per cent of total imports from Japan
Total imports from Japan.....................................	$117,963,573	100.00
Imports of 271 items valued at $12,000 or more................	116,391,752	98.7
I. Commodities imported free of duty........................	83,863,209	71.1
II. Dutiable imports..	32,528,543	27.6
A. Commodities of which there is no domestic production....	6,656,743	5.6
B. Commodities, the domestic production of which is insufficient...	3,924,498	3.3
C. Commodities imported due to special conditions, either temporary or permanent, and not competitive at time or place of sale....................................	363,726	0.3
D. Commodities of a type not produced in the United States, consumed mainly by Orientals.......................	1,059,898	0.9
E. Commodities sold in the United States chiefly on the basis of their Oriental or novelty nature...................	3,437,687	2.9
F. Commodities distinctly different in type or grade from those produced in the United States......................	5,013,197	4.2
G. Commodities which are competitive but imports of which are negligible in comparison with domestic production	2,359,038	2.0
H. Commodities which are substantially competitive........	9,713,756	8.2

Some American producers and workers would undoubtedly be adversely affected by lower tariffs, although the extent of these losses is often exaggerated, as we have seen. But three other groups of Americans are affected in an opposite way. Some American producers and workers will gain profits and find jobs because of purchases made in this country with the funds received by foreigners from the sale of their goods here. Many essential commodities can be bought more favorably in the United States than elsewhere. If therefore foreigners can secure dollars from the sale of their own goods to us they will eagerly make purchases here. And to this extent our producers and workers are benefited.

Americans as consumers will also receive benefits from the lower prices of foreign goods sold in this country. Every tariff is a form of taxation of the consumer. Except where tariffs are imposed for purely revenue purposes, the very objective is to help maintain high prices. That the net effect of high tariffs is to increase prices to consumers is unquestionable.

Americans as citizens will likewise be benefited by the diminishing of international tensions produced by increased prosperity in the handicapped countries. Because the relief of economic distress in Germany, Italy and Japan is a necessary condition of avoiding war, and because the reduction of tariff barriers by the United States and Great Britain especially is a prerequisite of the solution of the economic problem in the less favored nations, citizens of the United States would find it to their advantage to reduce obstructions to international trade. The financial savings due to smaller appropriations for armed preparedness made desirable by a less provocative international situation, and the increased likelihood of avoiding the colossal costs of war must be emphasized.

Ethically sensitive individuals will also take into account the effects of our high tariffs upon the peoples of the more distressed areas. Even if high tariffs do not cause war, they surely do increase the economic burdens resting upon the backs of millions of human beings in other lands. The fixing of tariff schedules with the single objective of increasing our own gain, without regard to disastrous consequences for other peoples, is an immoral practice.

From the perspective of a world view, the case against high tariffs is sound and convincing. *Over against the American producers and workers who lose profits and jobs because of*

*foreign sales in this country, stand other American producers
and workers who gain profits and find jobs because of increased
foreign purchases in this country with the funds obtained from
goods sold here, American consumers who profit from lower
prices due to imports from other lands, American citizens who
benefit in countless ways from a less provocative international
situation brought about by increased prosperity in the more
belligerent countries, as well as the peoples of the lands in which
economic misery is reduced by freer international trade.* The
heart of the situation is laid bare in the accompanying boxed
summary.

The Roosevelt administration is committed to a policy of
lowering tariffs through reciprocal trade agreements. By February, 1937, such agreements had become effective with sixteen
countries: Belgium, Brazil, Canada, Colombia, Costa Rica,
Cuba, El Salvador, Finland, France, Guatemala, Haiti, Hon-
duras, The Netherlands, Nicaragua, Sweden, Switzerland.
These agreements constitute steps in the right direction and
deserve popular support. The fact should be emphasized, however, that Germany, Italy and Japan are not included in the list
of countries with which reciprocal agreements have been made.

Ten years ago a leading American financial journal published an editorial entitled, "The Wars of the Tariffs." These
words have an even more valid ring now: ". . . never before
did the tariff stand out so prominently as an enemy to human
progress and an obstacle to peace. . . . All over the world the
Tariff is making trouble. . . . Does not this Tariff seem to be
as much an 'out worn creed' as war itself? . . . Tariff, start-
ing as a tax, as a revenue producer, ends as reprisal. A tit for
tat tariff breeds enmities that breed overt war. Reducing
tariffs, obliterating them, makes for peace. Tariffs sow the
seeds of war. Yet they are increasing in the earth—are a
constant source of turmoil and trouble. . . . There is no amity
or good-will in a barrier to the natural course of trade. Thus
a tariff is against the progress of the world. It is against the
happiness of mankind. It is against the Great Will that created

EFFECTS OF LOWER TARIFFS
UPON VARIOUS GROUPS CONCERNED

First Group:
American producers and workers who lose profits and jobs because of American purchases abroad.

Second Group:
American producers and workers who gain profits and find jobs because of increased foreign purchases here with dollars obtained from foreign sales in this country.

Third Group:
American consumers who profit through the lower prices paid because of foreign sales here.

Fourth Group:
Peoples of foreign lands who profit from the sale of their goods here and thereby obtain raw materials required for prosperity.

Fifth Group:
Government officials of foreign lands whose policies are made less provocative because of the easing of economic tensions through higher prosperity due to increased foreign trade.

Sixth Group:
American citizens who profit through lower taxes for armed preparedness and through the diminished likelihood that they will become involved in another world war.

the earth and distributed its varied resources and human energies. Yet all Governments employ it. To set it up, is to show at once the need of modifying it, of reducing its power to stop the flow of goods. Is it sacred, is it even sacrosanct? By no means. Only selfishness cries for a system which sustains better wages, better living conditions of one people (its alleged merit) at the expense of all others. It is a barbarism growing out of feudal times when the King, Prince or ruler took what he could by force of arms and kept his plunder in the same way. To sell, a people must buy. All now know this. Yet in the grasp of selfish politics this agency of spoliation continues to shatter the concord of the world. And will!" [23]

Seven years ago Professor Gilbert Murray wrote: "As I look towards the future of our civilization I see ahead only two causes that may bring it finally to ruin; one is another European War between the Great Powers; the other is a general resort to Protection. And in essence these are not two causes, but one." [24]

IV

It is not enough for the ten o'clock and the twelve o'clock robbers to share the economic advantages which have accrued to them as a result of aggression. They must bring to an end the looting system. *So long as they maintain imperialistic control over conquered territories, they will continue to stimulate Germany, Italy and Japan to extend their own empires.* The dynamics of imperialism are partly economic and partly psychological. Territories are seized not only because of supposed economic advantages, but also for prestige and power. Bowing down before the god of imperial grandeur is not confined to public officials, but is practiced also by millions of devotees among the rank and file of people. The glories of empire are constantly portrayed by Mussolini, but he had many predecessors. "Every Englishman," writes Bernard Shaw in his *Man*

[23] "The Wars of the Tariffs," *The Financial Chronicle*, Oct. 8, 1927, pp. 1891, 1892.

[24] Gilbert Murray, *Tariffs and Peace*.

of Destiny, "is born with a certain miraculous power that makes him master of the world. When he wants a thing he never tells himself that he wants it. He waits patiently till there comes into his head, no one knows how, the burning conviction that it is his moral and religious duty to conquer those who have the thing he wants. Then he becomes irresistible. Like the aristocrat he does what pleases him and grabs what he wants; like the shopkeeper he pursues his purpose with the industry and steadfastness that come from strong religious conviction and deep sense of moral responsibility. He is never at a loss for an effective moral attitude. As the great champion of freedom and independence, he conquers half the world and calls it Colonization."

The colonial system may be brought to an end by granting complete independence or by a genuinely international administration of mandates. The British Dominions are now almost entirely self-governing, with the privilege of withdrawing from the British Commonwealth of Nations if they should ever so desire. India should quickly be given full status as a dominion, or granted complete independence outside the British Commonwealth if this alternative is desired by the Indian people. The Philippine Islands should be granted complete independence, without reservations of naval bases by the United States and with economic agreements which are favorable to the Filipinos during a period of adjustment.

Certain backward regions of the earth may well be treated as mandates and administered by a genuinely international body in the interests of the peoples of these lands. The mandate system of the League of Nations constitutes a long step in the right direction but at present is characterized by grave weaknesses. It was devised as a means of dealing with Germany's former colonies and with parts of Turkey which were detached at the end of the war.

Under a satisfactory system, the mandate would be administered by an international body rather than by an imperialist power. The chief weakness of the prevailing system is found in the fact that a single nation acts as mandatory for a back-

ward area. Great Britain, the British Dominions and France
dominate the mandated territories. Japan obtained a mandate
over certain islands in the North Pacific, and Belgium became
mandatory power for Ruanda-Urundi in Africa. Thus it is
apparent that the two great imperialist powers increased their
predominance at the expense of Germany and Turkey. The
extent of the territories now governed as mandates is shown in
the following table: [25]

DATA ON MANDATED TERRITORIES

Mandate	Mandatory	Population (1931)	Area Sq. Mi.
A Mandates			
Palestine	United Kingdom	1,035,154	9,010
Transjordan	United Kingdom	305,584	15,444
Syria and Lebanon	France	2,656,596	62,163
B Mandates			
Cameroons	France	2,186,015	165,928
Cameroons	United Kingdom	774,585	34,236
Ruanda-Urundi	Belgium	3,450,000	20,541
Tanganyika	United Kingdom	5,063,660	374,085
Togoland	France	725,580	20,077
Togoland	United Kingdom	293,671	13,240
C Mandates			
Islands, North Pacific	Japan	73,027	830
Nauru	British Empire (Australia acting)	2,692	8.43
New Guinea and Islands	Australia	392,816	93,000
Southwest Africa	South Africa	242,290	322,393
Western Samoa	New Zealand	46,023	1,133

The mandatory powers do not exercise legal sovereignty over
the mandated territories and are supposed to govern under specific terms laid down by the League of Nations. These conditions are designed to protect the interests of the native peoples
and to prevent excesses of exploitation. "Nevertheless, there
are few people who will assert that each of the fourteen mandated areas is being administered today in every respect as a

[25] Denys P. Myers, *Handbook of the League of Nations*, p. 106.

'sacred trust of civilization.' The primary interest of the British Empire in Nauru seems to be in phosphates; the government of Australia seems to smile more benevolently upon the European plantations and gold fields of New Guinea than upon its native wards; the Union of South Africa is attempting to fasten the color bar upon the mandate of Southwest Africa, and the administration and the settlers of this mandate frankly regard the natives as a commodity; Belgium is using its over-populated mandate of Ruanda-Urundi as a labor reservoir for the Katanga mines in the Congo; the French have bled the Cameroons for administrative purposes; French misrule in Syria, culminating in the revolt of 1925, has been notorious. Even in Tanganyika, where an admirable native policy has been followed, an attempt is being made to introduce the plantation system already followed with such disastrous results in the neighboring colony of Kenya. If this attempt succeeds and Tanganyika is converted into a white man's colony, the principle of the mandate will have been violated." [26]

That there have been abuses is not surprising when the history of imperialism is kept in mind and when we remember the conditions under which the mandate system was inaugurated. "When the Peace Conference met Japan was in occupation of the North Pacific islands and had secret treaties made in February and March, 1917, with Great Britain, France, Russia, and Italy agreeing to support her claim to acquire them. Australian forces were in occupation of German New Guinea and Nauru and New Zealand forces were occupying German Samoa, while the secret treaty with Japan had recognized Britain's claim to the German islands south of the Equator. South African troops under General Botha had occupied German Southwest Africa and South African public opinion vigorously demanded annexation. British forces under General Smuts had occupied East Africa with the exception of a small region on the Congo border held by Belgians. The French and British had occupied Cameroons and Togoland and M. Simon, colonial minister of

---

[26] Raymond Leslie Buell, *The Mandates System After Ten Years*, published in *Current History*, December, 1929, p. 549.

that power, argued for 'annexation pure and simple.' British
forces under Maude and Allenby were holding Mesopotamia,
Palestine, and Syria but the British had invited French forces
under Gouraud to occupy the Lebanese and Syrian littoral and
Cilicia in 1919 in pursuance of various secret treaties distributing Turkish territory made in 1915 and 1916. These
states having sacrificed blood and treasure for the territories
were not inclined to accept internationalization. Independence
was barred by the same considerations." [27]

Professor David Hunter Miller reminds us that "the French,
or at least the French Colonial Office, wanted to annex part of
the Cameroons and Togo; and the three British Dominions interested wanted to annex respectively German South West
Africa, New Guinea and German Samoa." [28] Although General Smuts is credited with being the father of the mandate system, he did not want it applied to the former German colonies
in Africa but favored outright annexation of these territories.
Indeed C mandates may be "administered under the laws of
the Mandatory States as integral portions thereof." Later
General Smuts wrote: " 'C' mandates are in effect not far removed from annexation." [29] Concerning the inauguration of
the mandate system, Professor Quincy Wright says that it was
"mutilated in details, sullied by the spirit of barter, delayed in
confirmation, and minified by the mandatories." [30]

Notwithstanding its handicaps and weaknesses, the mandate
system is a vast improvement over the older forms of colonial
imperialism. It needs to be improved and extended. In sum-
marizing its advantages, Professor Wright says: "The system
has already resulted in wider recognition of the principle of
trusteeship, that dependencies should be administered in the
interests of their inhabitants; in the principle of tutelage, that
the cultivation of a capacity for self-government is such an interest; of the principle of international mandate, that states are

[27] Quincy Wright, *Mandates Under the League of Nations*, pp. 26, 27.
[28] *Foreign Affairs*, January, 1928, p. 280.
[29] Wright, *op. cit.*, p. 62.
[30] *Ibid*, p. 63.

responsible to the international community for the exercise of power over backward peoples even if that responsibility is not fully organized." [31]

Professor H. R. G. Greaves, of the London School of Economics, writes: "It is quite clear that much has been done by the League to apply the principles of the Covenant, that Mandatory Governments have always been anxious that their policy should appear to be in harmony with the terms of the trust they have undertaken, and that in many cases it has really been so. The existence of the Permanent Mandates Commission, the obligation to report to it, and its power to cross-examine in private and criticize in public, have formed an instrument of really practical value for ensuring the application of the principles contained in Article 22. But it must be remembered in all fairness to the administrators of mandated territory—and in particular of B and C Mandates—that the 'principle that the well-being and development of such peoples form a sacred trust of civilization' is too new to be easily applied. Such a revolution is not made in a day, or even in ten years. The theory that these peoples are mere barbarians—to use the words of General Smuts himself—cannot be destroyed by merely writing on paper such phrases as 'sacred trust' and 'well-being and development.' The tradition of race superiority and supremacy, and of its consequence, exploitation, dies hard. It dies particularly hard when the job of hastening its end is given to the type of expert colonial administrator for whom that very tradition has been a comforting thought in exile, or when the task is conferred upon army generals accustomed to autocracy, and suffering also, perhaps, from the disease of power, as it has been named." [32]

The intolerable character of the old system has been vividly outlined by Professor Leonard Barnes of the University of Liverpool: "An empire as a form of political organization is subject all the time to three kinds of friction, three kinds of

---

[31] *Ibid*, p. 588.

[32] H. R. G. Greaves, *The League Committees and World Order*, pp. 192, 193.

strain. First there is the resentment and the incipient revolt of the oppressed peoples in the colonies. Second, there is the friction generated between the controlling power and other powers who exercise or hope to exercise rival imperial controls themselves. And third, there is the class struggle waged by those wage-earners at home who are largely excluded from the benefits of the imperial system and of the economic order generally. Empire has always to resist these three destructive forces which challenge it from within and from without. . . . I submit there is a far more plausible and far simpler explanation than the special immorality of foreign nations, and that is the existence of exclusive armed commercial empires in the world. Take the British Empire, which most of us here happen to know best. Ever since the last war we have been busy organizing the Empire in accordance with an economic scheme by which the 65 millions or so of its white-skinned members have arranged for the systematic exploitation of its 430 millions of dark-skinned members. The Empire as it stands today is a plutocracy governed by a small white minority at the expense of an immense colored majority which lives for the most part at a level of primary poverty. Not only do we stand in those relations inside the Empire, but we have at the same time been building round the outside of it a wall more and more formidable of tariff restrictions, quota arrangements, embargoes, and the rest. We have been doing our best to exclude foreign nations from the benefits of economic and commercial contact with the coloured members of the Empire . . . our old-fashioned and out-dated Empires are threatening the world's peace. If you want to build up the guarantees of a stable peace based on agreement, I submit that you are obliged to attempt the reorganization of those Empires, . . . by reference to a world order and a world community, instead of by reference to the old destructive aim of exclusive national advantage." [33]

On the voyage to the Peace Conference, President Wilson suggested that "the German colonies should be declared the

[33] Leonard Barnes, "The Future of Imperialism," *Problems of Peace,* 11th Series, pp. 183, 184, 197.

common property of the League of Nations and administered by small nations. The resources of each colony should be available to all members of the League." Because the victors were unwilling to take this step, they subjected Germany, Italy and Japan to powerful stimulus to acquire additional territories for themselves. The ten o'clock and twelve o'clock robbers cannot end the looting system until they are willing to apply the mandate principle to the backward territories now in their own possession as the result of past conquests.

V

National sovereignty must be sufficiently abridged to make possible the effective functioning of world organization. So long as each nation attempts to determine its own basic policies without due regard for the interests of other countries, international friction will hold the peoples of the earth on the edge of the war-precipice. Year by year the degree of interdependence is becoming more extreme. The growth of industrialism and advances in the spheres of transportation and communication have made it impossible for the respective peoples to live aloof from the rest of the world. Exports and imports are the life-blood of industrialized and urbanized nations. Points of contact are therefore multiplying and occasions of quarrels are increasing. Imperialism offers no road of escape but rather leads straight to war. Mutual cooperation through world organization is absolutely essential.

The real nature of the world's present dilemma may be more clearly discerned from the perspective of history. Consider the situation which confronted the thirteen states in the days immediately following the Revolutionary War.[34] When the Constitutional Convention assembled in 1787, the calamitous effects of anarchy among the states were everywhere visible. "There are combustibles in every State," wrote Washington, "which a spark might set fire to." Shay's rebellion in Massa-

---

[34] A portion of this section is printed also in my pamphlet, *Patrick Henry and Senator Lodge.*

chusetts was merely the most ominous of a series of riots and uprisings. The impotence of the Confederation has long been apparent. The Continental Congress had been formed in 1774 as a means of taking common action against England, but not until after a delay of seven years were the Articles of Confederation signed by Maryland, as the thirteenth colony to ratify "the firm league of friendship." Each state had one vote in the Congress, and the consent of nine states was required to pass any important measure. Salaries of the delegates were paid by the respective states, and much of the time a quorum was not present and legislative activities were halted. During the seven months beginning with October, 1785, on three days only were representatives of nine states on the floor, and a similar condition prevailed during the following year.[35]

Sharp restrictions were placed upon the jurisdiction and power of Congress. It had no authority to raise money or to regulate commerce, and could only make requisitions and await responses from the 13 sovereign states. Even during the perilous days of the Revolutionary War, the states frequently failed to accede to its entreaties for troops and funds. At a critical period Washington recorded the fact that hardly a state had provided as much as one-eighth of its quota of soldiers. During 1781 financial requests of the states amounted to five million dollars, of which only $422,000, or less than one-tenth, was remitted. Not a cent came from Georgia, North Carolina, South Carolina, or Delaware. Paper money to the extent of over 400 million dollars was issued by Congress and the states, with the result that its rapidly diminished value gave rise to an expression which has lingered until this day: "It isn't worth a Continental!" Professor Schlesinger tells of a barber who

---

[35] Further details concerning the difficulties confronted by the Federal Government in its early days may be found in the following volumes: A. C. McLaughlin, *The Confederation and the Constitution;* Charles A. Beard and Mary R. Beard, *The Rise of American Civilization,* Volume I; Charles A. Beard, *An Economic Interpretation of the Constitution of the United States;* Breckinridge Long, *Genesis of the Constitution of the United States of America;* J. S. Bassett, *The Federalist System;* Louise Irby Trenholme, *The Ratification of the Federal Constitution in North Carolina.*

found it a matter of economy to paper his shop with Continental money.

Professor Beard has pointed out that the Continental Congress was "little more than a glorified debating society speaking for 13 independent states, each of which claimed to be sovereign and was deeply occupied with its own problems, civil and military." Professor Nevins reminds us that "nine States, from Massachusetts on the north to South Carolina on the south, organized their own navies, and some States established their own systems of privateering. Several States fitted out their own armies, and used them for State purposes." The prestige and authority of the Continental Congress degenerated to such a degree that in 1783 its members were compelled to flee from Philadelphia to Princeton, in order to avoid being seized as hostages by a band of mutinous soldiers. "Thus in a city of thirty-two thousand inhabitants, the largest city in the country," wrote John Fiske, "the government of the United States, the body which had just completed a treaty browbeating England and France, was ignominiously turned out-of-doors by a handful of drunken mutineers."

The cleavage between the Eastern and Southern states was sharp and bitter. One section was engaged in commerce and shipping, while the other region was covered with plantations operated by slave labor. Their economic interests were as antagonistic as those of present-day nations. In the Federal Convention the East contended that laws affecting navigation and commerce should be passed by a majority vote in Congress, whereas the South, wishing to block undesirable legislation, held out for a two-thirds vote. For economic and humanitarian reasons the Eastern states urged the abolition of the slave trade; while self-interest made the Southern states belligerent.

Mr. Pierce Butler considered the interests of the Southern and Eastern states "to be as different as the interests of Russia and Turkey"; while Mr. Elbridge Gerry could not restrain "his fears that a civil war may result from the present crisis of the United States." Territorial disputes, which have always been among the most dangerous of controversies, added fuel to the flames. When the Federal Convention opened its sessions there were eleven interstate boundary controversies outstanding. Tariffs and retaliatory measures still further embittered relations among the states. New York, for example, imposed a duty upon firewood, butter, cheese, chickens and vegetables from New Jersey and Connecticut, "just as was done by ships from London and Hamburg." In retaliation Connecticut merchants signed an agreement, under $250 penalty, not to send a dollar's worth of goods to New York for twelve months. James Madison recorded the fact that "Some of the States, Connecticut, taxed imports as from Massachusetts higher than imports even from Great Britain. . . ." John Fiske once expressed the opinion that if it had not been for the successful outcome of the Federal Convention, "another five years would scarcely have elapsed before shots would have been fired and seeds of perennial hatred sown on the shores that look toward Manhattan Island." Immediately after the signing of the Constitution, George Washington appealed in vain to Patrick Henry for support. "From a variety of concurring accounts," he wrote, "it appears to me that the political concerns of this country are in a manner suspended by a thread, and that the Convention had been looked up to, by the reflecting part of the community, with a solicitude which is hardly to be conceived; and if nothing had been agreed on by that body, anarchy would soon have ensued, the seeds being deeply sown in every soil."

The doctrine of sovereignty has always constituted one of the most formidable barriers to peace. In commenting upon the jealousy exhibited by the respective states, Washington deplored the "thirst for power, and the bantling—I had like to have said MONSTER—sovereignty." So reluctant were the states to impair the "precious jewel of sovereignty" that the Continental Congress was merely a "mutual court" where ambassadors gathered together to negotiate with "foreign" powers.

In 1787 the idea of a superstate was viewed with alarm. In one of his numerous speeches Patrick Henry complained:

"This Constitution is said to have beautiful features; but when I come to examine these features, sir, they appear to me horribly frightful. Among other deformities, it has an awful squinting; it squints toward monarchy. . . . Your president may easily become king. . . . I would rather infinitely, and I am sure most of this Convention are of the same opinion, have a king, lords, and commons, than a government so replete with such insupportable evils. . . . As this government stands, I despise and abhor it." Mr. Tredwell of New York expressed the opinion that "our lives, our property, and our consciences, are left wholly at the mercy of the legislature, and the powers of the judiciary may be extended to any degree short of almighty. . . . This government is founded in sin, and reared up in iniquity . . . and I fear, if it goes into operation, we shall be justly punished with the total extinction of our civil liberties." In quaint language, Mr. Holmes, of Massachusetts, expressed an apprehension that "we shall find Congress possessed of powers enabling them to institute judicatories little less inauspicious than a certain tribunal in Spain, which has long been the disgrace of Christendom: I mean that diabolical institution, the Inquisition."

The prestige and authority of the Federal Government was so low during its first decades that frequently men of high ability refused to accept office. Professor Bassett records the fact that "five men of Revolutionary distinction refused the secretaryship of state in 1795." President Jefferson found the task of securing a capable Secretary of the Navy so difficult that he laughingly suggested that it might be necessary to advertise for a candidate. De Witt Clinton resigned from the Senate of the United States to become Mayor of New York City. Chief Justice John Jay resigned from the Supreme Court in order to run for Governor of New York, and when in 1800 he was tendered a reappointment by President Adams, he declined because he was convinced that the Supreme Court "under a system so defective" would never "obtain the energy, weight, and dignity which were essential to its affording due support to the National Government, nor acquire the public confidence and respect which, as the last resort of justice of the nation, it should possess." In a recent interpretation of the Constitution, we read: "During the same interval there were also several resignations among the associate justices. So, what with its shifting personnel, the lack of business, and the brief semi-annual terms, the Court secured only a feeble hold on the imagination of the Country." John Randolph expressed the opinion that the judiciary had become a "hospital for decayed politicians." Alexander Hamilton once described the Constitution as "a frail and worthless fabric."

During the first three years of its history only five cases came before the Supreme Court, and only 55 cases were heard before John Marshall ascended the bench on February 4, 1801. In the famous Chisholm case which came before the Court in 1793, the first instance in which a decision against a state was handed down, the Court ordered Georgia to pay a judgment to Mr. Chisholm. Whereupon the Georgia Legislature met, and instead of making the required appropriation, passed a law to the effect that anyone who attempted to enforce the decision of the Court was guilty of a crime and would be hanged. A decade later Judge Todd of Kentucky, in referring to the Supreme Court, said: "We resist every idea of having our suits decided by foreigners."

From 1793 to 1795 the famous Whiskey Rebellion threatened the very foundation of the national government. Objection to the tax on liquor was so violent that the legislatures of North Carolina, Virginia, and Maryland passed resolutions against the law. In Pennsylvania armed resistance was offered, and President Washington found it necessary to send an expeditionary force to quell the rebellion. In 1800 one of John Jay's correspondents moaned: "Old Gates used to tell me in 1776 that if the bantling independence lived one year, it would last to the age of Methuselah. Yet we have lived to see it in its dotage, with all the maladies and imbecilities of extreme old age."

In the Cherokee case in 1831 Georgia again flatly refused

to abide by a decision of the Supreme Court and was supported by the President of the United States. It was on this occasion that President Jackson made his famous remark: "Chief Justice Marshall has made his decision; now let him come off the Bench and enforce it." In the same year the *United States Telegraph* thundered: "This court has no more right to meddle with our questions than has the court of King's Bench in London." About this time John Quincy Adams confided to his diary: "The union is in the most imminent danger of dissolution. The ship is about to founder." To his colleague, Justice Story, John Marshall wrote despairingly: "I yield slowly and reluctantly to the conviction that our Constitution cannot last. Our opinions are incompatible with a united government even among ourselves. The Union has been prolonged thus far by miracles. I fear they cannot continue."

This long citation of evidence reveals clearly the menace of interstate anarchy. In our day the threat of international anarchy is even more severe because the failure to create and utilize effective international agencies of justice may lead to the destruction of civilization in the conflagration of another world war. The economic interdependence of present day industrial nations is more pronounced than it was among the original thirteen states. Advances in transportation and communication have brought the peoples of Asia, Africa, Europe and America closer together than were the citizens of Georgia and Massachusetts. When President Washington in 1791 visited Charleston and Savannah, he traveled the round-trip distance of 1,800 miles on horseback and required three months' time for the journey.

International agreement, international administration and international adjudication are essential to the maintenance of world peace. World goverment in any marked degree similar to the Federal Government of the United States cannot be established within the near future, so deep rooted is the concept of national sovereignty and so virulent are national antagonisms. But the minimum requirements of the present situation are the limitation of national sovereignty and the acquiring of the habit of international cooperation.

The havoc being wrought by the prevailing dogma of national sovereignty can scarcely be exaggerated. Even a moment's sober reflection makes clear the menacing character of the doctrine that a nation is an ultimate political entity exercising the right to determine its own course of action without restraint from any external source. For surely it is obvious that in an interdependent world, with humanity divided into some sixty units, the conflict of interests among unrestrained nations leads to war. The full significance of this fact was hidden from the pre-war generation partly because the pioneering period of world expansion had not completely ended, and partly because the great powers of Europe had refrained from war with each other for four decades. But it will be criminal blindness if we longer refuse to look the present situation squarely in the face and then act upon the basis of understanding.

"Every one ought to know," writes W. Arnold-Forster, "as part of his historical equipment, how anarchic, how really lunatic, were the assumptions upon which responsible statesmen conducted international relations, at least so lately as twenty and thirty years ago. All the Foreign Offices were engaged in a deadly game of bluff and counter-bluff and genuine menace, with war as their ultimate instrument. The Kaiser described the game with refreshing candour when he wrote in 1899, apropos of The Hague discussions on arbitration, 'In practice I, at any rate, will henceforth rely and call upon God and my bright sword alone; and damn their resolutions.' The Kaiser was not alone: that is what they were all doing in greater or lesser degree—relying upon their own bright swords and their exclusive alliances with God." [36]

The inevitable consequences of the continuation of the old system are pointed out by the Marquis of Lothian: ". . . the ultimate cause of the war was the European anarchy in which

---

[36] W. Arnold-Forster, "Order and Self-Defence in the World Community," *Problems of Peace,* 5th Series, p. 231.

every state had to depend upon its own arms or its alliances
for its security, and it was nobody's business to think of Europe
as a whole. . . . In an anarchic world *macht-politik,* power
diplomacy, becomes inevitable. Nations must think in terms
of security rather than of merits. And all the time the soldiers
and sailors and airmen are whispering to the statesmen the
risks they run if they allow their neighbors to gain an advantage, in territory, in armament, in the diplomatic game
of bluff, because it may make the difference between defeat
and victory in the event of war. Then the decision begins to
pass out of the hands of statesmen and Parliaments. A knave,
a fool or an accident can precipitate an event in some corner
of the world which thrusts the diplomats on one side and puts
the military time-table in command and slides the whole world
into a war which nobody wants. Anarchy, not national
wickedness, was the villain of the tragic drama which ended
in the World War. The most sinister fact today is that this
time-table has begun to reappear, made immensely more dangerous by the air." [37]

"The state is irresponsible," writes Harold J. Laski. "It
owns no obligation save that which is made by itself to any
other community or group of communities. In the hinterland
between states man is to his neighbour what Hobbes says was
true of him in the state of nature—nasty, mean, brutish.
Politically, in its judgment of what it is entitled to do, a state
considers not the interest of humanity as a whole, not the
obvious precepts of judgment and right, but the basest considerations of expediency, as it chooses to interpret them. A
state becomes, in short, the judge of its own cause, and it is
elementary that that is a denial of justice. . . . If there is
one outstanding fact in the modern world it is that the fact
of a world-market has made a world-economy, and that everything that interferes with the movement of that world-economy
is so much taken from the prosperity of the world, and by
that amount so much taken from the standard of life of the
people. Things that are shared in common by one nation and

[37] The Marquis of Lothian, *Pacifism Is Not Enough,* pp. 23, 24.

another can only be decided in common by one nation and another.   The politics of power or the politics of prestige are in this connection fatal to the well-being of the world.   The national sovereignty that makes up its mind that its tariff laws or its immigration laws, or what you will, are matters upon which its own unaided and uncontradicted word is the final decision in the making of the ultimate result is thereby a traitor to the unification that we need . . . if any nation-state is entitled to regard itself as an isolated factor in an inter-connected world, and to use its rights as a sovereign power to enforce the consequences of its isolation, the result is the destruction of the civilization." [38]

The imperative necessity of opening the eyes of rank and file citizens to the significance of the dogma of national sovereignty has been emphasized by Professor Rappard: "That doctrine as an ideal is today condemned by most clear-sighted and in-dependent students; but it is still proclaimed and indeed extolled by practically all politicians. . . . A politician, if he be a practical democrat, talks with a view to being elected or re-elected.   This implies no criticism.   Such are the rules of the game to which he is obliged to conform.   If he failed to do so and thus forfeited his usefulness, he might be a brilliant student, but he would be a poor politician.   Now, to exalt national sovereignty as the guiding principle of future evolu-tion towards peace would be for the scholar the shortest road to disastrous error, but for the politician it is the safest road to success at the polls.   In other words, the people, the true sovereign in all so-called enlightened countries, while they want peace and prosperity, are insistent on committing their chosen representatives to an international philosophy which cannot but breed war and misery." [39]

The tenacity with which the nations cling to the dogma of national sovereignty and the zeal with which they seek isola-

---

[38] H. J. Laski, "International Government and National Sovereignty," *The Problems of Peace,* 1st Series, pp. 292-295.

[39] Professor W. E. Rappard, "The Beginnings of World Government," *The Problems of Peace,* 5th Series, pp. 3, 4.

tion and self-sufficiency are responsible for the tragic weakness of the League of Nations. We now recognize the folly of blaming the Continental Congress of the thirteen states for its impotence in the hour of crisis. It was the doctrine of state sovereignty which paralyzed cooperative action. And so today national sovereignty is strangling the effort to prevent war. And upon no country must heavier responsibility be placed than upon the United States. In smug complacency our people are doing their full share in perpetuating the armed anarchy that now threatens to destroy civilization.

In the next chapter consideration will be given to ways and means by which the League of Nations may be transformed into a more effective instrument for the prevention of war.

VI

Termination of the prevailing race of armaments is necessary if a great war is to be averted. Huge armies and navies are provocative sources of passion and fear. They render impotent pacific means of settling international controversies and expose the peoples of the earth to the mercy of an incident. The more acute fear becomes and the higher passions rise, the more dominant becomes the military mind. With the ascendency of general staffs, appropriations for war purposes mount, and to this end propaganda designed to generate suspicion and hostility pours like lava into the minds of patriots everywhere. Competent observers of world affairs recognize the terrifying menace of this race of armaments, but statesmen in all lands rise to heights of eloquence in disclaiming responsibility for this madness.

That Hitler and Mussolini and the Japanese military caste are responsible is the easy answer now being given in many quarters. The utterances and actions of leaders in Germany, Italy and Japan are cited as proof of the necessity of increased armaments in other lands. The re-arming of Great Britain is widely heralded as the strongest bulwark of peace. *But surely the evidence is incontestable that the re-armament of*

*Germany was directly due to the refusal of her conquerors to
reduce to her level their own armies and navies.* The terms
imposed at Versailles and executed with rigor disarmed Germany so far as heavy instruments of war were concerned and
reduced her fighting strength to that of a second-rate power. A
superb opportunity for general reductions of armaments was
thus presented. It was passed by, however, because the French
theory of security called for a heavily armed France and a disarmed Germany. Lack of perspective caused the French to
dash wildly down a blind alley. Armaments can never lead to
permanent security. Let the French ask themselves what they
would have done from 1919 onward if they had stood in German shoes. No great power will ever consent to disarmament for herself while her hereditary enemy is heavily armed.
There is simply no disputing the statement that the French
policy is directly responsible for German re-armament.

Listen to the German case as presented by official spokesmen.
In an address to the German people on May 17, 1933, following Germany's withdrawal from the Disarmament Conference
and from the League of Nations, Hitler said: "Germany has
disarmed and has carried out this disarmament under the strictest international supervision. Six million rifles and carbines
were handed over or destroyed; 130,000 machine-guns, enormous quantities of machine-gun barrels, 61,000 guns, 38.75
million shells and enormous stocks of other arms and ammunition had to be destroyed or handed over by the German nation.
The Rhineland was demilitarised, the German fortresses were
destroyed, our ships were handed over, our air-craft destroyed,
our military system abandoned and the training of reserves
thereby prevented. Even the essential defensive arms were
forbidden. . . . Germany has thus a completely justified moral
claim to the fulfilment by other Powers of their obligations
under the Treaty of Versailles. . . . What assurances has
Germany received in return for this? According to the figures
published by the League, France alone has 3,046 aeroplanes in
service, Belgium 350, Poland 700, Czechoslovakia 670. In
addition to this there are innumerable reserve aeroplanes, thou-

sands of tanks, thousands of heavy guns and all the necessary technical equipment for chemical warfare. Has not Germany greater justification in her state of defencelessness and disarmament in demanding security than heavily-armed States bound together in military alliances? Germany is, however, entirely willing to undertake further obligations of international security if all the other nations are ready on their side to do the same, and if this security is also to benefit Germany. Germany would also be perfectly ready to disband her entire military establishment and destroy the small amount of arms remaining to her, if the neighboring countries will do the same thing with equal thoroughness. But if these countries are not willing to carry out the disarmament measures to which they are also bound by the Treaty of Versailles, Germany must at least maintain her demand for equality . . . the German Government will not reject any prohibition of arms as being too incisive if it is applied in the same manner to other States. These demands do not imply rearmament but a desire for the disarmament of the other States. . . . I am obliged to state that the reason for the present armaments of France or Poland can under no circumstances be the fear of German invasion of those nations, for such fear would be only justified by the existence of modern offensive weapons. Germany, however, does not possess such modern offensive weapons; she has neither heavy artillery nor tanks nor bombing aeroplanes nor poisonous gases. The only nation therefore which has the right to fear invasion is the German, which not only may not possess offensive weapons but is also restricted in its right to defensive weapons and is forbidden to erect frontier fortifications. Germany is at all times prepared to renounce offensive weapons if the rest of the world does the same." [40]

Foreign Minister von Neurath, on September 15, 1933, said: "For fourteen years the victorious powers put up an attitude of platonic friendship and confined themselves to theoretical manifestations of sympathy towards the various democratic

[40] Quoted by Richard Schmidt and Adolf Grabowsky, in *Disarmament and Equal Rights,* pp. 202-206.

governments of Germany. In practice their policy tended on all essential questions to keep Germany in the fetters of Versailles, prevent any revision of the Treaty though this was declared capable of revision in 1919, and perpetuate the discriminating treatment of Germany. Just as at Versailles, any argument was good enough if it served to injure Germany, and just as principles of a moral, economic, historical and juridical nature were never applied in any single case on lines of equality but interpreted and exploited in perfectly one-sided fashion with their point ever directed against Germany, just as much is it at present intended to apply a different standard to Germany. Ladies and Gentlemen, it is about high time for the countries outside of Germany to wake up to the fact that Germany has the full right to defend itself against this spirit of Versailles with all the power at its disposal. . . . Does that mean that Germany wishes to re-arm? The heavily armed States continue with their armaments, and instead of disarmament talk about their security." [41]

German spokesmen constantly emphasize the fact that the Allied governments have failed to carry out definite promises to reduce their own armaments. Part V of the Treaty of Versailles begins with these words: "In order to render possible the initiation of a general limitation of the armaments of all nations, Germany undertakes strictly to observe the military, naval and air clauses which follow." Part V of *The Reply of the Allied and Associated Powers to the Observations of the German Delegation on the Conditions of Peace* contains these words: "The Allied and Associated Powers wish to make it clear that their requirements in regard to German armaments were not made solely with the object of rendering it impossible for Germany to resume her policy of military aggression. They are also the first steps towards that general reduction and limitation of armaments which they seek to bring about as one of the most fruitful preventives of war, and which it will be one of the first duties of the League of Nations to promote. They must point out, however, that the colossal growth in armaments

[41] *Ibid*, pp. 209-211.

of the last few decades was forced upon the nations of Europe by Germany. As Germany increased her power, her neighbours had to follow suit unless they were to become impotent to resist German dictation or the German sword. It is therefore right, as it is necessary, that the process of limitation of armaments should begin with the nation which has been responsible for their expansion. It is not until the aggressor has led the way that the attacked can safely afford to follow suit."

The Allies agreed to make peace upon a basis of the Fourteen Points, which included: "adequate guarantees given and taken that national armaments will be reduced to the lowest point consistent with domestic safety." Emphasis should be placed upon *domestic* safety.

Let American patriots ask themselves what their own country would have done if the United States had been placed in a position parallel to that of Germany since 1919. Indeed, the suggestion may reasonably be made that they examine the prevailing policy of national defense of their own land. Appropriations for the United States army and navy during the current year exceed a billion dollars, including certain amounts allocated from relief funds. What is the purpose of this huge expenditure? By what standard is "adequate" national defense measured?

The State Department and the Navy Department are following contrasting policies. The people of the United States should make up their minds which is the sounder policy and insist that their government in all its branches adhere to it. The State Department assumes that the United States means to observe the obligation imposed by Article II of the Kellogg-Briand Pact, namely: "The High Contracting Parties agree that the settlement or solution of all disputes or conflicts of whatever nature or of whatever origin they may be, which may arise among them, shall never be sought except by pacific means."

In line with this commitment, President Roosevelt and Secretary Hull have announced the abandonment of the practice of armed intervention by the United States in Latin America

U.S. NAVAL POLICY

Naval policy is the system of principles, and the general terms of their application, governing the development, organization, maintenance, training, and operation of a navy. It is based on and is designed to support national policies and national interests. It comprehends the questions of number, size, type, and distribution of naval vessels and stations, the character and number of the personnel, and the character of peace and war operations

FUNDAMENTAL NAVAL POLICY OF THE UNITED STATES

To maintain the Navy in sufficient strength to support the national policies and commerce, and to guard the Continental and overseas possessions of the United States

GENERAL NAVAL POLICY

To create, maintain, and operate a navy second to none and in conformity with Treaty provisions.
To develop the Navy to a maximum in battle strength and ability to control the sea in defense of the nation and its interests.
To organize the Navy for operations in either or both oceans so that expansion only will be necessary in the event of war.
To maintain the Marine Corps in strength sufficient to furnish detachments to vessels of the fleet, guards for shore stations, garrisons for outlying positions, and to provide expeditionary forces in immediate readiness.
To make war efficiency the object of all development and training and to maintain that efficiency at all times.
To protect American lives and property.
To support American interests, especially the development of American foreign commerce and the merchant marine.
To make foreign cruises to cultivate friendly international relations.
To encourage and to lead in the development of the art and material of naval warfare.
To maintain a definite system of progressive education and training for naval personnel.
To determine emergency material needs, and to plan for procurement.
To inspect systematically all naval activities and materials.
To cooperate fully with other departments of the Government.
To encourage civil industries and activities useful in war.

APPROVED May 10, 1933   Secretary of the Navy.

Claude A. Swanson.

for the purpose of protecting American property and life. Indeed, this Government has entered into a general treaty which contains the following provision: "The High Contracting Parties declare inadmissible the intervention of any one of them, directly or indirectly, and for whatever reason, in the internal or external affairs of any other of the Parties." This inclusive and drastic commitment was entered into at the Buenos Aires Conference in 1936 and has been ratified by the United States Senate.[42]

In his circular note of May 16, 1933, to the heads of fifty-four nations, President Roosevelt proposed: "That all the nations of the world should enter into a solemn and definite pact of non-aggression; that they should solemnly reaffirm the obligations they have assumed to limit and reduce their armaments, and, provided these obligations are faithfully executed by all signatory powers, individually agree that they will send no armed force of whatsoever nature across their frontiers." He restated this proposal to Congress in the following terms: "That subject to existing treaty rights no nation during the disarmament period shall send any armed force of whatsoever nature across its own borders." And in his Wilson Day address of December 28, 1933, the proposition was again stated in less qualified terms: "That no nation will permit any of its armed forces to cross its own borders into the territory of another nation. Such an act would be regarded by humanity as an act of aggression and as an act, therefore, that would call for condemnation by humanity."

The proposal was thus presented to the general disarmament conference by Norman H. Davis on May 22, 1933: "If we are to keep faith with these obligations (the Pact of Paris), we must definitely make up our minds to settle our disputes around a conference table instead of preparing to settle them on the battle-field. It was with such a thought that the President proposed an undertaking by the nations that, subject to existing treaty rights, armed forces should not be sent across national frontiers. In the long run, we may come to the

---

[42] See *Foreign Policy Reports*, July 1, 1937.

conclusion that the simplest and most accurate definition of an aggressor is one whose armed forces are found on alien soil in violation of treaties."

The Navy Department, however, adheres to a contrasting policy. Notwithstanding the fact that the United States has bound herself in the Kellogg-Briand Pact never to seek the settlement of any dispute except by pacific means, the Navy Department includes in its published basic policy the function of protecting American interests, commerce, property and lives in all parts of the earth. "To support the national policies and commerce" by armed action or threats of armed action is a policy that cannot be reconciled with the solemn renunciation of war as an instrument of national policy in Article I of the Kellogg-Briand Treaty: "The High Contracting Parties solemnly declare in the name of their respective peoples that they condemn recourse to war for the solution of international controversies, and *renounce it as an instrument of national policy* in their relations with one another."

Appropriations for the United States Navy are made on the assumption that the armed forces of the United States may be called upon to serve as instruments of national policy. The basic premise of the prevailing system of national defense is that we must be prepared to wage war in the enemy's country. In 1917 and 1918 a vast majority of the American people thought they were fighting a defensive war against Germany, yet they took it for granted that hostilities would be waged as near to Berlin as possible. Many years ago Mahan, America's greatest exponent of navalism, said bluntly: "War, once declared, must be waged offensively, aggressively. The enemy must not be fended off, but smitten down. You may then spare him every exaction, relinquish every gain; but till down he must be struck incessantly and remorselessly." [43]

Certain rebels within military and naval circles, however, challenge this dominant policy, notably Major General Hagood and Major General Butler. They maintain that an effective system of national defense should be based upon prepared-

[43] Mahan, *The Interest of America in Sea Power,* pp. 192, 193.

ness to defend our own soil and not upon preparedness to send our armed forces to distant lands.   They point out that with well-fortified harbors, a moderate navy and a moderate air force, the United States becomes impregnable against successful invasion by a foreign foe.   An invading army of enormous size would be required and would have to be supported by foreign naval forces of vastly greater strength in our waters than that of the American defensive fleet, since the effectiveness of a navy diminishes in ratio to distance from its bases.

Listen to the testimony of Major General Hagood of the United States Army: "Considered from a defensive standpoint America is the strongest military nation on earth—that is, it is the easiest nation to prepare for defensive warfare. It would not take much to make it invulnerable against any nation or any combination of nations that could possibly be brought against it. . . . Let's turn the problem around and examine the difficulties that we would encounter in sending a large expeditionary force to Japan, to Germany or to Russia. . . . British experience during the World War indicated that about forty pounds of general cargo per soldier per day was required to supply an army from an overseas base.   In the A.E.F. we started out with that figure.   We attempted to build up a ninety-day reserve for an army of two million men, but we did not get very far with it.   So we arbitrarily shortened our objective.   On the basis of two million men, we would have had to unload at the ports an average of forty thousand tons of cargo per day.   We shortened our objective to thirty thousand, but, as a matter of fact, we never reached twenty-five.   Our shortage was met by the Allies. . . . We had all of the French ports at our disposal.   Our line of communication across the ocean was never seriously threatened. And all we had to do was to run our ships back and forth like ferryboats.   But our difficulty was in getting the ships loaded at one end of the line and getting them unloaded at the other and, after that, evacuating the ports.   For this, we had the French railways and a magnificent system of highways, none of which was in any way interfered with by the enemy.

In order that the reader may get a physical conception of what is meant by forty thousand tons of cargo per day, I will say that there are only five ports in the United States that handle so much tonnage, and that if it could have been loaded on army trucks it would have required a daily truck train over 150 miles long. . . . If the United States has an adequate navy, plenty of submarines, an aggressive air force and all of our harbors sealed against enemy ships, the chances of an invasion must surely be very small. . . . It has long been understood that the American Navy cannot meet a serious opponent in the western Pacific. . . . In time of peace our shipping requires no protection. We do not have to protect it against pirates, and we would not risk war by forcing it into places where it was not wanted. In time of war we could not insure the safety of our shipping through the waters controlled by any of the Great Powers of western Europe. Trade routes would be infested with submarines, aircraft and surface vessels working from near-by bases and making these routes untenable. Even during the World War we had to depend upon Great Britain to help us guard our transports. . . . But if an enemy fleet did attempt such a thing and succeeded in avoiding ours, its position would be untenable when it got near our coast. The enemy, in slipping past, would have left our fleet on its line of communication, on its routes of fuel and supply. It would soon be located and brought to battle. Its situation then would be almost beyond hope. Thousands of miles from its docks, its repair, its fueling and its supply bases, fighting a superior fleet in close proximity to home bases, its fate would be like that of the Great Armada." [44]

In a volume of nearly 500 pages, Mauritz A. Hallgren presents the results of an extensive study of America's war policies. The following summary is taken from this illuminating book: "Step by step, as one examines the problem of invasion, one finds the impossible becoming ever more impossible. There is no enemy in sight and none is likely to appear. And even were this non-existent enemy miraculously to materialize, to

[44] Major General Johnson Hagood, *We Can Defend America,* pp. 3-35.

discover some now undiscoverable motive for attempting to invade the United States, the mathematical odds against his successfully moving a sufficiently large force against the United States to accomplish his purpose would be so overwhelming that he would never try it.   Rationalize and declaim as they may, the generals and admirals simply cannot show that America stands in any danger of being invaded. . . . Naval authorities concede, though usually only by implication, that a British fleet as powerful as or even more powerful than the American navy, cannot successfully invade American waters.   Captain Knox has pointed out that 'even with numerous adequate bases at hand the (British) Grand Fleet during the late war had great difficulty in maintaining enough ships in readiness at all times to meet with superior force a possible sally of the (German) High Seas Fleet, this notwithstanding the fact that theoretically the comparative strength between the Grand Fleet and the High Seas Fleet was in ratio of five to three.' It must be remembered that the German fleet was but a short distance off, while in trying to reach American shores a British fleet would have to travel almost three thousand miles. What proportion of its effective strength could it bring against the American navy if it were to make such an attempt? . . . Admiral Yarnell has said that in an Anglo-American war 'Canada would either declare her neutrality, or be invaded, and Canadian ports denied to the British fleet.   The other remaining British possessions in the western Atlantic and the Caribbean would be occupied by our forces.   Lacking bases, Great Britain could not send her battle fleet to the western Atlantic. . . .'   In sum, though the British had twice the naval strength of the United States, dwellers along the Atlantic coast would need have no fear of a British naval attack.   The chances of a successful attack are practically nil and Britain, therefore, would never attempt it.   Japan's chances of successfully investing the other coast are even less, for the Japanese would have twice as much open sea to cross, and they have no naval bases or other possessions on the American side of the Pacific. . . . 'When we come to discuss the problem of defending the Pacific coast,' Admiral Yarnell said, 'it is reasonable to assume that the enemy will require the same advantages and preponderance to come to our coast that we feel are necessary to us in advancing our forces to the western Pacific. Hence the inhabitants of the Pacific coast can sleep quietly in their beds until Japan builds a navy twice the strength of that of the United States.' In truth, as a number of authorities, including Admiral Yarnell himself, have shown, even with a navy more than twice as strong the task of the Japanese would be hopeless if they did not have also a place to rest and to repair their ships on the American side of the Pacific. . . . In sum, then, so far as territorial defense goes, the United States would be perfectly secure with half the navy that it has today. Indeed, it could get along with a good deal less than that." [45]

Admiral Sir Herbert Richmond points out that naval comparisons are often misleading: "No absolute comparisons of power can be made. Japan is stronger than America for war in Northern Asia, but weaker for a war in the Caribbean. England is stronger than America for a war in the Indian Ocean but weaker for one on the coasts of the Pacific. Any of the military states of the Continent is stronger than America, England or Japan for a war on the Continent. Is there not reason to suspect that many of our present troubles arise from refusal to recognise these facts? Are not the parallel growths of the fleets of the United States and Japan the result in some measure, perhaps a marked measure, of each trying to make itself stronger than the other in an area in which one possesses all the advantages of position." [46]

Major General Smedley D. Butler is advocating an "amendment for peace" with the following provisions:

"1. The removal of members of the land armed forces from within the continental limits of the United States and the Panama Canal Zone for any cause whatsoever is hereby prohibited.

---

[45] Mauritz A. Hallgren, *The Tragic Fallacy*, pp. 69, 170-176.
[46] Admiral Sir Herbert Richmond, *Sea Power in the Modern World*, p. 316.

"2. The vessels of the United States Navy, or of the other branches of the armed service, are hereby prohibited from steaming, for any reason whatsoever except on an errand of mercy, more than five hundred miles from our coast.

"3. Aircraft of the Army, Navy and Marine Corps is hereby prohibited from flying, for any reason whatsoever, more than seven hundred and fifty miles beyond the coast of the United States." [47]

Citizens of the United States should make up their minds which policy of national defense they desire and insist that all branches of their government adhere to it. The prevailing policy is unnecessary, ineffective and highly expensive. Let taxpayers study the accompanying tables.

NATIONAL DEFENSE EXPENDITURE OF THE WORLD, 1931–1936*
(in millions of dollars—1936 parity)

Regions	1931	1932	1933	1934	1935	1936
United States..	707.6	667.8	540.3	710.0	911.7	964.9
Britain........	449.0	426.1	455.5	480.6	595.6	846.9
France.......	694.8	509.2	678.8	582.7	623.8	716.4
Germany......	246.8	253.5	299.5	381.8	2,600.0	2,600.0
Italy.........	272.0	270.6	241.2	263.7	778.1	870.8
U.S.S.R......	280.8	282.5	309.5	1,000.0	1,640.0	2,963.1
Japan........	131.8	199.1	253.1	271.9	296.2	307.2
World Total....	4,067.2	3,815.7	3,992.0	5,064.1	8,810.1	10,730.7

(60 Countries)

MILITARY EXPENDITURES OF THE GREAT POWERS
(in millions of national currency)

Great Britain	Army	Navy	Air	Total
1913–14.............	....	....	....	77.2
1930–31.............	31.6	43.6	17.0	95.1
1936–37.............	47.8	71.6	49.5	173.9
France				
1913–14.............	....	....	....	9,035.0
1930–31.............	6,278.5	2,722.7	2,018.9	16,073.9
1937...............	10,078.0	4,460.2	3,688.3	19,238.7

[47] *Woman's Home Companion*, September, 1936, p. 4.

* William T. Stone & Helen Fisher, "The Rising Tide of Armament," *Foreign Policy Report*, February 15, 1937, pp. 283, 292.

MILITARY EXPENDITURES OF THE GREAT POWERS—(*Cont.*)
in millions of national currency

Germany	Army	Navy	Air	Total
1913–14.............	....	....	....	1,168.6
1931–32.............	....	....	....	617.0
1936–37.............	....	....	....	6,500.0
Italy				
1913–14.............	....	....	....	3,711.6
1931–32.............	2,828.0	1,489.7	695.1	5,439.6
1937–38.............	2,491.0	1,793.0	1,250.0	5,534.0
Japan				
1913–14.............	....	....	....	330.7
1931–32.............	227.5	227.1	....	454.6
1936–37.............	507.5	551.9	....	1,059.4
U.S.S.R.				
1913–14.............	....	....	....	869.5
1931.................	....	....	....	1,404.0
1937.................	....	....	....	20,012.0
U.S.A.				
1913–14.............	....	....	....	244.6
1930–31.............	345.3	354.1	....	699.4
1937–38.............	393.5	598.1	....	991.6

In a later section I shall present reasons for opposing the entire system of *armed* defense. But acceptance of the pacifist position is not the only justification for rejecting the present naval policy of the United States. Even with the premise that armed defense is necessary, the most that is required is armed preparedness to defend our own soil.

VII

The Peace Amendment introduced by Congressman Ludlow provides that war shall not be declared by Congress until previously approved by a nationwide referendum of American citizens. Surely the people have a right to decide the momentous question as to whether or not their sons and fathers and husbands and brothers shall be sent to wage war on foreign soil. The text of this proposed amendment to the constitution is as follows:

Section 1. Except in the event of an invasion of the United States or its territorial possessions and attack upon its citizens residing therein, the authority of Congress to declare war shall not become effective until confirmed by a majority of all votes cast thereon in a Nation-wide referendum. Congress, when it deems a national crisis to exist, may by concurrent resolution refer the question of war or peace to the citizens of the States, the question to be voted on being "Shall the United States declare war on . . . . ?" Congress may otherwise by law provide for the enforcement of this section.

Section 2. Whenever war is declared the President shall immediately conscript and take over for use by the Government all the public and private war properties, yards, factories, and supplies, fixing the compensation for private properties temporarily employed for war purposes at a rate not in excess of 4 per centum, based on tax values assessed in the year preceding the war.

VIII

The transformation of competitive capitalism into a cooperative commonwealth is essential to the abolition of war.[48] War may be delayed in the meantime and particular armed conflicts may be averted, but enduring world peace cannot be established upon the pillars of capitalism and nationalism. In a later section I shall deal briefly with the steps which must be taken if capitalism is to be supplanted by non-warlike means. Elsewhere I have written at length upon this subject.[49] At this point it seems desirable that emphasis be placed upon the ways in which a competitive economic society increases the likelihood of war among nations.

Gross inequality of wealth and income within a given country; the wielding of vast political power over foreign policy by rich industrialists and financiers; the mentality and habits created among the people at large by daily familiarity with ruthless economic struggle for private gain—these are significant factors which drive nations toward war. And all of them are inseparable from competitive capitalism.

[48] See Norman Thomas, *Human Exploitation;* Harry W. Laidler, *A Program for Modern America;* George Soule, *The Coming American Revolution.*
[49] See *Individualism and Socialism,* and *Living Courageously.*

Gross inequality of wealth creates a situation where the masses of workers do not receive sufficient income to purchase the volume of goods they produce; whereas a small minority of rich owners cannot spend their incomes upon themselves in a socially useful way and cannot find profitable sources of investment for their excess savings. This combination of surplus goods that cannot be sold at home and surplus capital that cannot be satisfactorily invested greatly intensifies the international struggle for foreign markets and domination of foreign fields of investment. The additional combination of glutted home markets and millions of unemployed workers reenforces powerfully the trend toward higher tariffs and other restrictions against foreign goods.

"It is the law of capitalism that it must engage in a ceaseless struggle against the tendency of the rate of profit to fall," writes Mauritz A. Hallgren, "for only by maintaining the rate of profit can production and exchange be continued and the elementary needs of the capitalist nation be satisfied. Capitalism must at the same time, however, and in consequence of this very struggle, strengthen the forces that tend to depress the rate of profit. For it is not by profit alone, but also and more essentially by the accumulation of capital, that capitalism lives. That part of the national income that goes into the purchase of consumption goods is spent, consumed; it earns no profit. It is and can be only that part which is invested in new capital goods upon which future profit can be earned. Hence capitalism must go on endlessly accumulating capital. But as capital is accumulated, as the facilities for turning out goods are improved and enlarged, the productivity of capital increases; and the more productive it becomes, the greater is the pressure on the rate of profit. . . . Were all of this surplus capital to be put to work in the domestic economy, it would tend to depress the rate of profit still further and eventually to wipe it out altogether. For this reason capitalism in each country is compelled in ever greater measure to look abroad for outlets for its surplus capital and for markets for its surplus goods." [50]

The wielding of vast political power over foreign policy by rich industrialists and financiers increases the belligerency of the state in its controversies with other states. The relatively small number of individuals who have a considerable financial stake in foreign trade and foreign investments are the same persons who have comparatively more control over foreign policy. Government is not neutral in the class struggle. With temporary exceptions, the powers of government are exercised in behalf of the most powerful economic groups. This power is exercised partly by direct control of individaul officials of government, and partly indirectly through domination of the press, the radio, the movies, the schools and other agencies of public opinion. Concentration of economic power therefore means that a financial oligarchy with the highest stake in foreign affairs exercises dominant control.

"The capitalism we know," writes Harold J. Laski, "is a system in which the effective motive to production is the profit made possible by such ownership. This system implies a special system of class-relations, and the essence of its habits lies in the fact that the power of the state is used to maintain the implications of these class-relations. The whole effort of the state, therefore, is directed to securing the owner's right to profit. . . . Exactly as it uses its force to protect the interest of the capitalist at home, so it uses force to protect his interest abroad. The value to it of its sovereignty in the international field is precisely that, in extreme cases, it can bring force into play against any rival which seeks to interfere with the expression of its will. If it surrendered that sovereignty, it would be subject to rules; and, so long as it observed them, it would not be able to make the might at its disposal the measure of the right it may seek to enforce. . . . An international order, to be effective, must control things like currency, tariffs, labour standards, migration, access to raw ma-

[50] Hallgren, *op. cit.,* pp. 336-338.

terials, the penetration of backward areas, and so forth. But to control these things, it must be able to override the existing vested interests which use the sovereignty of the state for their protection. It cannot override them, as the world is at present organized; for they arise inherently from the class-relations of a capitalist society. The forces which protect them are exactly the same as the forces which protect the power of the capitalist inside the national society to which he belongs. Exactly as the sovereign state protects, in the internal sphere, a system of legal rights intended to safeguard his supremacy, so, externally, its authority, by the sheer logic of his relationships with it, must be used to impose that supremacy, so far as may be, upon others. It is only as these class-relations are transformed that state-antagonisms become capable of any fundamental reconciliation. Upon the existing basis, the utmost goodwill in international relations can only postpone, without being able to avoid, the ultimately inevitable conflict.[51]

The mentality and habits created among the people at large by daily familiarity with ruthless economic struggle for private gain are in the last analysis responsible for the outbreak of international war. Powerful industrialists and chauvinistic patriots cannot wage war without popular support. Corruption of the minds and degradation of the characters of citizens in general are charges that must be laid at the door of competitive capitalism. It would be folly to say that capitalism alone must shoulder this responsibility. But the accepted principles and practices of a competitive economic society are constant incitations to greed and callousness and ruthlessness. The idea that an individual is entitled to all the privilege and power that he can lay hands upon; the glorification of grabbing as a method of distributing the necessities, comforts and luxuries of life; the division of society along lines of extreme wealth and extreme privation; the blindness that comes from wielding power and the numbness produced by prolonged exploitation; the degree of suppression and brutality used in maintaining vested

[51] Harold J. Laski, *The State in Theory and Practice*, pp. 208-218.

privileges and the ease with which workers follow this example of resorting to violence in their struggle for justice; the craving for excitement on the part of millions who are doomed to monotony and sordidness—all these make it easy for people whose lives are dominated by competitive capitalism to resort to war. Such individuals are easy prey for jingoists and militarists. With appalling enthusiasm they rush madly over the brink of international suicide.

The present threat of another world war is not due to lack of understanding of the prevailing malady, or to ignorance concerning remedies. The trouble is that the popular mode of life in capitalist and fascist countries makes effective action exceedingly difficult. Concerning the findings of the World Economic Conference of a decade ago, Professor Gilbert Murray says: "I think it is no exaggeration to say that if the advice of that Conference had been taken by the Governments there would be no crisis now, or, at any rate, the crisis would be vastly less acute. A great effort was made by two or three Governments and by important private societies in many countries, to try to get the Governments of the world to take that advice, but the attempt failed completely. Hence we have the present state of affairs. Each Government, instead of taking the advice of the economists of the world and trying to get some world order into economics, preferred to follow what seemed to be its own interest and to tackle the difficulty by means of economic war. Following upon that situation, there was the present World Economic Conference in London, and for perfectly simple reasons, that has been, with certain small allowances, a very great failure. I do not want to criticise any particular person, but I remember that in Canada one important minister, a very able and high-minded man, won his election on the cry 'Canada First'! I expect it was the same in other countries. Is it remotely probable that the Canadian electorate as a whole would *not* put Canada first? Of course they would. When a man comes to an electorate already disposed by every natural instinct to put their own interests first, and passionately urges them to put themselves first, the result is that they must put themselves quite wildly and unreasonably first. And so, having had a movement of this sort in most of their countries, the delegates went into an economic conference where one said, 'Now, we must all agree to put Canada first'; and another said, 'Australia first'—I confine myself to the British Empire in order not to be offensive to other nations—while another said, 'That's right, except, of course, that it ought to be South Africa first.' Naturally, the Conference broke. Each Government wanted to fight for itself. There was again the lack of the spirit of world order, the spirit which subordinates the nation's immediate interest to the interest of the whole community of nations." [52]

The law of the harvest is inexorable: whatever we sow that we reap. From the sowing of competitive struggle for private gain, civilization reaped a world war. Whether it is too late to prevent another harvest of desolation cannot now be told. But surely the evidence is indisputable that the only hope we have is to gain time in which the seed of a cooperative commonwealth will have an opportunity to grow into a ripe harvest.

[52] Professor Gilbert Murray, "A Survey of Recent World Affairs," *Problems of Peace*, Eighth Series, pp. 4, 5.

Chapter Four

Is an International Police Force Needed?

" JUST AS local government would be paralyzed without the presence of a police force, international agencies of justice cannot function effectively unless supported by an international police force." How valid is this oft-repeated analogy?

Significant characteristics of a police force should be stressed. The police are agents of a sovereign government and do not act on their own authority. Passing sentence upon or executing judgment against the lawless is not part of their legitimate function. Prisoners are turned over to judges for trial, and if found guilty, to prison wardens or to executioners. Police action is used against lawbreakers only, not against their relatives and neighbors. The police force of one city is not equipped and trained for attacks upon policemen of another community. In the exercise of their legitimate duties, the police do not bombard and demolish whole areas or massacre inhabitants wholesale irrespective of their guilt or innocence. Popular support of a police system would quickly be withdrawn if constantly it produced more casualties and fatalities among the innocent members of the community than among criminals.

A *bona fide* international police force must be the servant of a genuinely international government. Resort to armed action by one nation against another is not police action, even though the avowed purpose is to redress wrong, as for example armed action by the United States Marines in Nicaragua. An armed alliance of two or more powers does not constitute a truly international police force. When a score of nations engaged in

95

armed hostilities against Germany, they were not exercising
police power in any valid sense. The prevailing confusion of
thought and terminology is illustrated by the statement of the
author of a huge volume on this subject that "the action of
those nations which participated in the Great War in defence
of Belgium's neutrality and the maintenance of international
law approximated to a police function." [1] To be justified in
using the name, an international police force must be supported by practically all nations of the earth.

International police is a designation used with different
meanings. When armed soldiers from several different countries acted in behalf of the League of Nations as supervisors in
the Saar elections, many commentators used this as an illustration of successful action by an international police force.
More frequently, however, international police force is a term
used to designate an armed body of men gathered from several
countries by an international government for the purpose of
resisting aggression by a recalcitrant national government.
Concerning the first of these practices, no question is raised
as to the practicability of establishing and maintaining such a
body. But there are sharp divergencies of opinion with regard to the desirability and practicability of international police
in the latter sense.

Discussions of this question are entirely theoretical because
under modern conditions an international police force has never
been pitted against the lawbreaking government of a powerful
nation. There seems to be no question about the ability of a
united League of Nations to use armed force successfully
against a small country. But surely there is no reason to
doubt that other means than armed attack are available for
effective use against a weak government. Could an international police force operate successfully in restraining one or
more great powers? Is it desirable that an attempt be made to
establish and maintain a system of international police?

[1] David Davies, *The Problem of the Twentieth Century*, p. 7.

I

The essential condition of an effectively operating system of international police is that it should be under the control and direction of an international government possessing a wide range and high degree of sovereignty. Until this condition is fulfilled, nothing more than an armed alliance embracing several or many states can be achieved. So long as national sovereignty prevails in its present form and to the existing degree, an international agency will continue to be subject to the conflicting interests and whims and passions of national governments. Relinquishment of a sufficient degree of national sovereignty to make possible the creation of an authoritative and powerful international government is a prerequisite of effective international police action against a great power. "The fundamental fact is," writes Professor Rappard, "that peace cannot be guaranteed to and against sovereign states by an un-sovereign League. Only if the League were endowed with that kind of sovereignty to which all states, and particularly the great powers, still pretend today, could it enforce peace." [2]

Substantial reductions in national armaments must be brought about before an international police body will be able to enforce peace. Under prevailing conditions, millions of armed men equipped with the latest weapons of destruction would be required for successful armed action against a recalcitrant great power. To be effective, declares a British admiral, an international police requires the "existence of a permanent armed force in an unarmed world, whose certainty of action, readiness to act, and irresistible power, command confidence as completely as the confidence in the internal police forces of nations." [3]

In emphasizing this fact, Professor Clyde Eagleton, an ardent supporter of a system of armed international action against an aggressor nation, says: "We thus arrive at our final

[2] William E. Rappard, *The Geneva Experiment*, p. 111.
[3] Richmond, *op. cit.*, p. 238.

conclusion: that states must surrender some of their national sovereignty and accept such rights as are agreed upon by the community; that for this purpose an international organization is necessary; and that this international organization must be backed by an overwhelming physical force, strong enough to assure to each state the security which it seeks. Until such an international government is created, it is not to be expected that any state will surrender its right to make war; not until it can be assured that its disputes can be settled, its wrongs can be remedied, and its rights enforced." [4]

National governments must develop the will to pacific settlement of all disputes with other countries and must commit themselves to the use of international agencies of justice before international police power will be practicable. A beginning has been made in the Kellogg-Briand Treaty, but this commitment is purely negative. The signatories agree never to seek the settlement of disputes except by pacific means, but they do not bind themselves to use pacific agencies of international justice. The importance of this condition is stressed by Mr. David Davies, one of the most zealous and persistent supporters of an international police system: "When nations are prepared to refer all disputes, including the revision of treaties, to a world tribunal without any reservations, the International Force can be ushered on the stage, but not before." [5]

Another prerequisite is the creation of faith in international agencies on the part of governments and peoples. Lack of confidence in government always undermines security. Huge national armaments will be maintained and relied upon until the belief prevails generally that international government is able to provide security. "We know by now," writes D. Mitrany, another advocate of international police action, "that we have not the smallest chance of being successful in this unless we can offer the nations some assurance that in disarming they will not be left at the mercy of some international miscreant. Much more important it is to get arbitration accepted

---

[4] Clyde Eagleton, *Analysis of the Problem of War*, p. 122.
[5] *International Affairs*, January, 1932, p. 77.

as the normal method of settling international disputes. Without some guarantee, arbitration, even if formally accepted, will lead a precarious existence. Not that the nations are of bad faith, but in a time of crisis their temper is unreliable. One country, knowing that there is nothing to restrain the other from attack, and to aid herself against it, may be too fearful to face the risks of patience; and it may rush into 'defensive' actions, as Austria and Russia did in 1914, which only increase the panic in both camps until it grows beyond anyone's power to quench it. . . . If, then, we are to induce the States of Europe to renounce the explosive means by which they each provide nationally for their security, we must supply them in exchange with some all-round international protection, equally comforting." [6]

These various essential conditions will not be fulfilled until long strides have been taken in the direction of exalting common interests among the various peoples of the earth. The international mind and the international heart are required as foundations of authoritative and powerful international agencies of justice, without which a system of international police cannot function successfully. Suspicion and passion must be diminished substantially. In stressing these points, Professor John Dewey draws upon the experience of the American people: "I think no reasonable person will hold that the coercive force of the federal government is chiefly or in any large degree that which keeps the various states together; or that it is a factor of any great importance as compared with the bonds of common tradition, habits of mind, beliefs, information, intercommunication, commerce, etc., which tie the people of the states together. Nor can I imagine any sensible person today who, when he looks at rivalries of interest and latent frictions between sections which still exist, would urge as a remedy the strengthening of coercive force exercised from above upon them. (We tried 'force bills' after the Civil War.) I cannot imagine such a person proposing anything but means which will positively intensify the bonds of common interest and purpose

[6] D. Mitrany, *The Problem of International Sanctions*, pp. 2, 34.

which exist among sections. . . . Laws that are enforced are enforced because there is a community consensus behind them.
The threat of force does not bring about the consensus. . . . If
the population of New York State were practically unanimous
in refusing to obey a federal law, it would not be police which
would be called out if it were decided to use coercion, but the
army and navy. The result would be civil war, not the ordinary processes of courts and sheriffs." [7]

By way of summary, the prerequisites of the successful operation of an international police force against a great power
are these: the relinquishment of a high degree of national sovereignty by the respective countries in order to make possible
the functioning of an authoritative and powerful international
government; substantial reductions in national armaments; development of the will to pacific settlement of international disputes and commitment to the use of pacific agencies; the creation of faith in international agencies; and the willingness to
subordinate conflicting national interests to the common good
of all peoples.

II

That these essential conditions are far from being fulfilled
at the present time is clear. In fact, only the barest beginning
has been made in these directions, and just now the tides are
moving swiftly outward. National sovereignty has never been
prized more highly or clung to more tenaciously; the race of
armaments has never been more furious; confidence in and
willingness to rely upon pacific agencies for security and justice
are at a low ebb; and insistence upon the priority of national
interests has never been more pronounced.

The simple truth of the matter is that the great powers are
willing to fight only in behalf of their own interests and are
unwilling to support the League of Nations with armed action
against a covenant-breaking state. On three occasions member
nations have been declared by the League to be guilty of fla-

---

[7] Raymond Leslie Buell and John Dewey, *Are Sanctions Necessary to
International Organization?*, pp. 32, 33.

grant violations of international agreements: Japan in relation to Manchuria, Italy with regard to Ethiopia, and Paraguay in connection with the Chaco war.

The text of Article 16 makes unequivocally clear the duty of other member nations when a fellow member illegally resorts to war. Certain words deserve emphasis through the use of capitals: "Should any Member of the League resort to war in disregard of its covenants under Articles 12, 13 or 15, it shall *ipso facto* be deemed to have committed an act of war against all other Members of the League, which hereby undertake IMMEDIATELY to subject it to the severance of ALL trade or financial relations, the prohibition of ALL intercourse between their nationals and the nationals of the covenant-breaking State and the nationals of any other State, whether a Member of the League or not. 2. It shall be the DUTY of the Council in such case to RECOMMEND to the several Governments concerned what effective MILITARY, NAVAL OR AIR FORCE the Members of the League shall severally contribute to the ARMED FORCES to be used to protect the covenants of the League."

In spite of these binding obligations, members of the League have been wholly unwilling to provide armed forces to support the League in resisting flagrant aggression. Citizens of the United States should have no difficulty in understanding the reluctance of the great powers of Europe to assume this responsibility because their own government has manifested an even greater reluctance. The Committee on Economic Sanctions, under the chairmanship of President Nicholas Murray Butler, well says: "In the present state of world opinion, it is highly probably that no people whose government is signatory to the Pact of Paris will desire the use of their government's military and naval forces in the settlement of international quarrels arisen elsewhere in the world." [8] *Armed police action against a lawless great power is wholly impracticable under prevailing conditions.*

[8] Evans Clark, *Boycotts and Peace,* p. 8.

III

To what degree is it practicable to resort to economic measures in behalf of the League against a covenant-breaking great
power?   Many persons who recognize the impracticability of
armed sanctions are convinced that it is possible to make effective use of economic means of coercion.   Strong theoretical
arguments in favor of economic sanctions may be presented.
Under a combination of favorable circumstances, it is possible
that even a great power might be deterred or restrained by economic pressure.   But under prevailing conditions there is little
basis of expectation that the other nations would be willing to
adopt drastic measures of economic compulsion.   The history
of the Manchurian and Ethiopian crises is revealing.   The
text of Article 10 of the Covenant should be kept in mind.[9]
"The Members of the League undertake to respect and PRE-
SERVE as against EXTERNAL AGGRESSION the territorial integrity and existing political independence of ALL
Members of the League.   In case of any such aggression or in
case of any threat or danger of such aggression the Council
SHALL ADVISE upon the means by which this obligation
shall be fulfilled."   Both China and Ethiopia were members of
the League at the time of these crises.   Therefore, all members
of the League were obligated to preserve their territorial integrity.   In these instances the League declared that the invad-
ers had violated their obligations under the Covenant.   Did the
other members of the League exert themselves seriously and
vigorously to uphold Article 10?

Listen to a summary of the evidence as presented in one of
the *Foreign Policy Reports:* "Sanctions were never seriously
contemplated in the Sino-Japanese conflict, although the report
of the Lytton Commission and the final report on the dispute
adopted by the Assembly on February 24, 1933, clearly inti-
mated that Japan had violated Articles X and XII of the
Covenant.   Neither France nor Britain, both preoccupied with
domestic troubles and European politics, considered their in-

---

[9] Special use of capitals is mine.

terests sufficiently involved to warrant the risk of applying coercive measures to a country remote from Europe. The fact that no state of war in the strict legal sense existed at any time between Japan and China afforded them a welcome excuse for not regarding Japan as having illegally resorted to war in violation of its Covenant obligations. . . . In view of the League's failure to apply any but the mildest sanctions in previous cases, the invocation of Article XVI in the Italo-Ethiopian war seemed surprising. As the Italian delegate, Baron Pompeo Aloisi, asked in the Assembly on October 11: 'Why two weights and two measures?' The League's decision to enforce the Covenant against Italy was largely due to the energetic initiative taken by the British government. Hitherto Great Britain had been very reluctant to undertake definite commitments to check aggression. Italy's venture in Ethiopia, however, jeopardized important British interests and made the government realize that maintenance of the system of collective security was vital to the British Empire. The British had also become increasingly alarmed over the resurgence of a powerful and intensely nationalistic Germany, and apparently felt that unless Mussolini were checked, Hitler might also resort to arms . . . the French government was persuaded, not without reluctance, to stand by the Covenant, apparently because it realized that France would never be able to invoke collective action against Germany unless it also supported the League in cases where its interests were not vitally involved. . . . Italy is very poor in raw materials, lacking such essentials as coal, oil, iron ore, copper, rubber, cotton, manganese, nickel, tin, chrome and tungsten. Although nearly self-sufficient in cereals, it needs to import at least part of its food supply, especially vegetable oils. Yet if League members had stopped all their own exports to Italy, the result might merely have been the diversion of Italian import trade to other countries which would thus have benefited from their failure to apply sanctions. . . . The economic sanctions were therefore confined to an embargo on imports from Italy, supplemented by a measure prohibiting the exportation of certain 'key' articles useful in the prosecution of hostilities. From the list of banned articles League members had to omit such essential products and raw materials as iron and steel, of which Germany and the United States are large producers; coal, of which Germany controls a large supply; and copper, cotton and petroleum, which are exported in large quantities by the United States. . . . A number of countries consequently claimed exemption. The most important of these was Switzerland. . . . Certain Latin American members have also made reservations, although none, with the exception of Paraguay, has refused to apply all the sanctions. . . . Nor have the governments of Venezuela, Uruguay and Peru taken steps to carry out the economic sanctions. Although these abstentions—particularly in the case of Argentina and Switzerland—seriously weaken the efficacy of collective action against Italy, the Coordination Committee has seemed impotent to take any measures which might induce these delinquent League members to live up to their Covenant obligations. It could hardly invoke sanctions to enforce sanctions." [10]

The evidence was summarized as follows by M. Litvinoff: "It is a fact that not only was the whole admirable mechanism of Article 16 not brought into play, but from the outset there was a manifest striving to confine the action taken to the barest minimum. Four members had not applied sanctions at all. One, a State bordering on Italy, had refused to apply the most effective sanction—namely, the prohibition of imports from Italy—seven had not applied the embargo on arms, ten had not applied the prohibition of exports to Italy, and thirteen had not applied the prohibition of imports from Italy." [11]

In an illuminating article on "How Sanctions Failed," M. J. Bonn writes: "Economic sanctions have not failed as a measure for preventing war; they were not tried for that purpose. No-

[10] John C. de Wilde, "Testing League Sanctions," *Foreign Policy Reports,* Dec. 4, 1935, pp. 239-242.

[11] L. P. Jacks, "Alexander Hamilton and the Reform of the League," *International Conciliation,* December, 1936, p. 607.

body ever threatened Italy with expulsion from the League if she violated the Covenant, as laid down in Article XVI, Section 4. And she rightly assumed that the several governments concerned would not recommend to the Council, as in duty bound under Section 2 of the same article, 'what effective military, naval or air force the members of the League shall severally contribute to the armed forces to be used to protect the Covenant of the League.' Italy was declared the aggressor on October 9, 1935, and economic sanctions were adopted on October 19, but they were not enforced until November 18. They were not applied *immediately,* nor did they extend to *all* trade or financial relations between the League members and the Covenant-breaking state. . . . The League's policy was never complete. Not only were certain war materials, such as oil, left untouched, but shipping, the tourist trade and emigrants' remittances were not interfered with. The Italian attitude was simple and clear. 'We shall stand all sanctions which do not seriously hamper us; if they do more than inconvenience us, we shall fight.' The League had the choice either of accepting this challenge and imposing such sanctions as would make war hopeless for Italy; or of acknowledging that the independence of Abyssinia was not worth a world war. Quite possibly such a war would never have come; but this cannot be known for certain. It cannot be said that sanctions failed. For pressure which has not been exercised cannot have failed. . . . To brand Italy as the aggressor at a meeting of the League for having broken a solemn Covenant, and to implore this moral offender at the same time to remain within the League, whose statutes she had violated deliberately, was so incongruous that moral failure was inevitable even if material failure had not taken place. There might be reasons for maintaining diplomatic relations with Italy—they exist with non-members of the League, regardless of the moral principle which their governments represent. But to let Italy remain a member of the League Council, entitled to all its privileges, while at the same time breaking its fundamental law, was a mockery which Italy could not but look upon as an encouragement to go to the limit." [12]

An outstanding statesman of Czechoslovakia, who has attended every session of the League Assembly, thus interprets the failure of sanctions: "If you look at the conduct of the Members of the League you will find that since its foundation a three-cornered fight has gone on: some States strove to ensure their national acquired rights; others strove to gain what they lost or what they failed to gain by the World War; others again simply practised neutrality. . . . During sixteen years we had done our best to secure that the League should be unable to act in a conflict like the Italo-Ethiopian dispute. Italy was right when she complained that nothing in the conduct of the League during sixteen years had led her to expect that the whole machinery of the League would be put in motion against her for her conflict with Abyssinia. You can reply that what matters is not what was done during sixteen years, but the fact that Italy had signed the Covenant. This would be true if life were mechanical. Nations, however, are living organisms, moved and animated by interests, ideas, moral and spiritual forces. If you want them to act consciously and effectively, you must prepare them to do so. The fact is that we had done nothing to prepare them for such a great task. On the contrary, we acted as if our engagements contained in the Covenant were of no consequence. So much so that not only Italy was surprised, but Members of the League were no less surprised. Neither morally, nor intellectually, nor spiritually, nor politically were they prepared to accomplish their duties as Members of the League. Therefore they performed their duties as someone who had not expected them and was not prepared to carry them out. And as the accomplishment of the full duty under the Covenant requires not only a governmental decision but the active cooperation of the whole national collectivity of each Member, can you say that by deed and word we prepared them for such cooperation? Therefore, as against

---

[12] M. J. Bonn, "How Sanctions Failed," *Foreign Affairs*, January, 1937, pp. 353, 359.

those who say that in the Italo-Ethiopian conflict the League
proved that it could not accomplish the mission which nations
expected of it, I hold that what failed was not the League, nor
the collective system, but the egotistic, narrow ideas and conceptions which the nations wanted the League to serve. What
proved wanting were the pre-War conceptions, the continuation of the Great War under cover of the League." [13]

The fact that sanctions cannot be used successfully against
a great power under present conditions does not prove conclu-
sively that coercive measures can never be so applied. IF
national sovereignty were drastically diminished; IF substantial reductions were made in national armaments; IF nations
acquired the habit of utilizing pacific means of settling their
disputes; IF national interests were regarded as subordinate to
the general welfare of all peoples—THEN an authoritative and
powerful League of Nations could make use of economic sanctions.

In theory it is easy to devise types of economic pressure
which do not cause starvation and yet which make prolonged
resistance difficult. The Committee on Economic Sanctions,
for illustration, has published a detailed study of the problem.[14]
Their proposals "do not provide for an absolute boycott or for
a blockade or for the use of military force in any form." Under any conditions that can be visualized for the near future,
however, the application of drastic economic sanctions against
a great power is likely to provoke a general war. Mussolini
was blunt in his warning that he would resist with arms any
attempt to place an embargo on oil shipments to Italy. Under
the intense drive of national passions, any great power will
probably resort to war rather than submit to severe economic
pressure. *The hazard of economic sanctions is increased by
the fact that in the Covenant they are interlaced indissolubly
with military measures.*

This aspect of the problem is emphasized by George Soule:

[13] M. Stephan Osusky., "Central Europe and the Future of the Collective
System," *Problems of Peace,* 11th Series, pp. 44-47.
[14] Evans Clark, *Boycotts and Peace.*

"Clearly, Article 16 contemplates economic sanctions, not as a substitute for war, but *as an instrument of war,* to be backed up by other agencies of force. First, the League recognizes that the guilty nation has broken its pledge. Automatically this creates a state of war between that nation and the other members. Economic sanctions follow the recognition of the state of war; they do not precede it. Although the Council merely recommends to the several members what military, naval, and air forces shall be employed, it is assumed that use of these forces will be necessary as a consequence of the boy-cott. The members are also pledged to interrupt trade between the violator and any non-member of the League (such as the United States); and it is obvious that a measure of this kind would require a blockade or some equivalent use of navies. Even if the article were not phrased in just this way, it would be absurd to suppose that a boycott would not lead to the use of military force, or that it is in any essential respect different from other kinds of war activity. . . . What reason is there to suppose that an officially declared boycott would bring the Jap-anese or any other government and people to terms without actual hostilities? . . . Strange as it may seem to us, most of the Japanese do not think they are doing wrong. The people of a nation which has actually entered upon hostilities with an-other never does think so. The Japanese believe that the Chi-nese are in the wrong. To regard one's enemy as wicked is a trait of human nature, which no League of Nations or economic sanction can alter. The consequence is that anyone who tries to help the enemy becomes an enemy also. It is hardly con-ceivable that a boycott would be regarded in any other way by a warring people than as a supreme challenge to their powers of resistance, resting upon a judgment which was an insult to their patriotism. They would want to defeat it by any weapon they could seize." [15]

In commenting upon an address delivered on the subject "An International Police Force?", Professor H. A. Smith said "he

[15] George Soule, "The Fallacy of the Boycott," *Harper's Monthly Mag-azine,* May, 1932, pp. 704, 705.

thought that the title of the address had been rightly put with
a question mark, and in listening to the address that question
mark had generated a whole host of questions which time did
not allow him to put. His first question was, Where was the
International Police Force to be stationed? If at Geneva, how
was it to be transported to South America or Manchuria?
What were to be its lines of communication? How big was it
to be? If one entertained the idea of coercing Russia or the
United States, it would have to run into millions. If it was
to consist, not of the ordinary infantry, cavalry and ships, but
only of forces armed with the new weapons, submarines, tanks
and aeroplanes, it could not be effective. If an international
force was to have any military value it must consist of all arms,
sea, land and air, and then the problem became enormous—a
force of millions, which must be in some definite place, under
some one definite command, and capable of being moved to any
part of the world. These were not merely technical difficulties,
they were fundamental. Then, how far was the internationalism to go? It could not go through every unit. No admiral
would wish to command a ship the crew of which spoke ten
different languages. If the internationalism was to be only in
the higher command, then it meant substantially that States
were to keep their existing armies, navies and air forces, and
to cooperate together, when they wished, for common purposes, which they could do already. . . . A further and more
important point was that if the units of the International Police
Force were to remain as national armies, navies and air forces,
they would surely be animated by the same national spirit. It
would not be possible to order a French army against France,
or the Japanese Navy against Japan. And in the case of small
States, for example, the recent conflict between Paraguay and
Bolivia, the feeling of most people would be that they would
sooner see Bolivians and Paraguayans annihilating each other,
than sacrifice the life of one of their sons to stop them." [16]

So long as the governments of Germany, Italy and Japan

---

[16] David Davies, "An International Police Force?", *International Affairs*,
January, 1932, pp. 92, 93.

*look upon the continuation of the present international status
quo as a greater evil than war, it is folly to talk of deterring or
restraining them from acts of aggression by calling upon an
international police force.* Such action would probably provoke another world war. At present and for an indefinite time
to come, theories of sanctions are and will continue to be shat-
tered upon the jagged realities of international politics. As one
reads intricate details of plans of economic sanctions he is re-
minded of the remark made in another connection by Dupuis
that a certain proposal was "neat, complete, logical, chimerical,
and impractical." One also recalls the famous comment of
Frederick the Great: "The Abbe de St. Pierre sent me an excellent treatise on the means of restoring peace to all Europe
and on the manner of preserving it continually. The thing is
exceedingly practicable, nor is anything except the consent of
all Europe and some other such trifles wanting for its accomplishment."

IV

Nothing lacking except the consent of the two o'clock robber
to allow the ten o'clock and twelve o'clock thieves to retain
their loot![17] Sharing economic advantages and abolishing the
looting system of empire are requirements of an effective program of world peace. Until these steps are taken the League
of Nations will remain comparatively impotent in dealing with
recalcitrant powers and international peace will lead a precarious existence.

"Peace more important than justice," is the heading found
in an advocacy of sanctions. The writer goes on: ". . . there
is no grievance which justifies a state in embarking on
war. . . ." For citizens of dominant countries this argument
is convincing, and it *ought* to be accepted as valid in all lands.
There is no grievance which *justifies* a state in waging war.
But the governments of three handicapped powers look with
contempt upon this idea. *What the two o'clock robber thinks*

[17] See pp. 29, 30, 38 ff.

is as essential to peace as are the ideas of his predecessors in crime.

This towering fact vitiates much of contemporary discussion of international law and sanctions, as for example: "First of all, one must be clear that the rule of law inevitably brings with it stability. That, indeed, is its chief meaning, in national as in international life . . . unless we consciously prefer the habit of making changes by sporadic violence, which has been the rule hitherto, we must be prepared, when introducing the rule of law in international relations, to accept also its inevitable tendency to stabilize the actual state of things."[18] Such a discussion completely ignores the incontestable fact that Germany, Italy and Japan will not accept the stability of present international arrangements. *Talk of stabilizing things-as-are merely incites the handicapped to armed efforts to bring about changes which they regard as essential.* Let the fact be emphasized that the changes demanded by Germany, Italy and Japan cannot on their part be achieved peaceably. Pacific change is possible only for those who control privilege.

This fact is recognized and stressed by Professor Eagleton, an advocate of sanctions: "It is important to say, however, that forcible sanctions are not enough, and international government must provide more than this. For, after all, the use of force, whether as war by a nation, or as sanctions by the community of nations, is only a means toward an end. The end is to secure justice, in its widest sense, for the greatest number. If force is employed, in either sense, to maintain an unjust *status quo,* it will inevitably be met by force. Some states are far better equipped with natural resources than others; the latter will not submit to starvation. Nor will existing laws and treaties be allowed to continue an unjust situation, simply because they are law and are backed by sanctions. . . . In any system, there must always be provided means for change and progress; sanctions used to maintain an existing status, with no means of change, will lead only to a more violent explosion in the long run. In this respect, the League is defective—

[18] Mitrany, *op. cit.,* pp. 60, 61.

though it offers much more in this direction than was possible before it was created. It needs the authority to change a legal situation without the consent of those states which profit from that situation; and its authority must again be backed by force. The 'haves' will not divide up with the 'havenots' until they are forced to it." [19]

But the "haves" cannot be *forced* to divide their superior advantages—that is, not without a world war. Here is the heart of the world's dilemma: the status quo cannot be preserved by pacific means; and the status quo cannot be changed drastically by pacific means so far as Germany, Italy and Japan are concerned. The only possible escape from a world war is down the road of *voluntary change by the early robbers*. And the change required includes the sharing of economic advantages and the ending of the system of empires.

"It is axiomatic," writes Frank H. Simonds, "that law can be enforced effectively within a state only when it is backed by the public opinion of the community which lives under it. The attempt to compel a community to obey a law which is repugnant to its conscience, common sense, or material interest invariably leads to explosion. . . . Within a state, a government, confronted by three sectional phenomena like the Japanese, Italian, and German, would be constrained to undertake some amendment of the law which had thus been repudiated and defied. But the League can do nothing to amend the law because those who suffer by it are a minority, and nations which profit by it, and Great Britain and France in particular, have set their faces against revision. The three rebel countries are out to modify their own economic and territorial circumstances, which they find intolerable; but those countries whose security must be compromised, whose frontiers must be mutilated, or whose colonial monopolies must be abolished to satisfy the demand of the rebel nations can and will prevent all revision within the League. . . . Not merely to enforce old law, become obsolete and oppressive, as all law must with the passage of time and the change of conditions, but also to establish new

[19] Eagleton, *op. cit.*, pp. 130, 131.

laws and to repeal or revise ancient statutes, that must be the task of any institution charged with the task of preventing war. To succeed, in fact even to survive, Geneva must be a pacificator and not a policeman." [20]

The League of Nations is essential to the achievement of enduring peace. But it will continue to be comparatively impotent as a means of preventing war so long as its dominant members rely primarily upon Article 10 and Article 16. The hope of the future is found in Article 19, which opens the way to changes in prevailing arrangements. "Where the League has failed," writes Lord Lothian, "has been as a system of security resting upon the use of force. In point of fact the League, as a league, can never use force. The League has neither army nor navy nor air force nor the means with which to pay for them. As Lord Halifax has said, it has responsibility without power. There is the vice at the heart of the Covenant. . . . If the League is to recover the influence it can exercise in a world of sovereign States, it must—to use General Smuts' famous words—cease to be an international war office. This is not its function. The function of the League, so long as sovereignty resides in the States, is to act as a peace-promoting agency, standing at the heart of the world, bringing the nations constantly together, striving for unity, striving for social reform, in season and out of season, when there is war and when there is peace, the conscience of mankind and the nucleus about which may grow up a spirit which may some day enable it to assume the power without which it cannot exercise responsibility. Such a League may recover that universality which is the only real foundation for its influence. To commit it to the use of war is both inevitably to shrink it by resignations and to undermine it by further proofs that it cannot live up to its obligations. The first step to recovery is the excision of the compulsory and automatic obligation to use force under Articles 10 and 16." [21]

[20] Frank H. Simonds, "What Price Sanctions?", *Harper's Magazine*, Volume 172, February, 1936, pp. 264, 265.

[21] Lord Lothian, "New League or No League," *International Conciliation*, Dec. 1936, pp. 600, 601.

V

In spite of the present weakness of the League, I am strongly convinced that the United States should without delay become a member, with a clear understanding that this nation is not obligated to approve of or support sanctions. International agencies of justice are absolutely essential and the League is the most hopeful step yet taken in this direction. That the United States should become a member of the World Court, and should sign the optional clause, also seems highly desirable.

Nations signing the optional clause of the Statute of the World Court agree to accept the compulsory jurisdiction of the court, in relation to any other member likewise signing, in all legal disputes concerning:

(a) the interpretation of a treaty;

(b) any question of international law;

(c) the existence of any fact which, if established, would constitute a breach of an international obligation;

(d) the nature or extent of the reparation to be made for the breach of an international obligation.

This highly important obligation has been assumed by the following forty-two nations: [22]

Abyssinia	France	New Zealand
Union of South Africa	Germany	Norway
Albania	Great Britain	Panama
Australia	Greece	Paraguay
Austria	Haiti	Peru
Belgium	Hungary	Portugal
Brazil	India	Rumania
Bulgaria	Iran (Persia)	El Salvador
Canada	Irish Free State	Siam
Colombia	Italy	Spain
Denmark	Latvia	Sweden
Dominican Republic	Lithuania	Switzerland
Estonia	Luxemburg	Uruguay
Finland	Netherlands	Yugoslavia

[22] Manley O. Hudson, *By Pacific Means,* p. 146.

A proposed basis of membership in the League in the form of a Joint Resolution has been presented by Senator Pope: [23]

"Resolved by the Senate and House of Representatives of the United States of America in Congress assembled, That the President is hereby authorized to notify the appropriate authority of the League of Nations that the United States accepts its membership in the League of Nations on the following terms and understandings:

(1) That the obligation of the Pact of Paris not to resort to war as an instrument of national policy is recognized as the fundamental and guiding principle of the Covenant; and

(2) That the provisions of the Covenant of the League of Nations relating to cooperation in the prevention of war shall not be interpreted as obligating the United States to adopt measures which might involve the use of armed force; and that the decision as to what action shall be taken by the United States in case the peace of nations is threatened or violated shall rest with the Government of the United States acting according to the Constitution."

Eighteen years ago the United States was prevented from joining the League of Nations by fear, misrepresentation and partisan politics. Even under those circumstances, let it be remembered, 80 members of the Senate were on record as favoring entrance with reservations, and a considerable majority cast affirmative votes in the crucial ballot. The falling short by seven votes of the required two-thirds was due to the fact that the followers of President Wilson refused to vote for entrance with the Lodge reservations attached. On this ballot, if all Senators who were favorable to the League had voted accordingly, the negative vote would have totaled less than twenty.

In spite of a campaign of unrestrained vituperation, there is

[23] Senate Joint Resolution 119, 74th Congress, 1st Session, May 7, 1935.

an abundance of evidence to show that the nation as a whole favored our adherence with reservations. Senator Harding, later to be President, said on September 11, 1920: "It was the truth, last year, two years ago, three and four years ago, the people of this country were heedlessly and overwhelmingly for a league of nations, or society of nations. . . ." Senator Lodge recorded his opinion in memorable words: "I said to Senator Borah, it seemed perfectly obvious to me that any attempt to defeat the Treaty of Versailles with the League by a straight vote in the Senate, if taken immediately, would be hopeless, even if it were desirable. . . . He told me that he agreed entirely with my description of the situation, that he did not believe the treaty could possibly be beaten at that time by a direct vote. . . ."

During the Presidential campaign of 1920, an appeal was made by 31 distinguished Republicans—including Herbert Hoover, Charles Evans Hughes, Elihu Root, Henry L. Stimson and Ray Lyman Wilbur—to vote for Senator Harding as the quickest way to get the United States into the League, saying explicitly: "The question accordingly is not between a league and no league, but is whether certain provisions in the proposed league agreement shall be accepted unchanged or shall be changed." In his Des Moines address Candidate Harding promised to consult with the "best minds . . . to the end that we may have an association of nations for the promotion of international peace." Professor Irving Fisher of Yale has testified publicly that in July, 1920, Mr. Harding said to him: "I want the United States to get into the League just as much as you do. . . . My idea is to call the nations together and ask them to make such amendments as are necessary to secure the approval of the United States." After the election landslide, Calvin Coolidge, the newly elected Vice-President, said: "I doubt if any particular mandate was given in the last election on the question of the League of Nations and if it was the preponderant issue."

The urgent need for an authoritative League, which has renounced military coercion, is even more clearly discernible to-day than at the end of the World War. Changes in the League are required, but the United States can be more helpful in bringing about these changes from the inside. On some such terms as those of the Pope resolution, we should take our place at the council table of the nations and help to solve the common problems of an interdependent world.

VI

In any consideration of international police, the experience of the States of our Federal Union is illuminating. Fortunately, the evidence has been compactly and authoritatively summarized in a notable article by James N. Rosenberg in the *Columbia Law Review*, June, 1925. Most of the data presented in this section is taken from this illuminating discussion. Chief Justice White has stated that neither Madison's *Journal* nor the other scant contemporary records of the proceedings of the Constitutional Convention of 1787 disclose debate regarding the enforcibility of, or method or apparatus of enforcing, decrees of the United States Supreme Court against states.

The question of exertion of federal force "against a delinquent state" did, however, arise in the Constitutional Convention. The Virginia Plan for a Constitution provided for calling "forth the force of the Union against any member of the Union failing to fulfill its duty." Concerning this, Madison's timely observations deserve much thought from those who would create an effective world tribunal. "The more he reflected on the use of force, the more he doubted the practicability, the justice, the efficacy of it. . . . A union of states, containing such an ingredient, seemed to provide for its own destruction. The use of force against a state would look . . . like a declaration of war. . . ." The New Jersey Plan for a constitution also proposed force against states. But the counsels of such men as Madison prevailed. The Fathers excluded all such provisions from the Constitution.

James Wilson asserted, in the Pennsylvania debates, that the Constitution meant that the Supreme Court could enforce its decrees, urging this indeed as an especial reason for ratification.   Marshall and Ellsworth, on the other hand—whose opinions are entitled to special weight, since they both later became Chief Justices—were outstanding champions of a contrary view.   Marshall, in the Virginia Debates, speaking at the moment of suits by individuals against states, expressed the hope that ". . . no gentleman will think that a state will be called at the bar of the federal court. . . . It is not rational to suppose that the sovereign power should be dragged before a court."   And Ellsworth, before the Connecticut Convention, said: "This Constitution does not attempt to coerce sovereign bodies, states, in their political capacity."

Alexander Hamilton objected to the principle of coercion. "It is one of the maddest projects that was ever devised," he writes in the *Federalist*.   "Can we believe," he goes on, "that a (sovereign) State will ever suffer itself to be used as an instrument of coercion?   The thing is a dream.   It is impossible."   Further statements by Hamilton to the same effect are as follows: Addressing the Convention on June 18, 1787, he said: "A certain portion of military force is absolutely necessary in large communities . . . but how can this force be exerted on the State?   It is impossible.   It amounts to a war between the parties."   In the following year he writes in the *Federalist:* "Whoever considers the populousness and strength of the States singly at the present juncture, and looks forward to what they will become, even at the distance of half a century, will at once dismiss as idle and visionary any scheme which aims at regulating their movements by laws to operate upon them in their collective capacities and to be executed by a coercion applicable to them in the same capacities. . . . Even in those Confederacies composed of members smaller than many of our counties, the principle of legislation for sovereign States, supported by military coercion, has never been found effectual. . . . In most instances attempts to coerce the refractory and disobedient (States) have been the signals of bloody war, in which one half of the Confederacy has displayed its banners against the other half." [24]

In its entire history the Supreme Court has never attempted to use coercion as a means of securing observance of its decisions against states, in spite of repeated refusals to abide by its decisions on the part of various states. In 1792 an individual named Chisholm sued the state of Georgia and was awarded a judgment by the Supreme Court. Whereupon the legislature of Georgia not only refused to pay the money due but passed a law declaring that any person attempting to enforce the Court's decision would be "guilty of felony" and would "suffer death by being hanged." What did the Supreme Court do in the face of this insubordination and insult? Those who reason by analogy are likely to say that the law must be enforced at any cost, if necessary by calling upon the Federal Government for armed troops. What would have happened if a Federal army had started toward Atlanta? The result would have been war and the destruction of many lives. Under the circumstances the use of physical force would have been neither effective nor ethical. The Supreme Court simply waited. The other twelve states sided with Georgia. The result was the eleventh amendment to the Constitution declaring that the Supreme Court does not have jurisdiction in the case of a suit of an individual against a state.

In 1809, when a United States marshal attempted to enforce a federal court judgment awarding Olmstead prize money, to which the Pennsylvania court had previously decided he was not entitled, there was almost a small sized civil war. The Pennsylvania legislature passed resolutions which Chief Justice Marshall, directing the Federal District Judge in Pennsylvania to enforce his judgment, declared revolutionary. Pennsylvania militia surrounded the judgment debtor's house in her defense. The United States marshal summoned a posse of two thousand men. Again, the intensity of the conflict

---

[24] See an interesting article by L. P. Jacks on "Alexander Hamilton and the Reform of the League," in *International Conciliation*, December, 1936, pp. 605-621.

between states and court is indicated by the fact that four times—in 1822, 1831, 1847, 1858—bills were introduced in Congress for the repeal of that section of the Judiciary Act which enabled the Supreme Court to review the constitutionality of state legislation.   South Carolina for a decade enforced with impunity a "Negro Seaman's Act" which the federal court had declared unconstitutional.   It was in the Cherokee Indian cases that one of the greatest of these contests between Court and State occurred.   The Cherokee, seeking federal protection, sought to enjoin the state; the Georgia legislature instructed the Governor to ignore the subpoena of the Supreme Court.   A furious controversy developed throughout the country as to these acts of nullification by Georgia.   President Jackson was appealed to.   He refused to interfere.   It was, indeed, of this proceeding that President Jackson, then championing state rights, is said to have made his celebrated remark: "John Marshall has made his decision; now let him enforce it."

Just as Georgia, her state pride aroused, had defied the Court in 1832, so a quarter of a century later, Wisconsin challenged the court when the bitter issue of slavery aligned Court and State on opposite sides.   Two years after the *Dred Scott* decision, which had caused a large part of the North to look on the Supreme Court as the stronghold of slavery, the *Booth* cases arose.   Booth had been arrested and held by federal authorities in Wisconsin for a violation of the Fugitive Slave Law.   The Wisconsin court allowed Booth a writ of habeas corpus and caused his release.   Thereupon Booth was indicted by a federal grand jury for the same offense and convicted. He again applied to the state court for a writ of habeas corpus, which was again allowed and he was again taken from federal custody and released.   Writ of error was taken in both cases to the Supreme Court.   The Wisconsin court refused even to make return to the second writ.   Chief Justice Taney, in a powerful opinion, said that to grant the right assumed by the state court to annul the proceedings of the federal court would be to "subvert the very foundation of the Government."   The

Wisconsin legislature rejoined by declaring "the assumption of jurisdiction by the Federal judiciary an act of undelegated power and therefore without authority, void and of no force." Attempts by the United States attorney to file the mandates of the Supreme Court with the state court were unsuccessful.

In the case of Virginia against West Virginia there was a long delay before the decision of the Supreme Court was accepted. When West Virginia was formed into a separate state during the Civil War, it agreed to pay part of the Virginia debt. This promise was not carried out. In 1915 the case was brought before the Supreme Court and a judgment awarded against West Virginia. No action was taken by the latter. In 1918 Virginia sought a mandamus to compel payment. While the Supreme Court was considering the matter, West Virginia acted.

Mr. Rosenberg thus summarizes the record: "(a) Until 1918 the Supreme Court, which had by then sat in over forty cases where State sued State, not only never attempted to exert power over a State but, when called on to discuss that question, invariably declared it had no such power. (b) In 1918, however, Chief Justice White, in the West Virginia case, declared that 'judicial power essentially involves the right to enforce.' But did he try to enforce? Did he send a sheriff to the State of West Virginia? He did not. He pleaded with West Virginia to acquiesce voluntarily in the court's decrees and so save everybody from an embarrassing and disagreeable situation. If you doubt me, read his opinion. *So we find that there has never been an instance in our history where an attempt has been made to enforce a Supreme Court decision against a State by the exertion of power.*[25] During these one hundred and forty years all manner of interstate controversies have come before the Supreme Court—boundary disputes, economic quarrels, all the typical and favorite war-breeding issues; they have been resolved by the court and peaceably acquiesced in by the States, except in a few rare cases in our earlier history where, the

[25] Italics are mine.

States declining to acquiesce, the decrees were not enforced. Fortunately so, for an attempt to enforce would surely have resulted in war." [26]

From this record Dr. L. P. Jacks draws certain conclusions: "Such were the principles that triumphed in forming the Union of thirteen weak, quarrelsome, and disordered States in 1787, a union which has survived and promises to survive on the scale and with the results we now see. Are these principles applicable to the questions confronting us today? If coercion was a mad project then has it become a sane project now? Is the principle of national sovereignty less deeply rooted among the nations of the modern world than it was among those thirteen States? And does the fact that most of these nations are armed to the teeth, each in the determination to be sole master of its own destiny (and none more determined than the British), render them more or less amenable to coercion? Is it less true today than it was then that 'if these States will quarrel and want to fight no frame of government can possibly prevent it?' To be sure, the vast armaments now existing, if thrown into a common pool, would be so formidable that no dog would dare to bark in its presence. But where is the sovereign political State, determined to be master of its own destiny, which shows the slightest disposition to let the control of its armed forces pass out of its own hands by throwing them into a pool at the disposal of a central authority? Would not such an arrangement involve the surrender, by each of the contributing States, wholly or in part, of the power intended to make it master of its own destiny? Imagine the British Fleet taking its orders from Geneva!

"These questions may all be summed into one. Are the difficulties of union among the European States today, hard set in the assertion of national sovereignty, and armed to the teeth for asserting it, greater on the whole than those successfully overcome by the American statesmen of 1787? The answer is —*they are immensely greater for those who would base the*

---

[26] James N. Rosenberg, "Power to Decide, None to Enforce," *The Nation*, Vol. 121, December 9, 1925, p. 650.

League of Nations on coercion. What was a mad project for the American States in 1787 is a far madder project for the European States in 1936. 'It is a dream. It is impossible.' But for those who would embark the League on more profitable forms of cooperation, with a view to reducing the likelihood that these nations will 'want to fight,' the difficulties are less. Forms of international cooperation, and the means for achieving it, unknown and undreamed of in 1787, are now awaiting a statesmanship wise enough to make the most of them. It will be a tragedy if they are neglected, and the attempt made to restore the principle of coercion into a League of sovereign States each armed and still arming in the determination not to be coerced in any form or from any source. . . .

". . . The British Commonwealth of Nations is another and, in some respects, even more impressive. British statesmen who believe that a League of Nations is impossible without collective coercion may well be asked to consider what the reaction of the self-governing Dominions would be if the attempt were made to give the Commonwealth a constitution embodying a threat similar to that of Article 16? Would not that be a 'mad project'? . . . The result is that the British Commonwealth of Nations on the one hand, and the United States on the other, stand before the world today as object lessons revealing the only principle on which an enduring League of Nations can ever be founded. Both have solved the problem which the League of Nations has yet to solve on a greater scale. Both are non-coercive Leagues of Nations." [27]

VII

The meaning of all this seems crystal clear: military and economic sanctions cannot be used successfully against a great power until fundamental and far-reaching changes have been wrought in national attitudes and policies; if these basic changes are brought about, military and economic sanctions will not be required because more effective means of upholding international law will then be available.

[27] Jacks, *op. cit.,* pp. 617-619.

Chapter Five

Should the United States in an Endeavor to Preserve Democracy Be Willing to Engage in Armed Hostilities in Europe or Asia?

DEMOCRACY is now on the defensive, as contrasted with the aggressiveness of dictatorships in various parts of the earth. Widespread fear prevails that democratic countries are not only menaced from within but are also threatened from without by the expansionism of fascist nations. And since these black and brown dictatorships are heavily armed and extremely militaristic, the conviction is held by many that the democratic peoples must pool their resources in a war of defense against fascism. The statement is made frequently that Hitler and Mussolini and the Japanese military caste understand no language save that of force and that therefore their aggression cannot be restrained except by armed action. France and Great Britain and China, it is often asserted, deserve and require the armed cooperation of democratic United States.

The contrast between life in a democratic country and life under dictatorship is the theme of a small but impressive volume by Hamilton Fish Armstrong. Concerning the ominous threat to democratic peoples, Mr. Armstrong writes: "In a thousand ways the modern dictator is more formidable than the 'man on horseback' with whom their predecessors had to cope. He is mounted on swifter steeds and possesses more sudden and wholesale means of attack than were dreamed of by Attila or Napoleon or even von Kluck or von Mackensen. He is simultaneously the man in the aeroplane, the man in the tank, the man in the submarine, the man behind the gas waves, the man at the microphone. In no important instance in these last years has the effort to curb him succeeded. Not since Mussolini was balked in his Corfu adventure in 1923 has a ruthless militaristic government suffered direct defeat at the hands of the world community. . . . Can any nation on the face of the earth, wherever situated, however strong, pretend to itself that it is not affected by the rapid development of this portentous phenomenon?" [1]

In discussing the possibility that fascists may merely be bluffing, E. B. Ashton says: "For poker players, recent international history has been amusing to watch. Whenever one of today's 'aggressive' nations made a bold move frowned at by the others, the whole world talked about 'calling the bluff.' In one case the poker terminology was even adopted in the highest circles of diplomacy itself—when a prominent official of a great European power told the press, 'This time we have a royal straight flush and we know we can't lose.' Every time, however, it turned out that the supposedly bluffing nations meant every word they said—while the determination not to let them get away with it dissolved into thin air. . . . Between nations, a showdown means only one thing: war. The Fascists' willingness to accept war as a consequence of their acts is the decisive feature of their foreign policy . . . furthermore, we must realize that the Fascist nations will win future wars not because they are prosperous, or financially or culturally superior to their opponents. They will win because every fraction of their military, political, economic and cultural energies is prepared and available for, and adaptable to, the needs and purposes of the fighting community . . . there is now not a single major international aim of a Fascist nation which is not at least far on the way to realization. If the non-Fascists do not change their stand, the further outcome will be that the Fascists will continue to pursue a policy of following up increases in inner strength with 'balancing' expansion—through peace and war, *and for the duration of their existence as Fascist nations.* They will not be deterred by temporary set-backs—whether

[1] Hamilton Fish Armstrong, *We or They,* pp. 29-34.

they retract themselves or are beaten in a test of strength. They *cannot* change their fundamental attitude in international affairs as long as they remain what they are. To change it, it will be necessary either to end their Fascism or to end their national existence." [2]

Hitler and Mussolini have often stressed the irreconcilable conflict between their systems and democracy. In his autobiography, Hitler wrote: "Either the world will be governed by the ideology of modern democracy, in which case every issue will be decided in favor of the numerically stronger races; or it will be ruled by the laws of force, when the peoples of brutal determination, not those that show self-restraint, will triumph." While Mussolini announced in October, 1930: "The struggle between two worlds can permit no compromise. . . . Either we or they! Either their ideas or ours! Either our state or theirs!" [3]

Concerning war and peace, Hitler can be quoted to refute Hitler, and Mussolini can be cited against Mussolini. That is to say, there is no consistency whatever in their numerous public statements. ". . . the mistrust we feel," writes Hamilton Fish Armstrong, "as a result of witnessing actual deeds of bad faith are not to be wiped away by verbal assertions of peaceable intentions for the future, the more so as the dictatorial regimes which we regard most apprehensively have put us on notice that they consider such assertions mere diplomatic finessing. Listen, for example, to General Constantin Hierl, one of Chancellor Hitler's closest confidants, head of the Labor Service, Secretary of State in the Labor Ministry: 'There are two kinds of pacifism: true pacifism, which springs from a weak and sickly nature or from blindness, but which is honorably meant; and sham pacifism. This last is a political weapon and can serve for preparing for war. By putting the opponent to sleep with the help of pacifist declarations it seeks to induce him to neglect his armaments. The soporific fumes which it spreads

---

[2] E. B. Ashton, *The Fascist: His State and His Mind,* pp. 173, 174, 208, 211, 212.

[3] Quoted in Armstrong, *op. cit.,* p. 35.

over the enemy are useful to hide our own armament for war.'
General Hierl's idea is not new. Fichte phrased it succinctly:
'Promise peace, that you may begin war with advantage.'
When Hitler protests his innate pacifism, then, he should not
feel hurt if we refer him to his friend Hierl. When he says
that his foreign policy aims really at peace, he must wait for us
to believe him until he repudiates declarations like that of his
Minister for Propaganda and Public Enlightenment, Dr. Joseph
Goebbels: 'The only instrument with which one can conduct foreign policy is alone and exclusively the sword.' And
when he alleges that his vast rearmament is a gesture only for
the moral satisfaction of German dignity he need not be
surprised if we reply by quoting some words of his own
uttered in 1930 when he was not yet in office and did not feel
under any compulsion to dissimulate: 'It is impossible to build
up an army and give it a sense of worth if the object of its
existence is not the preparation for war. Armies for the preservation of peace do not exist; they exist only for the trium-
phant execution of war.' " [4]

The danger is not only real but terrifying. The spread of
fascism over the earth would be nothing less than the return of
an ice-age of liberty.[5] "It is well to remind ourselves of the
methods the new government has employed," writes Harold J.
Laski. "It has made terrorism a commonplace of daily life.
Assassination, torture, imprisonment without trial, the taking
of hostages, are now the normal environment of German existence. Criticism has been stifled; murderers have been glorified; men whose character would be intolerable in a civilized
society have been promoted to high office. A whole people has
been outlawed; property in goods and in occupation has been
ruthlessly expropriated. The spy and the *agent-provocateur*
are abroad; and they are encouraged to sow their poison in all
surrounding countries. The principle of the good neighbor is
cynically violated; and defeat in one war is advanced as the

---

[4] Armstrong, *op. cit.*, pp. 62, 63.
[5] See Gaetano Salvemini, *Under the Axe of Fascism;* Frederick L.
Schuman, *The Nazi Dictatorship.*

pretext openly to prepare for its successor. The state is made
an object of worship and sacrifice; and upon its altar are systematically immolated all the decent instincts of civilized mankind.   There is a terrorism in Germany today so widespread
that the study of its incidents reads rather like a page from
the records of an oriental tyranny than a sober account of the
effort of a people to affirm its essence." [6]

I

There is no denying that fascism gravely threatens democracy throughout the earth. If another great war comes, the
fascist powers will undoubtedly be the aggressors. Nevertheless, the governments and masses of people of Germany, Italy
and Japan look upon their own aggression as defensive in
character and absolutely essential to their security. "Justifiable
aggression" is an ancient argument that has been used many
times by all great powers. Aggression has often been justified
as a necessary means of removing a threat to security and as a
legitimate method of abolishing oppression.

Before me as I write is a full-page map published in the
Chicago Tribune.[7] In various colors it shows the original
thirteen colonies and subsequent acquisitions of territory by the
United States. Captions interpret different sections of this
map: Taken by Conquest, Organized 1787; By Conquest, Organized 1790; By Conquest, Spanish claim relinquished 1795;
By Conquest, Spanish Cession 1810; By Conquest, Spanish
Cession 1813; By Conquest, Spanish Cession 1819; Annexation 1845; Mexican Cession 1848; Philippines, By Conquest
1898; Hawaii, by Annexation 1898.

Aggression is written all over this map. Yet at the bottom are printed these words: "Making America. How this nation expanded from the original thirteen colonies to its present
vastness can be seen at a glance in the accompanying maps.
But what was back of this amazing national development is an-

[6] Harold J. Laski, "Freedom in Danger," *The Yale Review*, March, 1934,
pp. 536, 537.
[7] May 3, 1936.

other story. Who are the heroes whose sacrifices gave birth to this greatest of nations? Who are the patriots whose unfaltering courage has saved the country in every hour of peril? What thrilling exploits are hidden away in the yellowing pages of history that in their day were vital to the nation's progress? What deed of valor that an indifferent race of freemen has almost forgotten? The 'Making America' series, the first of which . . . appears on page eight of this section, will retell from time to time the stories—frequently unfamiliar—of America's heroes."

The aggressors of every great power are its heroes. To say that the governments and peoples of Germany, Italy and Japan are in a vigorously aggressive mood is merely to point out that they are now traveling a highway which is deeply grooved by the marching feet of conquering legions of many countries in all centuries. Calling them aggressors will never stop present-day dictatorships. Even democracies have found aggression as easy as breathing. Examine the British portions of a map of the world!

Over against their own aggression, Fascists set the oppression of their enemies. While security for France means maintaining the status quo; security for Germany is interpreted as requiring drastic change. Thus what the French regard as security is looked upon by the Germans as insecurity. *If another great war comes it will be interpreted respectively as a war against aggression and as a war against oppression.* Alibis are as easily found by two o'clock robbers as by ten o'clock thieves. Any other people placed in a position parallel to that of the Germans during the past twenty years would consider themselves victims of brutal oppression. And judged by their past records, Americans and Frenchmen and Englishmen would find it easy to justify an aggressive war against oppression and insecurity. Vivid awareness of this aspect of the prevailing international crisis is so essential to a sane program of war prevention that the German case should be stated again.

How would other peoples have felt and how would they have acted if they had suffered penalties equal to these? "The

Treaty of Versailles deprived Germany of 13 per cent of her territory (European), 13 per cent of her population and 14.3 per cent of her arable land.   In terms of her 1913 production, Germany surrendered 19 per cent of her coke, 74.5 per cent of her iron ore, 26.6 per cent of her blast furnaces, 19.2 per cent of her raw iron and steel, 15.8 per cent of her rolling mills, 68.5 per cent of her zinc foundries, 12 per cent of her livestock, her entire ocean-going merchant marine, 5,000 locomotives, 40,000 box cars, and other miscellaneous equipment.   More serious still, the Treaty and the subsequent decision of the League of Nations following the Polish Upper Silesian Plebiscite of 1921, split wide open two of the three major industrial centers of Germany, the Lorraine-Rhine-Westphalian and the Upper Silesian districts.   In the former and more important of these two centers, one section was placed under a temporary French mandate pending a plebiscite at a later date (the Saar), another section was removed entirely from the German customs union (Luxemburg), two small sections were given to Belgium (Eupen and Malmédy), and a final and highly important section (Lorraine) was ceded outright to France.   The principal losses were coal (Saar and Upper Silesia) and, especially, iron ore.   Lorraine ore had supplied about 75 per cent of the needs of the Ruhr iron and steel industry before the war.   In Upper Silesia practically all the iron ore and about 75 per cent of the coal were transferred to Poland.   In both areas the Treaty settlements destroyed the whole internal balance of the heavy industries remaining under German control.   Coal pits were separated from cokeries, cokeries from blast furnaces and steel mills, steel mills from rolling mills, and so forth." [8]

Mr. Ray Stannard Baker, biographer of Woodrow Wilson, thus summarizes French demands at the Peace Conference: "1. French military control of the Rhine; 2. A permanent alliance of the great Powers to help France to hold it; 3. A group of smaller allies to menace Germany from the east; 4. Territorial reduction of the German Empire; 5. Crippling of

[8] Robert A. Brady, *The Rationalization Movement in German Industry*, pp. xiv-xv.

the German political organization; 6. Disarmament of Germany but not of the Allies; 7. A crushing indemnity; 8. Deprivation of economic resources; 9. A set of commercial agreements preferential to France, prejudicial to Germany. Here we have exactly what was in the minds of the leaders of the Old Order, and their programme for the coming peace. It is easy, of course, to cry out, as the Germans do, that this was a purely militaristic and imperialistic programme. Strong militaristic and imperialistic elements there certainly were in it, but the dominating element first and last was fear and a passion for security." [9]

Imagine the feelings of patriotic Americans if they had been victimized in this way: "The revolution said, in effect, that the Kaiser and the Imperial system had been at fault. Now all that was gone, and with it the issues on which they had been duped into such an appalling waste of life. All this seemed clearer, too, since the Allied powers, which had won the war, announced their goals accomplished with the collapse of the Empire and the flight of the Kaiser to Doorn. The terms of the Armistice and of the fourteen points of President Wilson, on the basis of which arms had first been laid down, had served to bring this picture of things into still sharper relief. Then why the Treaty of Versailles? If the German people had been duped into fighting a fratricidal war by a ruler now fled and a caste of reactionary power now broken, on what basis could the Allied powers not only condemn the German people as a whole, but also lay upon their shoulders a burden which everybody knew they could not possibly bear—a burden which was intended not only to *punish* an admittedly innocent *people,* but which was also intended to beat them into a condition of servitude, generation after generation. The load of Versailles was, indeed, heavy. The bitter old men gathered together in the famous Hall of Mirrors had no intention to live up to the terms of the Armistice, the fourteen points, or any other promise. Their ethics were no different from those of the

[9] Ray Stannard Baker, *Woodrow Wilson and World Settlement,* vol. 2, pp. 20, 21.

acquisitive and completely amoral forces which had catapulted the world into the long-drawn-out slaughter just past and which it had been their mad fortune to command. Of what price an agreement? Of what worth a pledge scrawled on a 'scrap of paper'? With their ears finely attuned to the cheap magic of passing popular approval in coming-home elections— approval of deliberately inflamed and war-propaganda misled electorates—utterly oblivious to the grisly and terrifying implications of their decisions for the future, and dominated by the virulent, world-weary, and cynical old Clemenceau, they moved, not to salvage, but to crush, annihilate, and destroy." [10]

How would the British have reacted to the imposition of a staggering indemnity of more than six billion pounds sterling (132 billion gold marks)? Is there any doubt that the French would have regarded themselves as victims of intolerable oppression if the situation had been reversed and the Germans had seized the industrial heart of France in an endeavor to force the payment of impossible sums of indemnity? The last shred of doubt that they are sorely oppressed would be removed for any people by resultant inflation that destroyed the value of a nation's currency and wiped out the lifetime savings of an entire people. Look for a moment at the ghastly figures of German inflation: [11]

	Marks Note circulation	Number of Marks equaling one U.S. Dollar
Jan. 6, 1923.......	1,336,500,000,000	8,695
June 7, 1923.......	9,309,532,000,000	76,923
July 7, 1923.......	20,241,750,000,000	222,222
Aug. 7, 1923.......	62,326,659,000,000	3,125,000
Sept. 7, 1923.......	1,182,039,000,000,000	33,333,333
Oct. 6, 1923.......	46,933,600,000,000,000	909,090,909
Oct. 31, 1923.......	2,496,822,908,936,000,000	166,666,666,667
Nov. 7, 1923.......	19,153,087,468,804,000,000	2,500,000,000,000
Nov. 15, 1923.......	92,844,720,742,927,000,000	4,000,000,000,000
Nov. 23, 1923.......	223,927,315,083,796,000,000	5,000,000,000,000
Nov. 30, 1923.......	400,267,640,291,750,000,000	6,666,666,666,667

10 Robert A. Brady, *The Spirit and Structure of German Fascism,* pp. 8, 9.

11 From figures prepared by the National City Bank and published in *Nation's Business,* February, 1934, p. 27.

"Teetering on the edge of an abyss" is a literal description of the plight of the German people. Four and a half years of terrible suffering in wartime, followed by inflation and ruin, with a short period of comparative prosperity as a result of enormous loans and substantial credits by outside power, and then the world economic depression! ". . . . on one country in Europe," wrote G. D. H. Cole, "the reaction of the American boom fell far more disastrously than on the rest. Germany, since the stabilisation of her currency and the readjustment of reparations under the Dawes Plan of 1924, had been energetically reconstructing her industries on the basis of an intensive mechanisation which involved very heavy capital expenditure. . . . During these years the Germans borrowed from investors in other countries nearly fifteen thousand million reichsmarks (£750,000,000 at par). This was twice as much as she paid in reparations including deliveries in kind, and at least half of her total borrowings came from the United States. . . . When in the United States the boom broke and the slump set in, the situation in Germany at once became far worse. . . . Thus through the whole of 1930 and 1931 the German economic position became steadily more difficult and even desperate, although the German Government took the most drastic measures to deal with the situation. . . . The cost of maintaining the unemployed weighed more and more heavily on the German budget, and in the early months of 1931 Germany was absolutely at the end of her tether. Only the Hoover moratorium on war debts and reparations and the Berlin 'stand-still' agreement, under which Germany's creditors agreed to postpone repayment of their short-term loans, saved her from complete economic collapse; and as both these measures were purely temporary, whereas the causes which had made them necessary showed no sign of passing away, all that was secured by them was a brief respite. There was no restoration of confidence in the future, because no one knew what was to happen when the moratorium and the 'stand-still' came to an end. There was no recovery of the German home market or of the standard of life, which indeed was pressed down

further and further as the world situation became progressively
worse. Germany carried on, but only by desperate measures
of semi-starvation enforced by rigid governmental control at
the cost of stirring up among the German people a ferment of
resentment and despair." [12]

Only by desperate measures of semi-starvation! Seventeen
years after the beginning of the agony of the world war!
How would American patriots have responded to a similar
situation?

Is there any occasion for surprise that under these appalling
circumstances the German people should make a scapegoat of
the Social Democrats and other moderates who had signed
the Treaty of Versailles and attempted to carry out its provisions? Or that they turned to the man who symbolized in
the most extreme form hatred of the oppressors and who
made the most extravagant promises of relief and redemption
if he were placed in control of German policy? Is there the
slightest basis for surprise at German re-armament? If
the people of the United States, with unsurpassed security,
are spending this year more than a billion dollars in preparation for war, how much would they spend if they were subjected to the misery, insecurity and indignity which the Germans have endured throughout the entire lifetime of her youth
of seventeen?

What would the people of Great Britain or France do if
they had surrendered on a basis of definite commitments, one
of which was reduction of national armies to the status of
domestic police, only to find that disarmament was one-sided
against them and that their conquerors refused to carry out
their written pledge? Four years after the Armistice the armament budget of the world was nearly twice as much as in 1914,
and by 1930 the total was approximately three times that of
the pre-war figure. And this in spite of the disarmament of
the vanquished!

An outstanding British writer summarizes the situation in

---

[12] G. D. H. Cole, *The Intelligent Man's Guide Through World Chaos*,
pp. 86-94.

this way: "The story of the Disarmament Conference is a tragic one, not only because of its record of opportunities missed and genuinely well-meant intentions misunderstood, but also because it represents the second great disillusionment which we of the present generation have suffered in the last fifteen years. . . . It is true that the principle of democratic government was forced upon a Germany unprepared and, to a great extent, unsuited for it, but, this having been done, it was hoped that the older democracies of the West would at least extend a helping hand, and would play their part in that policy of fulfilment which first Rathenau, then Stresemann, and then Bruning strove genuinely and honestly to carry out. But it was here that there came the second disillusionment. The promises made to Germany under the Peace Treaties remained unfulfilled, and, having established a democratic form of government in Berlin, the Allies continued to treat it as though it were composed of the most dangerous Prussian War Lords. No measures were taken to remedy the harsh terms of the Treaty and no concession was made to Germany until it was wrung from the Allies by the sheer inexorability of facts. . . . Again and again, with all the eloquence and sincerity at their command, Stresemann and Bruning warned the Allied statesmen, and their warnings were repeated within the Allied countries themselves, that persistence in attempting to keep Germany permanently in subjection must inevitably end in national revolution and all that that implied. Again and again they assured us that it needed only a gesture of understanding from abroad to enable them to meet this new spirit of regeneration in Germany with an open hand, and to control and utilize it in building up a new State of which Europe might be proud. The warnings fell upon deaf ears. France could not, and England, apparently, would not, hear. Relentlessly they held on their same course, and in Germany the last Chancellors of the Republic, Bruning, von Papen, and von Schleicher, struggled vainly to keep in check the rising tide of National Socialism. The end came on 30th January, 1933, when Adolf Hitler was appointed Chancellor and the

Weimar System vanished in blood and recrimination. . . . The new situation must be faced, and it must be realized that the New Germany, the *Dritte Reich* of Adolf Hitler, born alike of the blindness and stupidity of Allied diplomacy and of the deep-seated passions of the revival of German Nationalism, is going to rearm to the fullest degree which she considers necessary, and, having done so, will set about revising the other provisions of the Treaty of Versailles which she considers unjust. . . . In taking account of the policies of the New Germany, dangerous and repulsive as they are, the fact remains that these policies would not have existed today if yesterday the Allies in their wisdom had seen fit to adopt a more friendly and a more sensible attitude towards the Germany which they themselves had created." [13]

Who is responsible for German re-armament? Which other great power would have refrained from re-arming as long as Germany did? These questions bring us back to the dilemma which was discussed in an earlier section.[14] The French have acted in about the same way that any other patriotic people would have acted in a similar situation; and the Germans likewise have responded in about the same manner that any other nation would have done under parallel circumstances. If there is another great war, it will be fought on one side with holy zeal against the aggressor, whereas soldiers on the other side will pour out their blood to free their land from the domination of oppressors.

Should the United States be willing to take up arms against Germany the aggressor in defense of France and Great Britain the oppressors?

II

What will happen to democracy if another great war sweeps over the earth? Merely to ask this question is sufficient answer. Millions of deluded victims imagined that the World War would make the world safe for democracy. Even Woodrow

---

[13] John W. Wheeler-Bennett, *The Pipe Dream of Peace*, pp. xiii, xiv, xv.
[14] See pp. 17-20, 75-79.

Wilson demanded the establishment of democratic government in Germany as a condition of the granting of an armistice. Tragic indeed is the evidence that democracy cannot be maintained or defended by resorting to war in its modern form. We have learned that militarism cannot be ended by militarizing its opponents. And another war should not be required to teach us the obvious and inescapable truth that totalitarianism cannot be ended by totalitarizing its threatened victims.

The very nature of modern war necessitates the abrogation of democracy as an essential condition of success. At least temporarily democratic processes must be set aside by nations that go to war against powerful enemies. Too much emphasis cannot be placed upon the fact that war has become a combat of entire peoples against entire peoples and that all the resources of a nation must be thrown into the struggle for victory. Totalitarianism is the very essence of war in our time.

In every great nation this fact constitutes the cornerstone of preparedness for war. The War Department and the Navy Department of the United States have collaborated in preparing and publishing a comprehensive Industrial Mobilization Plan.[15] This proposal was subjected to detailed analysis by the Special Committee on Investigation of the Munitions Industry (the Nye Committee).[16] From the Nye Committee's report the following comments are taken:

> "The following bills, prepared by the War Department for enactment immediately upon declaration of war by Congress, were introduced, without prejudice, by Senator Clark on February 6, 1935, and were referred to the Special Senate Committee Investigating the Munitions Industry. The purpose of their introduction was to secure public discussion of their merits before any emergency might arise.
>
> "1. S. 1716 (74th Cong., 1st Sess.) is a bill to create a capital-issues committee.

---

[15] This document may be secured for 15 cents from the Superintendent of Documents, Washington, D. C.

[16] *Munitions Industry,* Report No. 944, Part 4. Italics in this section are mine.

"2. S. 1717 is a bill giving the President *control over industry, the power to fix prices and wages,* establish priorities of manufacture and distribution, to purchase and sell any products, to requisition any products, to license production, sale, and distribution, to regulate speculation and profiteering, *and to suspend laws.*

"3. S. 1718 authorizes the President *to take over any personal or real property and to sell it.*

"4. S. 1719 is a bill to establish a marine war-risk insurance bureau.

"5. S. 1720 is a bill authorizing an administration of war trade with power to control exports and imports, secure their distribution, provide for ocean transportation, etc.

"6. S. 1721 is *a universal draft bill* for all male citizens above the age of 18, providing that all persons registered shall remain subject to induction into the public armed force of the United States, and placing under military law all persons who are called during and also *6 months after the emergency,* making all citizens over 18 liable to service in the armed forces, deferring liability to legislative and judicial officers and certain other public offices, giving courts martial concurrent jurisdiction to try registrants failing to report for duty, etc.

"7. S. 1722 is a bill creating a war-finance corporation with a capital stock of $500,000,000 authorized to issue bonds up to $3,000,000,000, to extend loans to banks to finance war needs, etc. . . .

"The committee notes the testimony of the War Department representative that he did not 'know how to take the profits out of war and get the material we have to get.'

"The committee finds little experience in the last war to indicate that this bill (S. 1719) will successfully take the profits out of war and much evidence to indicate that it will not do so.

"The committee finds that under this bill a strict censorship of the press is possible, and finds such censorship undesirable.

"The committee finds that this bill would give the President the power to fix wages throughout the country and that such fixing of wages could not, in fact, be accompanied by equally successful limitation of prices or profits, and that, in effect, the employees under this bill and under S. 1721, taken together, would suffer unequally as against owners and management. . . . S. 1721 is a proposed bill for a draft of men into military service which also allows for the extension of military control over all male citizens above 18 years of age in industry or elsewhere.

"In case of a major war, the cooperation of labor is very important to the successful functioning of the war machinery. The problem of securing such cooperation without necessarily infringing upon established liberties is a difficult one. Testimony covering the industrial mobilization plan indicates that the War Department expects to secure such cooperation by laws and rules which are in fact, although not in name, *orders to industrial and other labor to either work or fight or starve.*

"The industrial mobilization plan sets up as a controller of labor an administrator of labor who is to be an outstanding industrial leader.

"The war industries administration does not provide for any labor representation at all, except on an advisory council which has neither authority nor actual responsibility.

"S. 1721 and the industrial mobilization plan puts the entire male population of the Nation under military control by giving the War Department the power to cancel the deferment of men not inducted into the military force in case such men do not work 'continuously' in such places (at such wages as are fixed under S. 1717) as the Government finds they should work, under penalty of being drafted into military service or being cut off from food, fuel, and the other necessities of life.

"The committee finds that S. 1721, which puts all male labor under registration and provides for such penalties and also for courts martial in case any of the registrants 'fail or neglect fully to perform any duty required of him' *can be used to effect and enforce a draft of labor* and to remove, in effect, the right of any laborer to refuse employment in private industry under conditions or at wages which do not satisfy his needs. The power to call into military service any union or other representatives of labor who become spokesmen for other employees

in attempts to secure higher wages, is *the power to break strikes.*
This can also be done through the use of military force in removing the spokesman from the plant involved to other plants
or into active service or cutting off the food allowances of
all strikers.

"There is nothing in S. 1721 to prevent the use of men in
the military forces to operate industrial plants while in uniform,
which was done in at least one case in the last war. There is
also nothing to prevent the War Department from inducting
all the workers in any plant in the country into military service,
forcing them to work in that plant under military orders.

"The democratic treatment of labor, under the Constitution,
is essential to the survival of our institutions, and should
not be replaced by a military control over labor unless a change
in our institutions has been previously authorized by the people
in the form of amendments to the Constitution.

"In view of the increasing growth in the world of governmental dictatorship, enforced by the military powers, over
large groups of the population, and the constant temptation
therewith presented to certain elements in democracies, such
as ours, to solve their own problems by force, the committee
finds that it is not advisable in the permanent interests of
the Nation to attempt in wartime to draft civilian labor, directly or indirectly, nor is it advisable to continue military control over labor for a period of 6 months after any date which
the President shall in his judgment fix as the end of the
emergency. By deferring a proclamation declaring the emergency terminated (S. 1721, sec. 3) for several years, the President can, if he wishes, maintain an effectual military control
over the whole Nation long into the peace period. . . .

"The draft of men for the trenches will not, under the War
Department plans, be lifted *until 6 months after such time as
the President chooses to declare an end to the emergency.* The
draft of labor, under one name or another, will continue for
the same length of time. During all this period there will
be censorship of the press.

"In view of the growth of dictatorships in the world using labor under military control, it is very important that the people weigh the grave dangers to our democracy involved in the draft of manpower and labor under the conditions proposed. *The price of a war may be actual operating dictatorship, under military control, in this country.* Possibly, under certain circumstances, that price will not be too high for the people to desire to pay it.

"But in this matter the committee suggests that Congress consider putting a limitation upon its own powers, and submit a national referendum at the election in 1938 on the military draft of men for service outside continental America.

"The matter is certainly of sufficient importance to warrant Congress in asking the consent of the Nation before imposing the type of draft indicated to be part of the War Department plans."

The essentials of the Industrial Mobilization Plan, with certain modifications, are contained in a bill introduced by the chairmen of the House and the Senate Military Affairs Committees have introduced their bill (Hill-Sheppard H 1954-S25). commenting upon this bill, Stephen Raushenbush writes: "Democracies don't like a bloody struggle to assume the shape of 'a rich man's war and a poor man's fight.' The contrast between the creation of some thousands of new millionaires and the creation of some scores of thousands of corpses dead from lead and gas has bitten deep. The veterans' groups have been demanding that capital as well as men be drafted in the next war. Other groups are worried by the prospect of a really first-class post-war depression, and join in demanding the heaviest taxation bearable in order to avoid inflation and a real collapse. The gentlemen who run things have taken these feelings into consideration and assure us that the next war will not be marred by profiteering or any inequality of suffering. We now have their rough plans for the next war before us. The chairmen of the House and Senate Military Affairs Committees have introduced their bill (Hill Sheppard H1954-S25).

. . . The bill provides that immediately after Congress has declared war the President, without any further legislation by Congress, can draft the several millions of men between the ages of twenty-one and thirty-one. He can control business by licenses, priorities or shipments, price-fixing, and by inducting managers into the service as civilians. He can appoint all the agencies he deems necessary to carry out his orders and rules, and the fine for disobedience of the rules is $100,000 or a year in jail. Lastly, there is a tax of 95 per cent 'of all income above the previous three-year average.' In five short pages the President is given dictatorial powers which adequately meet Irenee du Pont's dictum, 'an absolute monarch is needed in war time.' *Once we have entered a major war we must expect something like this whether we like it or not.* It is our contribution to the 'totalitarian war,' and there is probably no valid technical objection to the military efficiency of this procedure. The objection comes to the claims made for the bill. Its stated purpose is 'to prevent profiteering in time of war and to equalize the burdens of war and thus provide for the national defense and promote peace.' But the claims made for it, unless they are promptly disproved, may sell to Congress and to the public a measure which actually drafts men in advance of any war, no matter how small, and which strangely 'equalizes the burdens of war' by letting capital make a larger profit in war time than it does in peace time. Capital was not drafted during the last war. It cannot and will not be drafted during the next one. The War Department is not equipped to do it, does not want to do it, and will not do it. Capital will be coaxed and flattered and given what it wants. It will be treated well behind closed doors because the War Department's duty is to win the war rather than save money. . . . Meanwhile the draft of men is not subject to behind-the-door evasion. It is to be taken out of the hands of Congress in 1937 and given to the President. A declaration of war against Mexico, for example, would automatically permit the President to call four million men to the colors. The draft is not something the boys can dodge. It is as real as death and far more real than taxes." [17]

Every possible effort should be put forth to prevent such a bill from being enacted into law. But we should be under no illusions; if the United States goes to war against a great power, even more drastic controls than those contemplated in the Industrial Mobilization Plan will be imposed.

There is little reason to believe that wartime abrogation of democracy will be temporary. Highly significant is the provision in the Industrial Mobilization Plan that conscription does not end with the armistice, but not until six months after the President shall have declared the emergency to be over. What emergency? War ends with an armistice. Why the provisions about six months after the termination of the emergency?

The fact that wartime centralization of power proved to be temporary in several belligerent countries and was abandoned soon after the armistice should not produce undue optimism about the future. Judgments based upon the experience of the older democracies during and following the World War may prove to be misleading. In the intervening years the class conflict has become more intense in all industrial countries, with the result that hereafter international warfare will deepen the cleavage within the respective belligerent nations. The Spanish War illustrates the problem. The sympathy and support of outside nations is determined in large part by their attitudes toward fascism and toward radical democracy. In another great war the cleavage will not only be along national lines but also along class lines.

There is abundant reason to anticipate the outbreak of civil war in belligerent countries in the event of a prolonged international conflict; or at least the possibility of civil war will be so serious that vested interests will be reluctant to relinquish the highly centralized powers of wartime. Perhaps this

---

[17] Stephen Raushenbush, "Kill the Conscription Bill!" *The Nation*, February 27, 1937. Italics are mine. See also his excellent volume, *The War Madness*.

thought was in the minds of the drafters of the Industrial
Mobilization Plan when they inserted the provision about six
months after the termination of the emergency. In commenting upon prevailing trends, Harold J. Laski says: ". . . war
means the creation all over Europe of either communistic dictatorships in alliance with Russia, or Fascist dictatorship in
alliance with great business enterprise, which thirty years ago
in this country, Jack London admirably called 'The Iron Heel';
. . . parliamentary government is incompatible with the possibilities that emerge out of the prospect of war. . . . May I say,
without one moment's hesitation, that in my judgment, constitutional government offers prospects of good to modern
society that are unequalled by any alternative, that the weapons
that are now at the disposal of violence are so disastrous in
their impact that if they are utilized, civilization may easily
become a legend." [18]

Many writers are emphasizing the extreme difficulty of stopping a great war. As an example, William Henry Chamberlin
says: "The World War has shown that any large-scale conflict between great powers is certain to turn into a bitter-end
struggle, with no quarter asked or given, because the penalty
for the leadership of the losing side is political, if not physical
destruction. Every defeated power in the World War experienced a revolution; most of them, to be sure, experienced
secondary revolutions, or counter-revolutions, which partially
restored to power the classes which had been ousted in the
first shock and bitterness of defeat. Russia, although it was
reckoned among the Allies, must also be considered a defeated
power, because the issue of its campaigns was almost invariably
disastrous. Italy also developed a somewhat defeatist psy-
chology, because its showing in the war was much weaker than
that of England and France and it came off very badly in the
distribution of the spoils. So, while a democratic regime would
probably survive a victory in a military struggle, it would almost certainly succumb to a defeat." [19]

[18] Harold J. Laski and Dr. Josef Redlich, *The Decline of Parliamentary
Government*, pp. 10, 11.
[19] William Henry Chamberlin, *Collectivism a False Utopia*, pp. 147, 148.

As citizens of the United States deliberate upon the desirability or undesirability of attempting to preserve democracy by armed action in Europe or in Asia, let them keep vividly in mind the nature of modern war. The mechanization of war which we discussed in an earlier section and the totalitarianism of modern war in combination mean devastation and slaughter on a scale hitherto unimaginable. It would be sheer madness to seek the preservation of democracy by making use of "an irrestible and uncontrollable run-away force of destruction—a Frankenstein monster set to devour its creators." No wonder, therefore, that even a severe critic of fascism writes: "The answer to the threats of the dictators is not a 'preventive war,' nor is it a crusade to help one of the dictatorial ideologies conquer another. We should collaborate with all of them on routine matters in a fair spirit, keep every engagement entered into with them to the letter, and show calmness and official reserve in the face of provocative gestures so long as they remain gestures only. But we should be under no illusions that a live-and-let-live relationship between democracies and dictatorships can last indefinitely. To recognize this does not imply a desire for war. Nobody who cares about the future of democracy wants war. The liberal states could fight, might win. But could their liberalism survive the wartime curbs that would be prerequisite to victory and the new waves of economic deterioration and social disorder that afterwards would overtake the victor along with the vanquished? Hardly. . . . The call is not for an attack on the dictators but for a general mobilization against all their conceptions and practices; for an increase in the sense of interdependence between free peoples; and for energetic efforts at home to broaden the social and economic bases that sustain a solid political union." [20]

The ominous prospect ahead of the nations and a hint as to the way of escape are thus presented by a distinguished Frenchman: "The future, certainly, is not very reassuring. The hopes of those who, following the war, believed in the advent

[20] Armstrong, *op. cit.*, pp. 45, 46.

of a humanity made wise by the great lesson of the world cataclysm, and in which there would be more justice and a better peace, have all gone up in smoke. The world remains a jungle in which peoples, retreating within themselves and armed to the teeth, struggle for their daily bread or for power, and where the triumph of the strongest seems to be the supreme law. The League of Nations, weakened by repeated checks, scarcely seems able to offer the weak any reliable guarantee. There are moments when its seems to be threatened even as to its own existence. We see a new iron age opening up before us." [21]

III

The world remains a jungle! So long as the economic activities of the peoples of the earth are organized on a basis of competitive struggle for private gain, man will continue to devour man and nation will continue to spring ferociously upon nation. But it is possible for the various peoples to transform competitive capitalism into a cooperative commonwealth. And to a consideration of this life-and-death endeavor the next chapter is devoted.

Democracy cannot be preserved by armed preparedness and by resort to war. Change is required, a fundamental change in capitalism and in nationalism. The jungle system must be brought to an end. In the meantime, measures must be adopted which will reduce economic tensions and diminish emotional strain in the handicapped countries. Superior advantages must be shared and steps taken quickly to assure a status of equality to Germany, Italy and Japan. "The German people have been told—and have believed—that the whole world is against them, a conviction which the events of the last twenty years do not seem to have disproved. They are convinced that they are encircled by an iron ring, and that the other powers are merely waiting a favorable opportunity to destroy them." [22] It will not be easy to dislodge this idea from the minds of peoples who look upon themselves as victims of oppression. But we dare not fail in this endeavor.

[21] Henri Lichtenberger, *The Third Reich*, p. 297.
[22] Mildred S. Wertheimer, *Germany Under Hitler*, p. 48.

Chapter Six

Can the United States Stay Out of Another Great War?

YES! IF! If the American people are willing to pay a sufficiently high price, and if in advance of the crisis they count the cost of refraining from war. One must hasten to admit, however, that we are not warranted in glibly assuming that the required conditions will be fulfilled. The odds are heavily against successful endeavor to stay out of a prolonged war involving great powers.

The will to keep out of armed hostilities on foreign soil is highly important. Even if the people were united in their determination to refrain from war, the task would be extremely difficult; and these difficulties will become more formidable just to the degree that peace advocates support a policy of American participation in the use of armed sanctions, or even to the use of economic sanctions against a great power under prevailing conditions.

An illustration is found in a leaflet, *A Constructive Neutrality Policy,* issued by the League of Nations Association, where we are told: "The essential feature of discretionary legislation is the grant of authority to the President to determine the aggressor nation, to apply embargoes against that nation only. ... A mandatory neutrality law which makes no distinction between aggressor and victim ignores or contradicts existing American treaties and the first principles of American diplomacy. ... Mandatory embargo legislation, contrary to the spirit of these treaties, implies the strict equality of aggressor and victim. ... Discretionary legislation would tend to prevent the outbreak of war by announcing in advance that the United

States will discriminate against the state which has been found to be the aggressor." [1]   The argument may be advanced that this is sound policy, *but surely it is not neutrality to take sides against one nation in favor of another nation.*

The impracticability of using sanctions against a great power under present circumstances has been discussed at length in an earlier section.[2]   A genuinely and comprehensively international tribunal cannot function so long as Germany, Italy, Japan, the United States and several other countries refrain from membership; and so long as *oppressor* nations look upon it as a means of freezing a status quo which is regarded as insufferable by *aggressor* nations.   During the critical next ten years there is only a remote possibility that armed sanctions can be used successfully, or even that economic sanctions can prevail, against a great power.

Therefore it would be the height of folly for the American people to base their neutrality policy upon the assumption that we may find it advisable to take sides against an aggressor in favor of an oppressor.   There is scarcely one chance in a hundred that during the next decade the citizens of this country will consent to participation in the imposition of sanctions against a great power.   Immense harm has been done in the United States to the cause of the League of Nations by the advocacy of sanctions.   Persons like myself who oppose all armed sanctions, and even economic sanctions under prevailing conditions, are not isolationists; on the contrary, *the surest way to continue the isolation of the United States from the League of Nations and to delay indefinitely acceptance of membership in the League by this country is through advocacy of a policy which would bind the United States to take sides in controversies in Europe and in Asia.*   Friends of the League will do well to exalt Article 19 and to minimize Articles 10 and 16, that is to place emphasis upon the necessity of bringing about changes in situations which entrench oppressors, and to abandon efforts

---

[1] For an elaboration of this point of view, see James T. Shotwell, *On the Rim of the Abyss.*
[2] See pp. 95 ff.

to preserve unjust and intolerable conditions through the use of sanctions. It is confusing therefore to place opponents of sanctions in the camp of isolationists; whereas there is more justification, so far as the United States is concerned, in designating advocates of sanctions as effective isolationists.

The will to keep out of all foreign wars is highly essential. To harbor the illusion that democracy and other high values may be preserved through resort to armed action in Europe or in Asia by the United States may prove fatal.

I

What are the primary features of existing neutrality legislation? To what extent is it satisfactory and adequate? On April 29, 1937, Congress adopted a neutrality act with the following provisions:[3]

1. In the event the President shall find that there exists a state of war between or among foreign States, or that civil strife of great magnitude exists in a State, he shall proclaim such fact, and it shall therefore be unlawful to export arms, ammunition, or implements of war to belligerent countries, or to neutral countries for transshipment to belligerent countries.

2. If under the circumstances the President shall find that the placing of restrictions on the shipment of certain other articles or materials is necessary to promote the security or preserve the peace of the United States, he shall so proclaim, and it shall thereafter be unlawful for any American vessel to carry such articles of materials to any belligerent State. When the President shall have issued such a proclamation, it shall thereafter be unlawful to export or transport such articles or materials to a belligerent State until all right, title and interest therein shall have been transferred to some foreign government or agency. Insurance written on such articles shall not be deemed an American interest therein and shall not be used as a basis of a claim put forward by the United States.

---

[3] See *International Conciliation*, June, 1937. Also *New York Times*, April 30, 1937.

3. In the event that the President proclaims the existence of a state of war, it shall be unlawful for any person within the United States to purchase, sell, or exchange bonds, securities or other obligations of belligerent governments, with the exception of certain commercial credits and short-time obligations.

4. This Act shall not apply to an American republic engaged in a war against a non-American State, provided the American republic is not cooperating with a non-American State in such a war.

5. There is hereby established a National Munitions Control Board to supervise the execution of these various provisions.

6. In the event that the President proclaims the existence of a state of war, it shall be unlawful for any American vessel to carry any arms, ammunition, or implements of war to any belligerent State.

7. Specifications are made for the use of American ports as base of supply during wartime.

8. Conditions are set forth which must be observed by submarines and armed merchant vessels during wartime.

9. In the event that the President proclaims the existence of a state of war, it shall be unlawful for any citizen of the United States to travel on any vessel of a belligerent State, with certain specified exceptions.

10. In the event that the President proclaims the existence of a state of war, it shall be unlawful for any American vessel engaged in commerce with a belligerent State to be armed or to carry any armament, arms, ammunition, or implements of war, except certain small arms.

II

This legislation constitutes a drastic reversal of policies which led to the entrance of the United States into the World War. A mandatory embargo is placed on the exportation of munitions and other implements of war, on loans and credits to belligerent government, on the transportation by an American vessel of munitions to a belligerent government, on travel by Americans on vessels of belligerents, and on arming American merchant vessels. Before considering the weaknesses of this act, it may be well to remind ourselves of the extent to which these mandatory provisions reverse policies long adhered to by the United States.

In the proclamation of neutrality issued on August 4, 1914, which "was taken as a matter of course without discussion," it was stated that "all persons may lawfully and without restriction . . . manufacture and sell within the United States arms and munitions of war." Never for a moment was President Wilson willing to abridge in the slightest degree this right of Americans to sell arms. In his memoirs Secretary Lansing included a chapter in which he defended with "moral considerations" the traffic in arms. His reasons were summarized in a quotation from a famous note sent to the Austrian government: "The principles of international law, the practice of nations, the national safety of the United States and other nations without great military establishments, the prevention of increased armies and navies, the adoption of peaceful methods for the adjustment of international differences, and, finally, neutrality itself are opposed to the prohibition by a neutral nation of the exportation of arms, ammunition or other munitions of war to belligerent powers during the progress of the war." President Wilson's biographer tells us that "the protests of pacifists and humanitarians regarding the trade in munitions were ignored or acknowledged perfunctorily."

There is much cumulative evidence that President Wilson was obsessed with the idea that American rights must be maintained even if this insistence dragged us into war. This conviction is set forth in a letter to Senator Stone: ". . . if the clear rights of American citizens should ever unhappily be abridged or denied . . . we should, it seems to me, have in honor no choice as to what our own course should be. . . . We covet peace and shall preserve it at any cost but the loss of honor. To forbid our people to exercise their rights for fear we might be called upon to vindicate them would be a deep humiliation indeed." In discussing the popular demand for firmness in upholding

American rights and the even more popular demand that he keep America out of war, the President, in Milwaukee said: ". . . there may at any moment come a time when I cannot preserve both the honor and the peace of the United States. Do not exact of me an impossible and contradictory thing." This basic idea was put bluntly in a note from the secretary of state to the American ambassador in Berlin: "No matter what England does to Germany or Germany to England, our rights are unaltered and we cannot abate them in the least." These words merely voiced patriotic sentiment throughout the nation.

So profound has been the change in public opinion that in 1937 the drastic embargoes listed above were passed by the House without a dissenting vote and with only 15 negative votes recorded in the Senate.

III

The chief weakness of the existing law is found in section two which deals with articles and materials other than munitions and implements of war. Coal and iron and oil and cotton are as essential to the waging of war as gunpowder and shrapnel. Discretion of action is given to the President in the 1937 act. He may decide that certain articles or materials, as distinguished from munitions and other implements of war, shall be placed on a cash-and-carry basis; that is, belligerent nations must come and get materials thus designated by the President.

The Senate bill contained a mandatory provision, which was later stricken out in conference with the House committee. The following provision was passed by the Senate, with only six negative votes recorded: "It shall be unlawful to export or transport to any belligerent country, or to any country wherein civil strife exists, named in said proclamation . . . or to any other country for transshipment to, or for the use of, such belligerent country or such country wherein civil strife exists, *any article or materials whatever until all right, title, and interest therein shall have been transferred to some foreign govern-*

ment, agency, institution, association, partnership, corporation, or national."

If this provision had been adopted it would have left the door wide open for vast purchases in this country by nations with command of the seas and with access to American securities. This means that Great Britain would be able in the event of war to buy billions of dollars' worth of American commodities. As a result, American financiers would again find themselves with a huge stake in the outcome of the war and for this reason the United States would find neutrality much more difficult. Therefore, many students of international problems are convinced that *it is highly desirable to limit the volume of purchases on a cash-and-carry basis to a quota equivalent to the average purchases of a given nation over the preceding five-year period.* In this way normal peacetime trade could be maintained with nations which are able to come and get their quotas, without involving this country deeply in the outcome of the war.

The deletion of this mandatory provision in the conference committee of the Senate and the House seems to me highly deplorable. Discretionary power will subject the President to terrific cross currents of political pressure in the hour of crisis and passion. Belligerent nations which consider themselves victims of the President's decisions will bitterly resent what they will interpret as discrimination. *Discretionary power is preferable if the objective is to induce the United States to take sides in a foreign conflict; mandatory provisions are preferable if the purpose is to keep the United States out of armed hostilities.*

Persons who desire to vest in the President such vast discretionary power will do well to remind themselves of the steps by which the United States became involved in the World War.[4] The extreme importance of the personal attitudes of high officials is made vividly clear by an examination of the relevant

---

[4] See Walter Millis, *The Road to War;* Edwin L. Borchard and William Potter Lage, *Neutrality for the United States.*

documents. The four individuals who acted as President Wilson's closest advisers were all strongly pro-British and anti-German in feeling: Colonel House, Secretary Lansing, Ambassador Page and Ambassador Gerard. The result was that British infractions of American rights were not regarded with the same resentment and abhorrence as were German violations. The Allied blockade produced far more suffering and caused many more deaths of women and children in Germany than were caused by German submarine warfare. But fatalities from blockade did not produce more than a tiny fraction of the revulsion that was caused by submarine warfare. If Germany had succeeded in starving the British and the latter had retaliated with unrestricted submarine warfare, the feelings of high American officials would have been vastly different.

Before the end of the first year of the war Secretary Lansing had written down his conviction that the United States should enter the conflict "in case it becomes evident that Germany will be the victor. A triumph for German imperialism must not be." Twelve months later he wrote: "I only hope that the President will adopt the true policy, which is, 'Join the Allies as soon as possible and crush down the German autocrats.' If he takes drastic measures against Great Britain, he will never be forgiven." [5]

No person was more acutely aware than Secretary Lansing that Great Britain was engaged in wholesale violations of American rights. "Under the accepted rules of international law these detentions and seizures were illegal and indefensible," he wrote, "as were the lists of contraband issued from time to time by the British government. . . . Many more Americans were directly affected by these British practices than were affected by the activities of German submarines." [5a]

Nevertheless, as secretary of state of a neutral nation, Mr. Lansing wrote: "Sympathetic as I felt toward the Allies and convinced that we would in the end join with them against the autocratic governments of the Central Powers, I saw with ap-

[5] *War Memoirs of Robert Lansing,* p. 173.
[5a] *Ibid,* p. 23.

prehension the tide of resentment against Great Britain rising
higher and higher in this country. . . . I did all that I could to
prolong the disputes by preparing, or having prepared, long
and detailed replies, and introducing technical and controversial
matters in the hope that before the extended interchange of
arguments came to an end something would happen to change
the current of American public opinion or to make the American people perceive that German absolutism was a menace to
their liberties and to democratic institutions everywhere. . . .
Short and emphatic notes were dangerous.   Everything was
submerged in verbosity.   It was done with deliberate purpose.
It insured continuance of the controversies and left the questions unsettled, which was necessary in order to leave this
country free to act and even to act illegally when it entered the
war." [6]

And the writer of these amazing words was President Wilson's secretary of state and most frequent counselor!   Yet this
pro-British official of the United States felt obliged to record
this opinion of the American ambassador in London: ". . . it
was useless to present protests and complaints through him, in
view of his manifest unwillingness to protect the rights of
Americans, if the exercise of those rights interfered with the
British war policies." [7]   That there was abundant justification
for this statement is evident from a notation in the British foreign minister's memoirs.   "Page's advice and suggestions,"
wrote Viscount Grey, "were of the greatest value in warning
us when to be careful or encouraging us when we could safely
be firm. . . . Page came to see me at the foreign office one day
and produced a long dispatch from Washington contesting our
claim to act as we were doing in stopping contraband going to
neutral ports.   'I am instructed,' he said, 'to read this dispatch
to you.'   He read, and I listened.   He then said: 'I have now
read the dispatch, but I do not agree with it; let us consider
how it should be answered!'" [8]

---

[6] *Ibid*, pp. 111, 112, 128, 171.
[7] *Ibid*, pp. 170, 166.
[8] Viscount Grey, *Twenty-five Years,* vol. 2, p. 110.

To favor discretionary legislation is logical for persons who desire to keep the United States free to take sides against an aggressor nation; and to support mandatory legislation is equally logical for persons who desire to keep the United States out of foreign conflicts.

The existing statute is incomplete in that it does not declare in specific terms that all trade and travel in a war zone by American citizens must be at the risk of the trader or traveler and that the Government of the United States assumes no responsibility for their armed protection. At the time of the Ethiopian crisis, President Roosevelt and Secretary Hull set forth this policy, but it has not yet been officially adopted as the permanent policy of this country. In his proclamation of October 5, 1935, the President said: "I do hereby give notice that any citizen of the United States who may travel on such a vessel, contrary to the provisions of said Joint Resolution, will do so at his own risk." [9] In a subsequent statement the President said: "By my public statement of October fifth, which was emphasized by the Secretary of State on October tenth, *we have warned American citizens against transactions of any character with either of the belligerent nations except at their own risk.*" [9] This policy was re-affirmed by Secretary Hull in his Note to the President of the Committee of Coordination of the League of Nations, as follows: "In addition to the three measures just mentioned, the President took a fourth and most important step by issuing a public statement definitely warning American citizens against transactions of any character with either of the belligerent nations except at their own risk." [10]

IV

Another weakness of the existing law is that the embargo against the exportation of munitions and other implements of war is not applicable until after the President has proclaimed that a state of war exists; and therefore does not shut off shipments to Germany and Italy for use in Spain or to Japan for

[9] Phillips Bradley, *Can We Stay Out of War?* p. 255. Italics mine.
[10] *Ibid*, p. 259.

use in China. Declarations of war are now out of fashion; nations simply start armed hostilities without the formality of a declaration of war. Therefore the only effective policy is to prevent all exportation of munitions in peacetime as well as in wartime; in spite of the fact that such a policy plays into the hands of the nations that are best equipped to manufacture their own implements of war. American foreign policy should not be determined with a view to aiding the armed action of some other nation, but with the avowed purpose of reducing the likelihood of its own participation in war. The weaker nations can never achieve justice and security by resort to arms and it would be folly for the United States to shape its own policy under the illusion that helping another country to wage war is effective.

Therefore, the American people will do well to support the following amendment to the neutrality law, as introduced by Congressman Fish:

> "Section 3. (a) It shall be unlawful to export, or attempt to export or cause to be exported, arms, ammunition, or implements of war from any place in the United States in peace or war." [11]

V

The people of the United States can stay out of wars in Europe and Asia if they have the will to do so. But they must be prepared to face serious economic difficulties and to endure substantial financial losses. Drastic embargoes are essential if this country is to keep out of a prolonged war involving great powers; and embargoes are costly to neutral countries, as well as to belligerent nations. It is of the utmost importance that the rank and file of citizens should open their eyes to the unavoidable necessity of paying the costs of peace if they are to avoid the far heavier costs of war and the yet greater costs of the consequent economic depression which follows in its wake.

The cost of refraining from war will be heavy, but it is easy

[11] Speech of Hon. Hamilton Fish of New York in the House of Representatives, March 18, 1937.

*to exaggerate these losses. Even a drastic policy of embargoes
on exports to belligerent countries would affect only a portion
of our total foreign trade. And if a cash-and-carry policy,
with a peacetime quota, were adopted, the loss of exports would
probably not exceed 15 per cent of our total annual exports.*
Normal trade with Canada, Central America and South America would be dislocated only to a slight degree. Even if Japan
were a belligerent, our normal trade with the Far East would
not be seriously affected. American exports to Europe would
suffer, but not disastrously, because Great Britain and her
allies would probably be able to come and get their normal
quota. Trade with European enemies of Great Britain would
be reduced drastically. But this loss would constitute only a
small fraction of the total American exports. Here are some
illuminating figures:

EXPORTS AND IMPORTS OF THE UNITED STATES BY COUNTRIES[12]
(Values in thousands of dollars; that is, 000 omitted)

Country	1921-25 Average Exports	Imports	1935 Exports	Imports
Grand Total	4,397,027	3,450,103	2,282,874	2,047,485
North America	1,071,959	910,902	531,331	494,557
Canada	619,017	393,771	323,194	286,444
Mexico	146,345	147,488	65,574	42,467
Central America	58,738	36,357	38,637	29,207
West Indies and Bermuda	239,494	330,388	97,577	129,734
South America	297,115	421,336	174,341	281,472
Europe	2,310,958	1,042,553	1,029,241	598,716
Denmark	42,615	6,029	12,481	3,337
France	265,196	147,875	117,013	58,107
Germany	383,219	132,496	91,981	77,792
Norway	28,081	18,498	13,624	16,502
Sweden	39,443	34,073	38,216	41,247
United Kingdom	939,412	355,781	433,399	155,282
Italy	185,237	79,141	72,416	38,674
Asia	505,839	949,820	377,940	604,537
Philippine Islands	51,927	80,108	52,640	96,999
China	104,175	142,035	38,153	64,164
Japan	241,877	335,384	203,283	152,902
Oceania	141,426	53,994	73,802	26,481
Africa	69,729	71,499	96,219	41,732

[12] *Foreign Commerce and Navigation of the United States,* Calendar Year 1935, pp. 701, 702.

From this table it will be seen that in 1935 American exports to Germany, Italy and other European countries likely to be arrayed against Great Britain in the event of a general war do not constitute as much as 10 per cent of the total foreign sales of the United States. And imports from these countries do not equal six per cent of all the commodities purchased abroad by this country. If Japan is included among the enemies of Great Britain, and Japan's trade with the United States should be reduced by half, the consequent loss of exports from the United States would be less than five percent, while the loss of imports from Japan would be less than four percent, of the total American exports and imports.

A realistic picture must include the effects of embargoes on special commodities, say cotton for illustration. What would happen to cotton-growing states in wartime if a drastic embargo were imposed on exports? Exports of raw cotton in 1935 to Germany, Italy and Japan were as follows:

Germany	$ 38,452,681
Italy	29,935,050
Japan	98,586,883
	$166,974,614

This figure constitutes approximately 44 percent of the total value ($383,398,427) of cotton exported in 1935 from the United States.[13]

Our total exports of petroleum and its products in 1935 amounted to $250,326,649, of which $49,468,099, or about 20 percent, went to Germany, Italy and Japan, as follows:[14]

Germany	$ 14,018,950
Italy	9,798,905
Japan	25,650,244

In 1935 the United States exported iron ore, iron and steel semi-manufactures, iron and steel advanced manufactures, and steel mill products to the value of $121,509,326, or which $22,-

[13] *Ibid*, pp. 402, 403.
[14] *Ibid*, p. 440.

745,518, or about 19 percent went to Germany, Italy and Japan, as follows: [15]

Germany.............................$	280,121
Italy.................................	5,078,753
Japan................................	17,386,644

Total exports of American automobiles and parts in 1935 amounted to $227,290,219, of which Germany, Italy and Japan bought $15,174,816, or seven percent of the total, as follows:[16]

Germany.............................$	1,159,007
Italy.................................	999,826
Japan................................	13,015,983

Machinery constitutes another principal export of the United States; and of various kinds only industrial machinery is exported on a substantial scale to Germany, Italy and Japan, these three countries buying a total of $10,481,775, or about nine percent of our total exports ($121,783,504) of industrial machinery.[17] Their purchases of other types of machinery represents a small proportion of our exports.

It thus becomes apparent that the combined purchases of Germany, Italy and Japan from the United States amount to a substantial proportion of the chief exports from this country *only in the cases of cotton (44 percent), petroleum (20 percent), iron and steel (19 percent).* The total value of their combined purchases of these three commodities from the United States in 1935 amounted to $239,188,231.

In the event of a general war in which these three countries were arrayed against Great Britain, with the consequence that their imports from the United States would be drastically reduced by the British navy, the economic effects upon this country would be serious, but not disastrous.

It would doubtless be advisable for the government of the United States to subsidize to some extent the industries which are especially hard hit by wartime embargoes and spread the

---

[15] *Ibid*, pp. 452, 453, 455, 456, 461.
[16] *Ibid*, pp. 510, 511.
[17] *Ibid*, p. 488.

losses over the entire population. *The total amount of these subsidies would constitute only a tiny fraction of the cost of waging war.*

VI

If the decision as to whether or not the United States should engage in armed hostilities depended upon a rational evaluation of the comparative costs of waging war and of taking the consequences of refraining from war, the American people could sleep peacefully. Two crucial factors however make a sane decision difficult: the prospect of making huge war profits; and the effects of a general war upon the judgments and emotions of the American people. Losses due to a drastic embargo would be much less than the failure to reap war profits. It is not enough therefore to convince the citizens of this land that it is cheaper and safer to subsidize industries seriously injured by embargoes than to wage war. Their eyes must also be opened to the consequences of attempting to reap excessive wartime profits.

In his Chautauqua address, President Roosevelt said:[18] "It is clear that our present policy and the measures passed by the Congress would in the event of a war on some other continent, reduce war profits which would otherwise accrue to American citizens. Industrial and agricultural production for a war market may give immense fortunes to a few men; for the nation as a whole it produces disaster. It was the prospect of war profits that made our farmers in the west plow up prairie land that should never have been plowed, but should have been left for grazing cattle. Today we are reaping the harvest of those war profits in the dust storms which have devastated those war plowed areas. It was the prospect of war profits that caused the extension of monopoly and unjustified expansion of industry and a price level so high that the normal relationship between debtor and creditor was destroyed.

"Nevertheless, if war should break out again in another continent, let us not blink the fact that we would find in this coun-

[18] August 14, 1936.

try thousands of Americans who, seeking immediate riches—
fools' gold—would attempt to break down or evade our neutrality. They would tell you—and, unfortunately, their views
would get wide publicity—that if they could produce and ship
this and that and the other article to belligerent nations, the
unemployed of America would all find work. They would tell
you that if they could extend credit to warring nations that

*Would these gentlemen, whose eagerness for juicy war orders and fat war profits finally involved the
United States in the World War, be as shortsighted in the next war?*

*Or have they learned from bitter experience that their temporary gains from fat war orders are but
a drop in the bucket compared to their losses if their country becomes entrapped in war?*

credit would be used in the United States to build homes and factories and pay our debts. They would tell you that America once more would capture the trade of the world.

"It would be hard to resist that clamor; it would be hard for many Americans, I fear, to look beyond—to realize the inevitable penalties, the inevitable day of reckoning that comes from a false prosperity. To resist the clamor of that greed, if war should come, would require the unswerving support of all Americans who love peace. If we face the choice of profits or peace, the Nation will answer—must answer—'we choose peace.' It is the duty of all of us to encourage such a body of public opinion in this country that the answer will be clear and for all practical purposes unanimous."

The accompanying cartoon by McCutcheon vividly illustrates the American dilemma. And no person with a keen memory of what happened to the minds of our people during 1914 to 1917 will minimize the difficulties ahead if a general war breaks out in Europe and Asia. The adoption in peacetime of a comprehensive policy of mandatory embargoes would help American citizens to hold steady. Abandonment of the policy of armed intervention abroad and of armed preparedness to fight in distant lands and waters would reduce substantially the likelihood of our becoming involved in a general war. The building up of a reserve fund with which to subsidize industries severely injured by wartime embargoes would make it easier to stay out of a general war. The present expenditure of approximately a billion dollars annually for the army and navy could be reduced by half through abandonment of the policy of preparedness to fight abroad and thus make available half a billion dollars per year for this reserve fund.

If the decision is made on financial grounds, this country will never again go to war. If we become a belligerent it will be because of illusions and passions; the illusion that war can be made a source of profit for people in general; and the illusion that war can be used successfully as an instrument of international policy for the preservation of democracy and other high values. Passion may play a decisive role; hatred of one set of belligerents or the other; and hatred of fascism or of communism.

Legislation will help; education which clarifies the issues will help. But success in the endeavor to keep this country out of war and to promote world peace depends upon our ability to shatter illusions and to restrain passions which blind and infuriate. Therefore the odds are heavily against us.

Chapter Seven

What Should Church and Synagogue Do About War?

WHAT CONTRIBUTION has religion to offer in helping to prevent war? Which basic principles of religion shed light upon the problem of participation or non-participation in war? Why have church and synagogue so often sanctioned and supported war? What would be the effects of entire excommunication of war by organized religion?

High regard for human personality; deep concern for human welfare; recognition of kinship with every other individual; craving for comradeship; zealous striving to do justice; reliance upon active goodwill as the effective means of overcoming evil; courageous and sacrificial willingness to run risks and accept consequences of faithful allegiance to the way of love; worship of God and trust in His wisdom and love and power—these are characteristics of men and women who dwell on the highest level of religion.

I

In his scale of values Jesus places human personality at the pinnacle. Because they are children of God, human beings possess inherent and inestimable value. Created in the spiritual image of the Eternal, they constitute the highest achievement of the creative process. Every person is an object of God's concern, irrespective of his ability and achievement. The sick and the afflicted, the dull and the ignorant, the vicious and the depraved—all are sons and daughters of a loving Father and as such are of great worth in themselves. Therefore human beings should always be looked upon with reverence and treated with the respect which is their right.

165

"Then God said, 'Let us make man in our image, after our likeness, and let him have dominion. . . .' So God created man in his own image; in the image of God he created him." [1] "Do you not know that you are God's Sanctuary, and that the Spirit of God has His home within you?" [2] "For we are the Temple of the ever-living God." [3] ". . . the very hairs on your heads are all counted. Away with fear: you are more precious than a multitude of sparrows." [4] If any one causes one of these "lowly ones" to stumble, "it would be far better for him if he had been thrown into the sea with a great millstone round his neck." [5] ". . . it is the will of my Father who is in Heaven that not one of these lowly ones should be lost." [6] "One day a leper came to Jesus and, falling on his knees, begged him for help. . . . Moved with compassion, Jesus stretched out His hand and touched him, saying as He did so: 'I am willing; become clean.' " [7] "And when He saw the crowds He was touched with pity for them, because they were distressed and were fainting on the ground like sheep which have no shepherd." [8] "So Jesus went out and saw an immense multitude, and felt compassion for them, and cured those of them who were out of health." [9] "And when he saw the city, as he approached, he wept over it. . . ." [10]

II

Concerning relationships, the message of high religion is that every man is kin to every other man; all are children of

[1] Gen. 1:26, 27, *The Bible: An American Translation,* published by the University of Chicago Press.

[2] I Cor. 3:16, *The New Testament in Modern Speech,* by Richard Francis Weymouth, published by James Clarke & Co., London.

[3] II Cor. 6:16, Weymouth.

[4] Luke 12: 7, Weymouth.

[5] Mark 9:42, *The Twentieth Century New Testament,* published by Fleming H. Revell Company, New York.

[6] Matt. 18:14, Twentieth Century.

[7] Mark 1:40, Twentieth Century.

[8] Matt. 9:36, Weymouth.

[9] Matt. 14:14, Weymouth.

[10] Luke 19:41, *The New Testament, A New Translation,* by James Moffatt, published by Harper and Brothers, New York.

one Father, so all are brethren. Kinship extends across boundaries of race, nation, class. Men of every tongue and condition possess in themselves great worth and should be recognized as beloved relatives.

"In this manner therefore pray: Our Father. . . ."[11] "I see quite plainly that God has no favourites. . . ."[12] "Then an expounder of the Law stood up to test Him with a question. "Rabbi," he asked, "what shall I do to inherit the Life of the Ages?" "Go to the Law," said Jesus; "what is written there? how does it read?" "Thou shalt love the Lord thy God," he replied, "with thy whole heart, thy whole soul, thy whole strength, and thy whole mind; and thy fellow man as much as thyself." "A right answer," said Jesus; "do that, and you shall live." But he, desiring to justify himself, said, "But what is meant by my 'fellow man'?" Jesus replied, "A man was once on his way down from Jerusalem to Jericho when he fell among robbers, who after both stripping and beating him went away, leaving him half dead. Now a priest happened to be going down that way, and on seeing him passed by on the other side. In like manner a Levite also came to the place, and seeing him passed by on the other side. But a certain Samaritan, being on a journey, came where he lay, and seeing him was moved with pity. He went to him, and dressed his wounds with oil and wine and bound them up. Then placing him on his own mule he brought him to an inn, where he bestowed every care on him. The next day he took out two shillings and gave them to the innkeeper. 'Take care of him,' he said, 'and whatever further expense you are put to, I will repay it you at my next visit.' Which of those three seems to you to have acted like a fellow man to him who fell among the robbers?" "The one who showed him pity," he replied. "Go," said Jesus, "and act in the same way."[13]

"Then the King will say to those on his right, 'Come, you who are blessed by my Father, enter upon possession of the

---

[11] Matt. 6:9, Weymouth.
[12] Acts 10:34, Moffatt.
[13] Luke 10:25-37, Weymouth.

Kingdom prepared for you ever since the beginning of the world.   For, when I was hungry, you gave me food; when I was thirsty, you gave me drink; when I was a stranger, you took me to your homes; when I was naked, you clothed me; when I fell ill, you visited me; and when I was in prison, you came to me.'   Then the Righteous will answer 'Lord, when did we see you hungry, and feed you? or thirsty, and gave you drink?   When did we see you a stranger, and take you to our homes? or naked and clothe you?   When did we see you ill, or in prison, and come to you?'   And the King will reply 'I tell you, as often as you did it to one of these my Brothers, however lowly, you did it to me.' " [14]

III

High religion calls for justice and more than justice.   Because every man regardless of race, nation, class or condition, is a beloved kinsman of priceless worth in himself, he must be treated with fairness and equity.   But this is not enough; an esteemed brother deserves magnanimity and generosity.   Beyond justice is affection and fellowship.

> "Even though you bring me your burnt-offerings,
> And your meal-offerings, I will not accept them . . .
> But let justice roll down like waters,
> And righteousness like a perennial stream." [15]

"And treat men just as you wish them to treat you." [16]   "Then Peter came to him and said, 'Master, how many times am I to forgive my brother when he wrongs me?   Seven times over?' Jesus said to him, 'Not seven times over, I tell you, but seventy-seven times over!' " [17]   "For the whole Law is summed up in one saying: 'You must love your neighbor as you do yourself.' But if you bite one another and eat one another, take care, or

[14] Matt. 25:34-40, Twentieth Century.
[15] Amos 5:22, 24, An American Translation.
[16] Luke 6:31, *The New Testament, An American Translation,* by Edgar J. Goodspeed, published by The University of Chicago Press, Chicago.
[17] Matt. 18:21, 22, Goodspeed.

you will be destroyed by one another. . . . But what the Spirit produces is love, joy, peace, patience, kindness, goodness, faithfulness, gentleness, self-control. . . . If we live by the Spirit, let us be guided by the Spirit. Let us not in our vanity challenge one another or envy one another. But if a man is caught doing something wrong, brothers, you are spiritual, and you must set him right, in a spirit of gentleness. Think of yourself, for you may be tempted too. Bear one another's burdens, and in that way carry out the law of the Christ. . . . Let us not get tired of doing right, for at the proper time we shall reap, if we do not give out. So then whenever we have an opportunity, let us do good to all men, especially to those who belong to the family of the faith." [18] "We, the strong, ought to take on our own shoulders the weaknesses of those who are not strong, and not merely to please ourselves. Let each of us please his neighbour for his neighbour's good, to help in the building up of his character. Even the Christ did not please himself!" [19]

> Blessed are those who feel their spiritual need, for the
>   Kingdom of Heaven belongs to them!
> Blessed are the mourners, for they will be consoled!
> Blessed are the humble-minded, for they will possess the
>   land!
> Blessed are those who are hungry and thirsty for up-
>   rightness, for they will be satisfied!
> Blessed are the merciful, for they will be shown mercy!
> Blessed are the pure in heart, for they will see God!
> Blessed are the peacemakers, for they will be called
>   God's sons! [20]

IV

The ultimate test of any way of life is found in its practice of dealing with opponents and enemies. Unrestrained retaliation in course of time was tempered by the doctrine of only an

---

[18] Gal. 5 :14-6 :10, Goodspeed.
[19] Rom. 15 :1, 2, Twentieth Century.
[20] Matt. 5 :3-9, Goodspeed.

eye for an eye and only a tooth for a tooth. And on the highest levels of religion, revenge is never sought; reliance is
placed in the method of overcoming evil with active goodness.
Because every man is a son of God and a revered kinsman,
possessing in himself great worth and high capacity to respond
to the appeal of kindliness and magnanimity, the way of untiring goodwill should be followed unswervingly, even when
confronted with enemies. Therefore we are called upon to
live now as if we are already in God's Home; to refrain from
ways of thinking and acting which disrupt bonds of affection
and cooperation; to incarnate attitudes and practices which
build up the family spirit; to run risks and accept consequences
of loyal devotion to the way of love.

"You have heard they were told, 'An eye for an eye and a
tooth for a tooth.' But I tell you not to resist injury, but if
anyone strikes you on your right cheek, turn the other to him
too. . . . You have heard that they were told, 'You must love
your neighbor and hate your enemy.' But I tell you, love your
enemies and pray for your persecutors, so that you may show
yourselves true sons of your Father in heaven, for he makes
his sun rise on bad and good alike, and makes the rain fall on
the upright and the wrongdoers. For if you love only those
who love you, what reward can you expect? Do not the very
tax-collectors do that? And if you are polite to your brothers
and no one else, what is there remarkable in that? Do not the
very heathen do that? So you are to be perfect, as your heavenly
Father is." [21] "Your love must be genuine. You must hate
what is wrong, and hold to what is right. . . . Bless your persecutors; bless them; do not curse them. . . . Do not pay anyone back with evil for evil. See that you are above reproach
in the eyes of everyone. If possible, for your part, live peaceably with everybody. Do not take revenge, dear friends, but
leave room for God's anger, for the Scripture says, 'Vengeance belongs to me; I will pay them back, says the Lord.'
No! If your enemy is hungry, feed him! If he is thirsty, give
him something to drink! For if you do, you will heap burn-

[21] Matt. 5:38-48, Goodspeed.

ing coals upon his head! Do not be conquered by evil, but conquer evil with good." [22] "Master, how often shall my brother act wrongly towards me and I forgive him? Seven times?" "I do not say seven times," answered Jesus, "but seventy times seven times." [23] "And now I will point out to you a way of life which transcends all others. If I can speak with the tongues of men and of angels, but am destitute of Love, I have but become a loud-sounding trumpet or a clanging cymbal. . . . Love is patient and kind. Love knows neither envy nor jealousy. Love is not forward and self-assertive, nor boastful and conceited. She does not behave unbecomingly, nor seek to aggrandize herself, nor blaze out in passionate anger, nor brood over wrongs. She finds no pleasure in injustice done to others, but joyfully sides with the truth. She knows how to be silent. She is full of trust, full of hope, full of patient endurance. Love never fails. . . . And so there remain Faith, Hope, Love, these three; and of these the greatest is Love." [24]

> "Now is the ends of the days
> The mountains of the Lord's house will be
> Established on the top of the mountains
>   And lifted above the hills.
> And all the nations will stream to it,
> Many peoples will go and say:
> 'Come! let us go up to the mountains of the Lord,
> To the house of the God of Jacob;
> That he may instruct us in his ways,
> And that we may walk in his paths;
> For out of Zion goes forth instruction,
> The word of the Lord out of Jerusalem.'
> Then will he judge between the nations,
> And will arbitrate for many peoples;
> And they will beat their swords into plowshares,
>   And their spears into pruning-hooks:
> Nation will not lift up sword against nation,
> And they will learn no more the art of war." [25]

---

[22] Rom. 12:9-21, Goodspeed.
[23] Matt. 18:21, 22, Weymouth.
[24] I Cor. 12:31-13:13, Weymouth.
[25] Isaiah 1:2-4, An American Translation.

V

Dealing with enemies is dangerous irrespective of weapons used; and not less perilous when active goodwill is relied upon to overcome evil. Men and women who dwell on the highest level of religion must therefore be prepared to run risks and accept consequences. To the degree that they refuse to accept prevailing customs and habits, to the extent that they endeavor even by pacific means to transform the actual into the ideal, they will be looked upon as threats to the existing society and will be persecuted as subversive agitators. Courageous and sacrificial willingness to live dangerously is required on the part of those who scale the heights of religion.

"Here I am sending you out like sheep among wolves. So you must be wise like serpents, and guileless like doves. But be on your guard against men, for they will give you up to their courts, and have you flogged in their synagogues, and you will be brought before governors and kings on my account. . . . One brother will give up another to death, and a father his child, and children will turn against their parents, and have them put to death. You will be hated by everybody on my account, but the man who holds out to the very end will be saved." [26] "And he called the people and his disciples to him and said to them, 'If anyone wants to go with me, he must disregard himself, and take his cross and follow me. For whoever wants to preserve his own life will lose it, and whoever loses his life for me and for the good news will preserve it.' " [27] "After this, the Master appointed seventy-two other disciples, and sent them on as his Messengers, two and two, in advance, to every town and place that he himself was intending to visit. 'The harvest,' he said, 'is abundant, but the labourers are few. Therefore pray to the Owner of the harvest to send labourers to gather his harvest. Now, go. Remember, I am sending you out as my Messengers like lambs among wolves.' " [28] "Truly,

[26] Matt. 10:16, 17, 21, 22, Goodspeed.
[27] Mark 8:34, 35, Goodspeed.
[28] Luke 10:1-3, Twentieth Century.

truly I tell you, unless a grain of wheat falls into the earth and dies, it remains a single grain; but if it dies, it bears rich fruit. He who loves his life loses it, and he who cares not for his life in this world will preserve it for eternal life." [29] "What I command you to do is to love one another. If the world hates you, remember that it hated me first. If you belonged to the world, the world would love what was its own. But it is because you do not belong to the world, but I have selected you from the world, that the world hates you. Remember what I said to you: No slave is greater than his master. If they have persecuted me they will persecute you too. . . . They will exclude you from their synagogues; why, the time is coming when anyone who kills you will think he is doing religious service to God." [30]

"It was then that Jesus Christ for the first time explained to his disciples that he had to go to Jerusalem and endure great suffering there at the hands of the elders, high priests, and scribes, and be killed, and be raised to life on the third day. And Peter took him aside and began to reprove him for it, saying, 'God bless you, Master! that can never happen to you!' But he turned and said to Peter, 'Get out of my sight, you Satan! You hinder me, for you do not side with God, but with men!' " [31] "On leaving there they passed through Galilee. He did not want anyone to know of their journey, for he was teaching his disciples, telling them that the Son of man would be betrayed into the hands of men, that they would kill him, and that when he was killed he would rise again after three days. But they did not understand what he said, and they were afraid to ask what he meant." [32] "But I must go on today and tomorrow and the next day, for it is not right for a prophet to die outside Jerusalem. O Jerusalem! Jerusalem! murdering the prophets, and stoning those who are sent to her, how often

---

[29] John 12:24, 25, Moffatt.
[30] John 15:17-20, 16:2, Goodspeed.
[31] Matt. 16:21-23, Goodspeed.
[32] Mark 9:30-32, Moffatt.

I have longed to gather your children around me, as a hen gathers her brood under her wings, but you refused!" [33] "As they went on their way to Jerusalem, Jesus walked ahead of them, and they were in dismay, and those who still followed were afraid. And he took the Twelve aside again and began to tell them what was going to happen to him. 'See!' he said, 'we are going up to Jerusalem, and the Son of man will be handed over to the high priests and scribes, and they will condemn him to death and hand him over to the heathen and they will ridicule him and spit on him and flog him and kill him; and three days after he will rise again.' " [34] "Then they came to a place called Gethsemane, and he told his disciples, 'Sit here till I pray.' But he took Peter and James and John along with him; and as he began to feel appalled and agitated, he said to them, 'My heart is sad, sad even to death; stay here and watch!' Then he went forward a little and fell to the earth, praying that the hour might pass away from him, if possible. 'Abba, Father,' he said, 'Thou canst do anything. Take this cup away from me. Yet, not what I will but what thou wilt.' " [35] "But they persisted with loud outcries in demanding that he be crucified, and their shouting won. . . . Two criminals were also led out to execution with him. When they reached the place called the Skull, they crucified him there, with the criminals one at his right and one at his left. . . ." [36] "At noon darkness spread over the whole country, and lasted until three in the afternoon. And at three o'clock Jesus called out loudly, 'Eloi, Eloi, lama sabachthani?' which means, 'My God, my God, why have you forsaken me?' " [37] . . . "And the curtain before the sanctuary was torn in two. Then Jesus gave a loud cry, and said, 'Father, I intrust my spirit to your hands!' With these words he expired." [38]

---

[33] Luke 13:33, 34, Goodspeed.
[34] Mark 10:32-34, Goodspeed.
[35] Mark 14:32-36, Moffatt.
[36] Luke 23:23, 32, 33, Goodspeed.
[37] Mark 15:33, 34, Goodspeed.
[38] Luke 23:45, 46, Goodspeed.

VI

The highest trails of religion cannot be traveled except by those who trust in the wisdom and love and power of God, and who through worship and comradeship draw upon reservoirs of spiritual sustenance. To overcome evil with goodness, and to accept the consequences of relying upon active friendliness, are beyond the power of man unaided in the hour of severest crisis. To refrain from the passion which seeks revenge, and to overcome the fear which infuriates, surpass the limits of self-control unless a person keeps in tune with the Eternal. The ethical teaching of Jesus requires the religion of Jesus to make it practicable; the way of the cross can be followed only by loyal sons and daughters with vivid awareness that their Father journeys with them every step of the way. "Nothing less than the sustained conviction that one is *God's* child," writes Walter Bell Denny, "that the supreme worth of life lies in a relationship deeper than any human life measurement of goodness or success, deeper than any failure, shame, opposition or hardship can reach, a relationship that even death itself can only bring into clearer realization, for it is a relationship to a living and deathless God,—only such a conviction can support the high and costly enterprise that Christian discipleship involves. Humanistic ethics can promise its own type of culture and self-realization, without religion. But the ethics of Jesus is hopeless apart from the inspiring, energizing life of God in the soul of man, diligently cultivated by love and worship, by thought and prayer." [39]

"All who are guided by the Spirit of God are Sons of God. For you did not receive the spirit of a slave, to fill you once more with fear, but the spirit of a son which leads us to cry 'Abba, Our Father.' The Spirit himself unites with our spirits in bearing witness to our being God's children, and if children, their heirs—heirs of God, and joint-heirs with Christ, since we share Christ's sufferings in order that we may also share his Glory. I do not count the sufferings of our present life

---

[39] Walter Bell Denny, *The Career and Significance of Jesus*, p. 410.

worthy of mention when compared with the Glory that is to be
revealed and bestowed upon us. All Nature awaits with eager
expectation the appearing of the Sons of God. . . . But we
do know that God causes all things to work together for the
good of those who love him. . . . If God is on our side, who
can there be against us? . . . Who is there to separate us from
the love of Christ? Will trouble, or difficulty, or persecution,
or hunger, or nakedness, or danger, or the sword? . . . Yet
amidst all these things we more than conquer through him who
loved us! For I am persuaded that neither Death, nor Life,
nor Angels, nor Archangels, nor the Present, nor the Future,
nor any Powers, nor Height, nor Depth, nor any other created
thing, will be able to separate us from the love of God revealed
in Christ Jesus, our Lord!" [40]   "Which of you men when his
son asks him for some bread will give him a stone? Or if he
asks for a fish, will he give him a snake? So if you, bad as
you are, know enough to give your children what is good, how
much more surely will your Father in heaven give what is good
to those who ask him for it!" [41]   "Look at the wild birds.
They do not sow or reap, or store their food in barns, and yet
your heavenly Father feeds them. . . . See how the wild flow-
ers grow. They do not toil or spin, and yet I tell you, even
Solomon in all his splendor was never dressed like one of them.
But if God so beautifully dresses the wild grass, which is alive
today and is thrown in the furnace tomorrow, will he not much
more surely clothe you, you who have so little faith." [42]   "I
tell you, who are my friends, have no fear of those who kill the
body, and after that can do no more. . . . Do not sparrows
sell five for two cents? And yet not one of them is forgotten
in God's sight. . . . Do not be afraid, little flock, for your
Father has chosen to give you the kingdom." [43]

"Therefore, surrounded as we are by such a vast cloud of
witnesses, let us fling aside every encumbrance and the sin that

---

[40] Rom. 8 :14-39, Twentieth Century.
[41] Matt. 7 :9-11, Goodspeed.
[42] Matt. 6 :26, 29-31, Goodspeed.
[43] Luke 12 :4-6, 32, Goodspeed.

so readily entangles our feet. And let us run with patient endurance the race that lies before us, simply fixing our gaze upon Jesus, our Prince Leader in the faith, who will also award us the prize. He, for the sake of the joy which lay before Him, patiently endured the cross, looking with contempt upon its shame, and afterwards seated Himself—where He still sits —at the right hand of the throne of God. Therefore, if you would escape becoming weary and faint-hearted, compare your own sufferings with those of Him who endured such hostility directed against Him by sinners. In your struggle against sin you have not yet resisted so as to endanger your lives." [44] "But to God be the thanks who in Christ ever heads our triumphal procession, and by our hands waves in every place that sweet incense, the knowledge of Him. For we are a fragrance of Christ grateful to God in those whom He is saving and in those who are perishing." [45] "And his commands are not irksome, for whatever is born of God conquers the world. Our faith, that is the conquest which conquers the world. Who is the world's conqueror but he who believes that Jesus is the Son of God?" [46] "Now to him who is able to keep you from slipping and to make your stand unblemished and exultant before his glory—to the only God, our saviour through Jesus Christ our Lord, be glory, majesty, dominion and authority, before all time and now and for all time: Amen." [47]

High regard for human personality; deep concern for human welfare; recognition of kinship with every other individual; craving for comradeship; zealous striving to do justice; reliance upon active goodwill as the effect-means of overcoming evil; courageous and sacrificial willingness to run risks and accept consequences of faithful allegiance to the way of love; worship of God and trust in His wisdom and love and power—these are characteristics of men and women who dwell on the highest level of religion.

---

[44] Hebrews 12:1-4, Weymouth.
[45] II Cor. 2:14-15, Weymouth.
[46] I John 5:3-6, Moffatt.
[47] Jude 24, Moffatt.

VII

In endeavoring to reach a valid decision as to whether or not a Christian should ever go to war, it is necessary that we remind ourselves of the real nature of warfare under prevailing conditions.   The reader may care to review the evidence presented fully on pages 3 to 16 of an earlier section.   War is planned devastation and organized slaughter.   War is atrocity, "a deed of violence or savagery; great cruelty or reckless wickedness."   War cannot be waged without atrocity.   Bombardment, air raid and blockade are orthodox weapons of warfare and certainly will be used in the event of another great conflict. War is now totalitarian in nature and no distinction can be made between belligerents and non-combatants, nor between men and women.   War is a combat of entire population against entire population.   Deceit and falsehood also are orthodox methods of warfare.   The doctrine of military necessity reigns supreme.   Passionate appeals to war gods supplant worship of the universal Father of all peoples including the enemy.

Wise and good people differ in judgment as to whether or not war is ever justifiable.   But they ought not to differ in their descriptions of the inherent and ineradicable characteristics of the war method.   The premise is debatable that the perpetration of atrocities is sometimes a patriot's duty; that the poisoning of the public mind with distortion and falsehood designed to inflame passions is sometimes a patriot's duty; that the sidetracking of ethical ideals in favor of the practice of military necessity is sometimes a patriot's duty; that the banishment of a loving Father of all men and the bowing down before a god of war is sometimes a patriot's duty.   But if these be obligations resting upon patriots, let them be proclaimed as such in plain unvarnished language.

"During the World War," writes Philip C. Jessup, "the Allies did not seek to disguise the fact that they placed great reliance on their plan to starve the German people into submission.   The United States sought the same objective after it entered the war.   Germany, on the other hand, eventually resorted to the unrestricted submarine campaign as a means of bringing like distress to England, always vulnerable if her lines of ocean communication can be cut. 'If England,' wrote the German Foreign Minister to the Government of the United States in 1915, 'invokes the powers of famine as an ally in its struggles against Germany with the intention of leaving a civilized people the alternative of perishing in misery or submitting to the yoke of England's political and commercial will, the German Government are today determined to take up the gauntlet and to appeal to the same grim ally.' " [48]

Precisely so! In wartime every belligerent nation endeavors to use starvation of civilian populations as a grim ally. In explaining his reasons for sending to Great Britain "long and exhaustive treatises" which were "submerged in verbosity," Secretary Lansing confided in his memoirs: "If my conviction was right as to the United States' entry into the war, and I never doubted it after the sinking of the *Lusitania,* it was of the highest importance that we should not become a belligerent with our hands too tightly tied by what we had written. We would presumably wish to adopt some of the policies and practices, which the British had adopted, though certainly not all of them, for our object would be the same as theirs, and that was to break the power of Germany and destroy the morale of the German people by an economic isolation, which would cause them to lack the very necessaries of life. If we went too far in insisting that Great Britain must cease certain practices as violative of our neutral rights, our utterances would certainly be cited against us by other neutrals if we, as belligerents, attempted to do the same thing. While our conduct might be illegal, we would not be flagrantly inconsistent. That reason was never lost sight of during the correspondence which passed between the two governments concerning the British restraints upon American trade. The notes that were sent were long and exhaustive treatises which opened up new subjects of discussion rather than closing those in controversy. Short and emphatic notes were dangerous. Everything was submerged in

[48] Philip C. Jessup, *Neutrality,* vol. IV, pp. 34, 35.

verbosity. It was done with deliberate purpose. It insured
continuance of the controversies and left the questions unsettled, which was necessary in order to leave this country free
to act and even to act illegally when it entered the war." [49]

Economic isolation! Cause them to lack the very necessaries
of life! Bluntly speaking: starvation. And even to act illegally. Not only starvation, but illegal starvation! That is the
method of war. And there is no basis for doubt that if the
United States goes to war against a great power, it will endeavor to starve into submission the peoples of enemy lands.
Mr. John Galsworthy, in a letter to the Disarmament Conference in 1932, made this appeal: "When a child is outraged or
done to death in time of peace, the whole nation is stirred. In
wartime, millions of children are outraged and done to death,
in manner not the same, but as horrible. On them are forced
slow starvation, illness, deformities, orphanage, death from
disease, gas and bombs. . . . Let those men therefore who
will soon meet for the avowed purpose of considering how far
they can minimize the chances and the scope of war put, each
one to himself, this question: If I were incited to outrage and
murder a child, what should I say and do to him who incited
me? And let them remember that, however far from their
thoughts it be that children should suffer, war will inevitably
outrage and destroy them." [50]

To recoil in horror from retail atrocities, while committing
wholesale atrocities, is not justifiable. The only realistic view
of war is to recognize IT as atrocity. Listen to a blunt ap-
praisal by General Sir Henry F. Thuillier: "To come back to
submarines: it is argued that submarine attack on merchant
vessels is inhumane since it violates an old and excellent sea
custom that non-combatants should be taken off in safety. . . .
But is it more so than to bombard a town with heavy artillery,
regardless of the civilians and the women and children in it?—
a practice which has prevailed for centuries, and no one makes
any protest against it. Is it more inhumane than blockading a

---

[49] *War Memoirs of Robert Lansing*, p. 128.
[50] Quoted by Leyton Richards, *Realistic Pacifism*, p. 244.

besieged town and starving the civilian inhabitants, including women and children? Is it more inhumane than cutting off the food supply of the whole of Germany and Austria, knowing full well that those countries could not produce sufficient food and milk for their own population? . . . All war is terribly inhumane. It is very splendid of our Navy to have kept up its chivalrous custom of ensuring the safety of civilians at sea right into the XXth century, but their less sensitive comrades on land have for long been in the habit of firing at railway trains or into towns without asking any questions about who are in them. We are more or less accustomed to these forms of inhumanity, but to send a few people adrift in open boats is a form which was new to us and so excited our horror and anger." [51]

Consider also the significance of bayonets in wartime. Mr. H. M. Tomlinson quotes from a suppressed speech delivered during the war by a British sergeant-major to cadets: "You've got to get down and hook them out with the bayonet; you will enjoy that, I can assure you. (Laughter.) You will want the bayonet to clear the trench. And it is because I know the value of the bayonet that I want you to forget sympathy. You should have no sympathy for any damned Germans; I have none, nor has anybody else that I know in France. If at any time you should be sympathetic, let it be to put a squarehead out of his misery—you will be doing him and yourself a good turn at the same time. (Laughter.) You will certainly know what it feels like to drive that bayonet home and get it out again; you will feel that you will like to go on killing. You are here to work on that idea and to work damned hard. . . . Don't forget that the Germans, when they advance, do not come on in tens and twenties, but in their thousands, and you have got to kill or be killed. Get sympathy out of your head. We washed sympathy out of the service years ago. We go out to kill. We don't care how, so long as they are killed." [52]

---

[51] General Sir Henry F. Thuillier, in *Journal of the Royal United Service Institution*, May, 1936, p. 267.

[52] Quoted by H. M. Tomlinson, *Mars His Idiot*, p. 135.

Major Reginald Barlow, in discussing the instruction of junior officers during the war, said bluntly: "We've got to teach these men to be mean, they must look mean, act mean, because they are going against a dirty enemy, an enemy that recognizes no sportsmanship, but who uses every means in his power to kill—in order to combat that spirit we've got to make our men just a little bit more proficient in the art of killing than they are, we've got to put the spirit of kill in our men, and so put the fear of Christ in the Germans. . . ." [53]

We go out to kill! We've got to make our men more proficient in the art of killing! That is the real business of war.

American religionists should also remember that if the United States goes to war against Germany, or Italy, or Japan, our fellow citizens will go out to kill those peoples for doing substantially what American patriots would do under parallel circumstances.[54]

Should followers of a religion based on reverence for every person and recognition of kinship of all peoples seek justice and security by resorting to planned devastation of extensive territories and organized slaughter of men, women and children indiscriminately? Should they endeavor to starve entire populations and to burn whole cities? Should they deal in falsehood and devote themselves to the engendering of hatred and fury?

If premeditated and deliberate planning to perpetrate the countless atrocities of war is not a flagrant violation of Jesus' way of life, then no method of resisting aggression and tyranny can be contrary to that way. To say that the method of war may be consistent with his teaching and example is to say that he could consistently have joined the zealots and taken up arms against the invading Romans. But surely it is indisputable that if he had resorted to the sword against tyranny he would not now be revered as the noblest of all religious leaders. He could not have manifested active goodwill toward the Romans

---

[53] Reginald Barlow, Major 302nd Infantry, Camp Devens, Mass., Sept. 28, 1917, Quoted in *The Outlook,* Oct. 10, 1917.

[54] See pp. 17 ff.

by plunging a dagger to their hearts.   He could not have set
an example of forgiveness seventy times seven by calling upon
his fellow countrymen to massacre the Romans.   The way of
Jesus and the method of war stand in utter opposition to one
another.   We can choose the road of atrocity or the way of
the cross, but we cannot at the same time travel both highways
since they lead in opposite directions.   War with its atrocities
is irreconcilable with the religion of Jesus and this incontestable
truth has been widely proclaimed by numerous religious bodies:

The General Conference of the Methodist Episcopal Church
in 1936 said officially: "War as we now know it is utterly destructive.   It is the greatest social sin of modern times; a denial
of the ideals of Christ, a violation of human personality and a
threat to civilization.   Therefore, we declare that the Methodist
Episcopal Church as an institution does not endorse, support
or purpose to participate in war. . . . We therefore petition
the government of the United States to grant to members of
the Methodist Episcopal Church, who may be conscientious
objectors to war, the same exemption from military service as
has long been granted to members of the Society of Friends
and similar religious organizations."

The College of Bishops of the Methodist Episcopal Church,
South, in 1935 issued an official statement on war: "We shall
hold in contempt this entire nefarious war business.   War as a
method of settling international disputes has not one single de-
fensible argument in its behalf.   We reiterate what we said
a year ago to the General Conference: 'It is archaic, belongs to
the jungle period of human development and should be branded
as an iniquitous and inhuman procedure. . . . It is an unhal-
lowed thing utterly contrary to the genius of Christianity.' . . .
We shall teach our children and youth to despise the unclean
thing and to swear eternal loyalty to the ways of peace and to
the sacred honor of their brother man."

The General Convention of the Protestant Episcopal Church
said: "As stated by the last Lambeth Conference: 'War, as a
method of settling international disputes, is incompatible with
the teaching and example of our Lord Jesus Christ.   We be-

lieve that as the Christian conscience has condemned infanticide
and slavery and torture, it is now called to condemn war as an
outrage on the fatherhood of God and the brotherhood of all
mankind.' " [55]   In a Pastoral Letter issued by the House of
Bishops of the Protestant Episcopal Church the statement is
made that "war is murder on a colossal scale. . . . The Christian Church cannot and will not deny loyalty and fealty to its
Lord by being partner in any scheme, national or international,
that contemplates the wholesale destruction of human life." [56]
The Northern Baptist Convention went on record: "War is the
supreme social sin, and so long as the war system is maintained
there can be no safety for our homes or for our civilization and
no realization of the kingdom of heaven on earth." [57]   The
Synod of the Reformed Presbyterian Church declared: "War
is essentially and inherently a supreme violation of the teachings and spirit of Jesus . . . as a method for securing national
ends, however just and right, is antichristian." [58]

The International Convention of the Disciples of Christ
said: "We believe that war is pagan, futile, and destructive of
the spiritual values for which the churches of Christ stand . . .
we therefore dissociate ourselves from war and the war system,
and hereby serve notice to whom it may concern that we never
again expect to bless or sanction war." [59]   The Universalist
Convention of California resolved: "That the Universalist
principles of the Fatherhood of God and the Brotherhood of
Man cannot be reconciled with the deliberate taking of life in
war.   That, since our country has renounced all war, we urge
our people to adopt the historical position of the Friends, and
take the attitude of conscientious objection to all war.   That
the faith of the Universalist Church should be recognized by
all governmental agencies in the same way as they accept the
belief of the Society of Friends."

The General Council of Congregational and Christian

---

[55] Protestant Episcopal Church, General Convention, 1931.
[56] Quoted in the *Living Church,* Nov. 3, 1934.
[57] Northern Baptist Convention, 1928.
[58] Reformed Presbyterian Church, Synod, 1924.
[59] Quoted in *The Christian Century,* October 31, 1934.

Churches thus went on record: "The cleavage between the way of Jesus and the system of war is clear. We of this council are convinced that we must now make this declaration, 'The church is through with war!' We of this council call upon the people of our churches to renounce war and all its works and ways and to refuse to support, sanction or bless it." [60]   The 1934 General Assembly of the Presbyterian Church in the U. S. A. "declares anew its break with the entire war system. . . . Christians cannot give their support to war as a method of carrying on international conflict." The Southern Presbyterian Church asserts that "the church should never again bless a war, or be used as an instrument in the promotion of war." [61]

A *Manifesto Against War* was released on Armistice Day, 1934, under the auspices of the Church Peace Union. This forthright declaration was signed by more than 200 outstanding citizens of the United States, *including 60 bishops and 45 college presidents*. Here is a quotation from this pronouncement: "The time has come when organized religion must proclaim that never again shall war be waged under the sanction of the Church. . . . With the ruins of the last war piled high at its feet the Church should solemnly declare herself the implacable enemy of war. . . . We have had in our generation an appalling revelation of the true nature of war. War is not what it was. When science added the airplane, the submarine and poison gas, warfare entered on a new stage. With the advent of poison gas and bacteriological germs it laid aside the last vestige of decency. War has always been bloody and brutal. It is now an atrocity. . . . War is as futile as it is barbarous. . . . There is no victor. All are defeated. . . . Modern war is suicide. The sword is so sharp that a nation can cut not only the throats of its neighbors but its own throat also. Civilization itself is in jeopardy."

The Ohio State Pastors' Conference asserted: "We are convinced that war is un-Christian, futile, and suicidal, and we renounce complete the whole war system. We will never again

[60] General Council, 1934.
[61] General Assembly, 1929.

sanction or participate in any war. We will not use our pulpits
or classrooms as recruiting stations. We set ourselves to edu-
cate and lead youth in the principles and practice of goodwill, justice, understanding, brotherhood, and peace. We will
not give our financial or moral support to any war." [62]   The
National Study Conference on the Churches and World Peace
declared: "War denies the fatherhood of God, scorns the
brotherhood of man, mocks the sacredness of human life, is
merciless to helpless women and children, uses falsehood, ignores justice, releases the passions, and cultivates hate. War
means everything that Jesus did not mean, and means nothing
that he did mean. We therefore hold that the Churches should
condemn resort to the war-system as sin and should henceforth refuse, as institutions, to sanction it or to be used as
agencies in its support." [63]   While the Commission on International Justice and Goodwill of the Federal Council of the
Churches of Christ in America said bluntly: "The war system
of the nations is the outstanding evil of present-day civilization.
It is the most ominous antichristian phase of modern life." [64]

Out of 20,870 clergymen who in 1934 replied to a questionnaire, 12,904 said "yes" to this question: "Are you personally
prepared to state that it is your present purpose not to sanction
any future war or participate as an armed combatant?"   While
13,997 answered affirmatively: "Do you believe that the
churches of America should now go on record as refusing to
sanction or support any future war?" [65]

VIII

If the method of war is so manifestly contrary to Jesus' way
of life, why have majorities of Christians in every country and
in every century since the fourth given their approval and their
support to all wars waged within Christendom? [66]   Parallel

[62] *The Nation,* February 10, 1932, p. 158.

[63] National Study Conference on the Churches and World Peace, 1929.

[64] *A Message to the Churches of Christ in America from the Federal
Council's Commission on International Justice and Goodwill,* 1924.

[65] See *The World Tomorrow,* May 10, 1934, for an exhaustive analysis
of the replies to 15 questions on international and economic questions.

[66] See C. J. Cadoux, *The Early Christian Attitude Toward War.*

questions instantly flash into mind: why did so many Christians for so many hundreds of years uphold the system of chattel slavery? why did adherents of a religion of mercy found the Inquisition and resort to every form of diabolical torture? [67]

Acceptance of the doctrine that the end justifies the means, and ethical blindness due to compromise with unjust social systems—these are the primary reasons why Christians have so often acted with cruelty and ferocity. The extent to which well-intentioned people have resorted to evil in order that good might be done is simply appalling. There are hardly any extremes of cruelty to which they have not gone. How did it happen that the Christian church, in many of its branches, officially used torture in dealing with heretics? A false assumption and the doctrine that the end justifies the means were responsible for the shedding of rivers of blood. Consider the Inquisition, for example. For the most part, the men who administered this terrible institution were conscientious and zealous churchmen. Like most other Christians of that age they believed that membership in the church was essential to salvation. Acceptance of the beliefs and practices of the church were required of all members. Heresy was punished with excommunication, and if a man died while outside the church it was assumed that he would go to hell, a literal lake of fire, and burn throughout all eternity. Since nothing could be worse than this awful fate, the church mercifully sought to prevent heresy and thus save a precious soul from eternal torment. If persuasion failed, then coercion was used; if mild forms of punishment were unavailing, then extreme measures were adopted. In the end the church which was founded on the corner stone of love toward God and man was starving men in foul dungeons and burning them at the stake for the good of their souls. Not the Catholic church alone but various branches of Protestantism practised diabolic cruelty for several centuries on the ground that high and holy ends justified any means.

---

[67] See Kirby Page, *Jesus or Christianity.*

Out of the literally thousands of other examples available let us consider a recent one, the defense of atrocities during the World War alike by German and Allied Christians. In both cases we find the same false assumption and the same deadly doctrine. The vast majority of Germans thought they were fighting in self-defense. Victimized by propaganda and obsessed with fear, they thought the war was necessary. For decades they had been warned by their nationalists and militarists against the aggressive designs of barbarous Russians, decadent Frenchmen, and perfidious Britons. Finding themselves and their allies far outdistanced by the combined armies and navies of their potential enemies, they endured the staggering burden of taxation and conscription occasioned by the race of armaments. When the war came they thought they were fighting in defense of country, civilization, and the Kingdom of God. None save a few extreme militarists wanted war or relished the idea of killing their fellows. But it was necessary, they reasoned, and so they exhibited great valor and sacrificial devotion. At all costs the war must be won, otherwise their culture and civilization would be swept away by the enemies they had been taught to despise. When all other weapons failed they resorted to unrestricted submarine warfare. It is a melancholy fact that the resultant atrocities were defended on grounds of necessity by many German Christians. A friend of mine told me that during the war one of his relatives stayed in the home of relatives of one of the best-known German theologians and that on the Sunday following the sinking of the *Lusitania they went to church and participated in a public cel*-ebration because they thought they were winning the war.

If this seems incredible to some readers let them remind themselves how Christians in England, France and the United States felt and acted during those terrible days. Most Christians in Allied countries thought they were fighting in self-defense. This is the way they reasoned: for forty years the Huns have been preparing; their plans were all blueprinted; they were bent on world conquest or downfall; it was to be first Belgium, then France, Russia, England, Europe, the

United States, and other distant countries. What can you do when confronted with barbarians determined on conquest? One English divine expressed it this way: "You might as well tickle a tiger as attempt to plead with a German." War was horrible but necessary, they said. Otherwise civilization would be destroyed and the Kingdom of God set back by centuries. And so most Allied Christians made use of or approved the various weapons of war, including the most terrible instrument of all, the blockade. To the extent that was possible the Allies put an arm of steel about Germany and strangled multitudes to death. More men, women, and children were starved to death by the blockade than were killed by all the submarine attacks and air raids. And all the while multitudes of Christians in Allied lands were assembling in their churches and thanking God they were winning the war and saving civilization. To this tragic end will a false assumption and a pernicious doctrine lead the followers of Jesus.

Lest we forget, it may be well to remind ourselves of the extremes to which Christians went in glorifying war. An appalling mass of evidence has been assembled by Ray H. Abrams in a volume entitled *Preachers Present Arms*. Believe it or not, ministers of churches offering allegiance to the Prince of Peace uttered these words: "It is God who has summoned us to this war. It is his war we are fighting. . . . This conflict is indeed a crusade. The greatest in history—the holiest. It is in the profoundest and truest sense a Holy War. . . . Yes, it is Christ, the King of Righteousness, who calls us to grapple in deadly strife with this unholy and blasphemous power (Germany)." [67] "I would not enter this work till I could see Jesus himself sighting down a gun barrel and running a bayonet through an enemy's body." [68] "As Christians, of course, we say Christ approves (of the war). But would he fight and kill? . . . There is not an opportunity to deal death to the enemy that he would shirk from or delay in seizing! He would take bayonet and grenade and bomb and rifle and do the work

[67] p. 55.
[68] p. 69.

of deadliness against that which is the most deadly enemy of his Father's kingdom in a thousand years. . . . That is the inexorable truth about Jesus Christ and this war; and we rejoice to say it." [69] ". . . a thirty-centimeter gun may voice the edict of God as truly as the notes of a cooing dove. . . . The sword of America is the sword of Jesus." [70] ". . . nowhere has the Sermon on the Mount, the embodiment of the Spirit of Christ, exercised more visible and amazing power than in the matter of war . . . this war, when carried by the Allies and America to the right issue, will be another proof of the divine power of the Sermon on the Mount." [71] "We will fight pacifism not only because it is contrary to the teachings of Christ, but because its whole tendency is to make a yellow streak where you want a man." [72] "No boy goes through the hell of fire and suffering and wounds that he does not come out newborn. The old man is gone from him, and a new man is born in him. That is the great eternal compensation of war and suffering." [73] "I look upon the enlistment of an American soldier as I do on the departure of a missionary for Burma." [74]

Compromise with the war system and with unjust social systems produces ethical blindness and insensitivity. ". . . be not conformed to this world: but be ye transformed by the renewing of your mind. . . ." [75] "If, therefore, your very light is darkness, how deep the darkness will be!" [76] Conformity to the slave system brings blindness with regard to human relations; and conformity to the war system destroys vision of its iniquities. If Christians declare that atrocity is mercy, and if they assert that planned devastation and organized slaughter are acts of holiness, they become blind leaders of the blind, and civilization plunges over the precipice.

[69] p. 68.
[70] p. 65.
[71] p. 66.
[72] *Ibid*, p. 63.
[73] *Ibid*, p. 60.
[74] *Ibid*, p. 57.
[75] Rom. 12:2.
[76] Matt. 6:23, Goodspeed.

Therefore, the least that the churches can do is renounce war without qualification and refuse ever again to approve or support it in any way. Members of churches should be admonished never to commit the terrible sin of engaging in war.

Civil war, as distinguished from non-warlike class struggle, is the most revolting kind of war and is therefore irreconcilable with the way of Jesus. The ferocity with which the combined civil and international war in Spain is now being conducted reveals the true nature of civil war. It has been estimated that a million persons have already been killed. Civil war in the United States would pile atrocity upon atrocity in an appalling manner.[77]

IX

Does this mean that the churches should also abjure all use of force and all police action? Was Tolstoy correct in maintaining that every use of force and coercion is contrary to the spirit of Jesus and therefore immoral? That all depends upon whether or not coercion is necessarily a violation of the family spirit. If the answer is in the affirmative, the only consistent philosophy for a follower of Jesus is that of anarchism, and the only logical procedure that of withdrawal from all responsibility for and participation in organized society.

But the evidence does not drive us to such a conclusion. It is possible that coercion may be administered in such a way as to prove restraining and redemptive. Wherever in a home there is immaturity, lack of self-control, and anti-social stimuli, coercion may be necessary in order to safeguard the other members of the family, and to prevent remorse for irreparable wrongdoing. To say that restraint administered in love and with the welfare of all concerned vividly in mind is immoral, is to reduce society to anarchy and chaos.

For many decades to come certain criminals will have to be restrained by force if society is to be safeguarded and they are to be kept from evil-doing. The victims of greed and ex-

[77] See pp. 272 ff.

ploitation will never get justice solely by relying upon the vision and generosity of those who hold power and seek their own gain. Power is blinding and corrupting and causes the slave-owner to imagine that it is his duty to perpetuate slavery. The victims of imperialism, in a world where national egotism and greed are rampant, must resort to non-warlike coercion if they are to secure freedom and justice. The British imperialist is conscientious in his determination to continue British rule in India, and Japanese militarists honestly consider themselves to be the saviors of Manchuria. Unless effective non-violent means of coercion can be devised and utilized, the victims of injustice will, in blindness and desperation, take up weapons of violence. In our kind of world, to rely upon anarchy and inaction, is to turn the reins over to violence.

With this dilemma in mind, let us turn again to Jesus' concept of God and his attitude toward wrongdoers. The God of Jesus is no soft, flabby sentimentalist. Jesus' picture of the judgment scene is terrifying in its severity. His own condemnation of the scribes and Pharisees is one of the most rigorous on record. His indignation flames in the presence of callous hypocrisy and cruelty. His whole life is a burning denunciation of iniquity and an indomitable resistance to evil.

If the family circle is to be extended beyond blood relatives and made to embrace men of all classes and races, effective social organization must be created and maintained by mutual goodwill, supported in emergencies and abnormal instances by ethical and effective restraints. Here we are confronted with one of the most urgent problems of our day. How can society restrain criminals, and restore them to right relations with their fellows, without vengeance in the form of a noose or an electric chair? How can the workers utilize the strike and other forms of economic coercion, and at the same time avoid hatred and violence? How can Mahatma Gandhi exert sufficient pressure through non-violent non-cooperation to secure freedom for India, without stimulating hatred and resorting to violence?

It is obvious that Jesus has no detailed solutions for these modern problems. But he does shed brilliant illumination upon every such critical situation. If true to his way of life, the state will avoid capital punishment and ruthlessness, and will be chiefly concerned with the protection of society and the rec-lamation of the evildoer. The workers will continue to regard their oppressors as kinsmen, and will refrain from unbrotherly attitudes. They will avoid covetousness and will be motivated solely by the desire for justice and for a wider sharing of the opportunities for the good life. The people of India will har-bor no animosity against the British and will seek no revenge, being driven solely by the desire to secure that freedom which is essential to self-respect, and the independence required for the redemption of India from her iniquities. The supporters of the League of Nations will manifest no bitterness toward Japan, or Italy, but only a righteous determination to resist military imperialism by effective non-violent methods.

Moreover, if Jesus' experience of God and his trust in man can be extended on a wide scale, this generation's ability to re-frain from hatred and violence will be increased enormously. The thought that God loves even his enemies, and seeks to re-strain them only that he may redeem them, helps to hold men steady in periods of strain and stress. Furthermore, followers of Jesus in our day will, by their compassionate concern for the victims of greed and blindness, be stimulated to search more diligently for means of increased persuasiveness of wrong-doers, on the one hand, and for ethical means of restraint, on the other. They will be prepared also to rely exclusively upon means which are consistent with the worthy ends sought, and to take the consequences of following Jesus' way of life.

Experience soon demonstrates that love and forgiveness and non-violence are not always immediately and completely effec-tive in restraining wrongdoers. In such a circumstance, what is an ethical procedure? Shall we resort to violence, on the ground that the end justifies the means? The answer of Jesus seems conclusive. There is no place in the home for warlike actions—as distinguished from the less extreme forms of co-ercion—and the killing of a beloved kinsman.

Our difficulty comes, of course, in deciding where ethical

coercion ends and unethical violence begins. The only person who is able to escape from this dilemma is the complete anarchist who repudiates every form of restraint and compulsion—and such a man has no solution to offer for the imminently menacing problems of the hour. All other persons are obliged to draw the line somewhere, and orderly progress depends upon the intellectual keenness and ethical sensitiveness with which this situation is confronted.

None of the three ways of dealing with social injustice can entirely prevent or remove human suffering. Resistance by violence tends to increase and intensify suffering; inaction or failure to exert effective restraint perpetuates the misery of the victims of crime or exploitation; non-warlike coercion likewise often results in suffering. We are driven, therefore, to the conclusion that, in an imperfect and developing world, suffering is inescapable. The policy of wisdom is to use that method which involves a minimum of suffering, and which offers a maximum of redemption.

What, then, is the meaning of all this? Is coercion ever consistent with the family spirit, and may it be administered in a manner that is constructive and redemptive, rather than destructive and debasing? I am fully persuaded that the answer is in the affirmative. If this is sound reasoning, Jesus can aid us at three points: by helping us to avoid hatred, to repudiate violence, and to increase our willingness to accept whatever suffering comes from this combination of refusing to submit to evil and of refraining from hatred and violence.

X

In this setting the cross of Calvary assumes new meaning. Jesus refuses to accept the *status quo,* with all its injustice and misery. He refrains from hatred and violence, but attacks entrenched iniquity with the utmost vigor and abandon, thereby incurring the relentless hostility which results in his own crucifixion and the ruthless persecution of his followers. That is to say, acquiescence and inactivity would have been safer for him, but would not have removed the misery of the people. On the other hand, his non-violent assaults upon evildoing cause his own early death and produce terrible havoc among his friends. He lives every day as a good member of God's Home, and is nailed to a tree.

The problem confronting present day followers of Jesus can thus be summarized: If we acquiesce in the presence of injustice and misery, we not only fail to remove exploitation and poverty, but we abdicate in favor of those who seek deliverance by violence. On the other hand, if we offer effective non-warlike resistance, we may bring suffering upon both evildoers and victims. If we are able to keep ourselves free from bitterness and vindictiveness, our procedure in every situation will be determined by our judgment as to which type of persuasiveness and which method of non-violent restraint are under the circumstances most ethical and most effective. We will then go forward, even if the journey leads to a cross. Without suffering there can be no redemption.

If we are to oppose evildoers, especially if we are to make use of none-warlike methods of restraining wrongdoers, we must not only refrain from animosity, but must reveal our devotion to mankind by exhibiting a willingness to endure suffering, rather than submit to the exploitation of our fellows, or to retaliate with weapons of violence. The menace inherent in any form of coercion is greatly reduced if those who act in behalf of the victims of oppression voluntarily submit to suffering. Mahatma Gandhi, of course, furnishes the most illuminating contemporary example of vicarious suffering.

So we gain illumination as to the immensity of Jesus' contribution in setting before us a vision of the new society, and indicating ways and means of bringing it to pass. By his own experience of God and his estimate of man, by his emphasis upon and practice of brotherhood, by his repudiation of hatred and violence, while attacking with audacity deeply entrenched iniquities, and by his vicarious suffering on the cross, Jesus awakens, challenges and inspires us to take up our cross and follow in his sacrificially redemptive steps. Thus we are saved and thus society must be redeemed.

Chapter Eight

What Would Happen If a Million Americans Became Resolute War Resisters?

RAPIDLY increasing numbers of men and women are making up their minds that they will never again approve of or actively support any future war. Many of these individuals are basing their decision upon the judgment that war is a colossal social sin; while other persons rest their case upon the conviction that the method of war is unnecessary, ineffectual and suicidal. On grounds of religion, patriotism and common sense, numerous individuals are becoming resolute war resisters.

If this movement should assume substantial proportions in the United States, what would the probable effects be upon our government, upon other nations, upon international organization, and upon organized religion? [1]

I

Before attempting to assess the probable influence of a substantial number of war resisters in the United States, it may be well to raise a question concerning the practicability of the endeavor to enroll a million Americans in this movement. It is obvious at the outset that the aid of various organizations will be required if success is to be achieved. Churches, synagogues, colleges, women's clubs, and labor unions are the most fertile sources; and in combination they offer immense possibilities. The churches alone could easily recruit half a million

[1] See Devere Allen, *The Fight for Peace;* Richard Gregg, *The Power of Non-Violence,* and his *Training for Peace.*

war resisters if they took the task seriously. Nearly 13,000 clergymen indicated by their replies to a questionnaire in 1934 that they would not sanction any future war. National polls by the Congregational and Christian Church and by the Disciples of Christ revealed a substantial minority of members taking the position of war resisters. Evidence is available showing that tens of thousands of college students have already gone on record against participation in any war waged by their government. By no means fantastic is the proposal that a million American war resisters be enrolled in a powerful movement.

In the British Isles the Peace Pledge Union, under the leadership of Dick Sheppard and George Lansbury, is conducting an extensive campaign for members on a basis of this declaration: "We renounce war and never again will we support or sanction another." To date some 165,000 persons have been enrolled, including Lord Arthur Ponsonby, the late General F. P. Crozier, Aldous Huxley, Beverley Nichols, Gerald Heard, Canon Raven and J. Middleton Murry.

II

A million determined war resisters could exercise tremendous influence on public opinion and governmental policy. All governmental action is determined by the decisions of minorities, since the mass of citizens are always inarticulate and inactive in public affairs. All government is pressure government. Various determined minorities exert counter pressure upon administrations. The total number of American citizens actively interested in heavy appropriations for armed preparedness is not large; but this small company brings terrific pressure to bear upon public officials. A million war resisters operating steadily throughout the nation could quickly make a profound change in public attitudes toward war.

Steady pressure from a powerful peace movement is required not because the President and Congress of the United States desire to go to war, but because government officials often feel obliged to continue policies which they deem necessary to the safeguarding of national interests and national honor, even at the risk of war. President Roosevelt, for example, is devoted to peace and equally devoted to a big navy; and apparently he holds the view that the occasion may arise when it will be necessary to use the navy in war against another great power. No President was ever more zealous in the cause of world peace than President Wilson; yet it was he who carried us into the World War. Citizens dare not leave the momentous decision of war or peace to public officials; mass pressure must steadily be brought to bear upon them.

A powerful war resisters' movement is needed also to counteract the influence of chauvinistic newspapers and jingoist patriots. In hours of crisis when passions are inflamed and fears aroused, the drift toward war cannot easily be checked, but the vigorous and courageous activity of a million war resisters might turn the tide in favor of peace.

The influence of a substantial number of war resisters would not only cause the government to be more cautious in deciding upon war, but would undoubtedly stimulate public officials to more vigorous activity in removing the causes of international hostility and in strengthening pacific alternatives to war. So long as the war method is accepted as valid and so long as masses of citizens are victimized by the delusion that armed preparedness offers security and justice, adequate consideration will not be given to the remedying of situations which produce war and appropriate action will not be taken to undergird pacific agencies of international justice.

"Against war resistance organised in advance," writes Bertrand Russell, "it may be urged that, if it becomes common in any one country, it is a source of military weakness, and therefore makes that country more likely to be attacked. No doubt in certain circumstances military weakness on one side may precipitate a war. . . . But all such arguments rest upon the naive assumption that the whole responsibility for a war is on one side. In fact, wars occur when what are considered vital interests are at stake, and each side thinks it can win. Whatever weakens one side diminishes its will to war as much as it increases that on the other side; on the balance, therefore, it has no more tendency towards war than towards peace. The fallacy is just the same as is involved in the contention that we shall make peace more secure by increasing our armaments." [2]

The vitality of church and synagogue will be intensified to the degree that they take seriously the principles and obligations of high religion. Compromise with the atrocity of war not only reduces their influence upon government, but also dims ethical vision and reduces spiritual strength. Unqualified excommunication of the war method would have the effect of removing a paralyzing cancerous growth.

III

The methods by which war resistance may be made effective include actions by individuals, by groups and by corporate bodies. Individuals who have reached a mature and resolute conviction that they will never approve of or participate in any future war should make a public declaration of this determination in one or more of the following ways: announcement to relatives and friends; signing a local register of individuals who are unwilling to engage in war; notifying the President of the United States and the Secretary of State of this determination not to support any future war; joining an organization of pacifists, local or denominational or national.

The Fellowship of Reconciliation is an international society of religious pacifists.[3] It is made up of individuals in many countries who are attempting seriously to follow Jesus' way of life. It began in England soon after the outbreak of the World War as a movement of protest against war and of faith in a better way than violence for the solution of all conflict. Although its members do not bind themselves to any exact form

[2] Bertrand Russell, *Which Way to Peace?*, pp. 212, 213.
[3] The office of the Fellowship of Reconciliation in the United States is located at 2929 Broadway, New York City; with branch offices at 252 Winona Drive, Decatur, Georgia; and at 553 South Western Avenue, Los Angeles, California.

of words: "They refuse to participate in any war, or to sanction military preparations; they work to abolish war and to foster good will among nations, races and classes; they strive to build a social order which will suffer no individual or group to be exploited for the profit or pleasure of another, and which will assure to all the means for realizing the best possibilities of life; they advocate such ways of dealing with offenders against society as shall transform the wrong-doer rather than inflict retributive punishment; they endeavor to show reverence for personality—in the home, in the education of children, in association with those of other classes, nationalities and races; they seek to avoid bitterness and contention, and to maintain the spirit of self-giving love while engaged in the struggle to achieve these purposes. It is intended that members shall work out these purposes in their own ways. There is no uniform program of social reconstruction to which all are committed. The movement depends not upon a large number of nominal adherents, but upon those who, accepting the principles fully for themselves, will give time individually and in groups to thinking out what is implied, and will set themselves seriously to apply their conclusions. Such an endeavor inevitably brings a consciousness of insufficiency; but strength and wisdom, far beyond the limits of our present experience, are available to all who open their lives to the leading of the Spirit of God."

The War Resisters' League has members in many lands who have signed this declaration: "War is a crime against humanity. I therefore am determined not to support any kind of war, international or civil, and to strive for the removal of all the causes of war." [4]

Group declarations of determination not to support war are effective means of influencing public opinion. These may take the form of manifestoes signed by men and women from all parts of the nation; or by outstanding leaders of a particular religious body or by officers of various other national or regional organizations; or by outstanding citizens of a local

[4] The American address is 171 West 12th Street, New York City; Miss Jessie Wallace Hughan, Secretary.

community. Official statements from religious assemblies and other organizations renouncing war and refusing to approve or support it are helpful.

Potentially most powerful of all is war resistance on the part of organized labor, because labor possesses the economic strength to prevent war whenever so determined. Organized labor wields tremendous political power and is in a position to influence foreign policy; and through the weapon of the strike it may prevent the waging of war. At the present time in the United States organized labor is far from being committed to war resistance. The conservative wing of the labor movement is now highly nationalistic and is committed to armed preparedness; while a radical wing is willing to fight against fascism and in behalf of Soviet Russia.

IV

Another practical form of war resistance is open to individuals who are unable to accept the full pacifist position. They may go on record as refusing to approve of or participate in any war waged by the United States in Europe or in Asia; that is to say, even though they may feel obliged to support their government in repelling an actual armed invasion of the United States by a foreign foe, they may consistently declare their purpose not to support a war on foreign soil.

Wide use has been made throughout the nation of an enrollment card which reads as follows:

> I agree to take part in peace education and peace action directed toward the removal of the causes of war and the strengthening of pacific means of settling international controversies.
>
> And as a further means of helping to prevent war, in company with many other individuals in all sections of the nation:
>
> Check (A) or (B)
>
> (A) I hereby record my mature and resolute determination never to approve of or participate in any war, except to repel an unprovoked armed invasion of continental United States by a foreign foe.

(B) I hereby record my mature and resolute determination
never to approve of or participate in any war.

The National Peace Conference and its various member
organizations are conducting a national roll call which is open
to individuals of varying convictions on war and peace.[5]

V

Refusal to approve of war or to engage in it is not enough;
war resistance is not a panacea. When looked upon as a sup-
plement rather than as a substitute, however, war resistance has
an extremely vital contribution to make in helping to avert war.
Negative as well as positive action is required. It is not enough
to say, "I will work for peace." Highly patriotic is the endeavor to persuade a maximum number of citizens to say also,
"I will not go to war, and I will never give my consent to the
waging of war."

"To the ordinary man or woman," writes Bertrand Russell,
"it seems a hopeless task to influence the policy of the Government. The drift towards war is observed in a mood of despairing apathy, but is thought to be as inescapable as bad weather.
. . . This apathy can only be cured if each individual who does
not wish his children gassed, his city laid in ruins, his country
devastated, and the civilization of Western Europe wiped out,
can be shown something definite to do about it. There is one
very simple and very definite thing to be done: to join the body
of men and women pledged to abstain from fighting and from
war work, and to support whatever efforts they may collectively
make to keep their country out of war. Such an action by one
man or one woman will not have much effect, it is true; but if
it were taken by a million men and women, it would begin to
influence policy, and if it were taken by several millions it
would become an irresistible argument for the preservation of

[5] Detailed information may be secured by writing to the National Peace
Conference, 8 West 40th Street, New York City; Dr. Walter Van Kirk,
Executive Director.

peace. War is an act of the organised community, and the organised community can prevent it. I believe that, if once the paralysing sense of impotence were removed, the desire for peace in Great Britain would soon express itself in such a form that no government could go against it. But to express the desire for peace effectively, it is essential to show that, whatever the nominal issue, you will oppose any and every war that the folly of governments may be tempted to provoke. Nothing less drastic can be expected to stand firm against the excitement which the approach of war invariably produces. . . . The only wise course, therefore, is to be prepared in advance by an absolute renunciation of war. . . .

"What is needed now is action by individuals, in unison, inspired by reason and passion intimately combined. The best passions to which, in the past, those who waged defensive war were able to appeal—love of home, the desire to protect one's children, the wish to preserve, for civilisation, the work of one's country and whatever has been good in the national traditions —all these, to those who have understood modern war, can no longer be invoked to sanctify even the most righteous conflict; they can be invoked only in favour of peace. The defence of what we value may be difficult, it may have become in part impossible, but in so far as it is possible it is possible only through peace. Of the things that make life tolerable to a lover of peace, none are likely to survive on either side in a great war between technically efficient States. A brutalised and much diminished population, made with hunger and fear, and kept from anarchy only by a military tyranny more extreme than any yet known; the disappearance of the arts and sciences, except as subsidiary to war; the extinction of affection and trust and all voluntary cooperation; the sudden descent into an ancient world of superstition and terror—these are the effects to be expected, on the victorious side as on that of the vanquished. If I am right in this—and the reasons which I have set forth, on the basis of official and expert pronouncements, are overwhelming—the duty of every friend of mankind, of every man who cares for any aspect of civilised life, of every patriot, and of every parent who desires the survival of his children, is simple and clear:

"To abstain from fighting, and from all voluntary participation in war between civilised states; to use every effort to persuade others to do likewise; to bring all possible influence to bear to prevent the participation of his country in war; and, within the limits of his capacity, to aim at similar results in other countries also." [6]

---

[6] Russell, *op. cit.*, pp. 214-223.

Chapter Nine

What Can I Do To Help Prevent War?

IT IS necessary to influence governmental policy if war is to be averted. The United States is one of the countries in which it is possible for rank and file citizens to exert substantial influence on decisions of government. The voters of the nation have it within their power to decide which public officials are sent to Washington, and through various devices they can let their demands be known to their public servants. Literally dozens of ways of exerting direct and indirect influence are open to them. By personal contact or personal communication they can set forth their views on public questions; and in numerous ways they can help to create the public opinion which dominates governmental action.

Public opinion is made up of ideas, traditions, myths, illusions, frustrations, passions, interests, loyalties, and ideals. And every individual can have an effective part in shaping and directing these potent forces. The minds of other individuals can be changed, their motivations and loyalties can be shifted, their emotions can be directed into new channels. Judgments and feelings form public opinion; public opinion in the long run decides governmental action; governmental action determines whether we are to have war or peace. From the following list of suggested courses of action, every reader will find a dozen or more that are open to him.

I

1. Study of international problems is required of persons desiring to be effective participants in the peace movement. Through books, magazines, lectures, classes and radio programs

one must keep informed. To the person who insists that he does not have the time needed for this study, the question should be put: is every hour of your daily program now being spent in ways that are more important than in helping to prevent the suicide of civilization in another world war? Are the lives and destinies of all those you love worth the time required to equip yourself for effective action against war?

2. Take membership in one or more peace societies and thus secure additional access to information and suggested courses of action; and, moreover, strengthen much needed cooperative agencies of persons determined to prevent war. Literature received from these societies will help one to evaluate the significance of news in the morning paper.[1]

3. Persuade other individuals to inform themselves more thoroughly concerning international problems through reading, attendance at lectures and classes, and through careful selection of radio programs.

---

[1] *The peace agencies which compose the National Peace Conference are as follows:*

American Association of University Women, 1634 I St., N.W., Washington, D. C.

American Friends Service Committee, 20 So. 12th St., Philadelphia, Penn.

American Unitarian Association, 25 Beacon St., Boston.

Carnegie Endowment for International Peace, 405 W. 117th St., New York City.

Catholic Association for International Peace, 1312 Massachusetts Ave., Washington, D. C. (Consultative).

Central Conference of American Rabbis, 117 Gibb St., Rochester, N. Y.

Church Peace Union, 70 Fifth Ave., New York City.

Committee on Militarism in Education, 2929 Broadway, New York City.

Council for Social Action of the Congregational and Christian Churches, 289 Fourth Ave., New York City.

Council of Women for Home Missions, 105 E. 22nd St., New York City.

Department of International Justice and Goodwill of the Federal Council of Churches, 105 E. 22nd St., New York City.

Emergency Peace Campaign, 20 So. 12th St., Philadelphia.

Fellowship of Reconciliation, 2929 Broadway, New York City.

Foreign Missions Conference, 156 Fifth Ave., New York City.

Foreign Policy Association (Consultative), 8 W. 40th St., New York City.

General Federation of Women's Clubs, 5295 Waterman Ave., St. Louis, Mo.

Institute of International Education, 2 W. 45th St., New York City.

International Society of Christian Endeavor, 41 Mt. Vernon St., Boston

League of Nations Association, 8 W. 40th St., New York City.

4. Cooperate with the National Peace Conference and its member organizations in promoting the national roll call of peace workers.[2] Help to enroll at least a million American citizens in the peace movement.

5. Help to organize and strengthen peace committees in local organizations, including churches, synagogues, clubs, fraternal orders, commercial organizations, labor unions, educational societies, etc. Help to increase the effectiveness of these committees as agencies of peace education and peace action.

6. Aid in the formation and undergirding of a city peace council, composed of representatives of various peace agencies, as a clearing-house for united peace education and peace action. Suggest the desirability of having the local peace council affiliate with the National Peace Conference.

National Board of the Y.W.C.A., 600 Lexington Ave., New York City.

National Committee on the Cause and Cure of War, 1641 Grand Central Terminal Bldg., New York City.

National Council of Federated Church Women, R. A. Long Bldg., Kansas City, Mo.

National Council of Jewish Women, 221 W. 57th St., New York City.

National Council for Prevention of War, 532 17th St., N.W., Washington, D. C.

National Council of the Y.M.C.A., 347 Madison Ave., New York City.

National Executive Board of the Woman's Auxiliary, Episcopal Church, 281 Fourth Ave., New York City.

National Federation of Business and Professional Women's Clubs, 1819 Broadway, New York City.

National Federation of Temple Sisterhoods, Merchants' Bldg., Cincinnati, Ohio.

National Student Federation, 8 W. 40th St., New York City.

Public Action Committee, 4412 R.C.A. Bldg., Rockefeller Plaza, New York City.

United Synagogue of America, 3080 Broadway, New York City.

Woman's Christian Temperance Union, 1730 Chicago Ave., Evanston, Ill.

Woman's International League for Peace and Freedom, 532 17th St., N.W., Washington, D. C.

World Alliance for International Friendship Through the Churches, 70 Fifth Ave., New York City.

World Peace Commission of the Methodist Episcopal Church, 740 Rush St., Chicago.

World Peace Foundation, 40 Mt. Vernon St., Boston.

World Peaceways, 103 Park Ave., New York City.

[2] Full information may be obtained from the National Peace Conference, 8 West 40th St., New York City.

7. Send telegrams and letters to Senators and Representatives. Concerned citizens should file their names, addresses, and telephone numbers with some local peace agency, and indicate a willingness to communicate with Washington promptly upon notification that a timely moment has arrived for communications dealing with specific legislative measures. Similar communications should also be sent to the President of the United States and to the Secretary of State, since they exercise great influence on legislation. In such communications the asking of questions which call for a definite answer is desirable. Volume is what counts in sending communications to public officials. An individual should not feel that his telegram or letter is unnecessary or futile, any more than he regards his individual ballot on election day as negligible in significance. Frequency in communicating with governmental officials is desirable. Alert citizens may wisely write or telegraph Senators and Representatives several times during a session of Congress. An effective practice is to take time at a public meeting or session of a discussion group then and there to write letters to public officials. Foresight in making available stationery, postcards, and stamps is required.

8. Pass resolutions and circulate petitions. Copies of resolutions and petitions should be sent to local newspapers, as well as to United States Senators, Representatives, the President, and the Secretary of State. Care should be taken to indicate the nature and place of the meeting and the number of persons present. It is highly desirable that resolutions calling for specific legislative action be passed by a wise variety of local organizations and sent to Washington. Volume, variety and frequency are needed.

9. Visitation of public officials in behalf of peace legislation is helpful. Wherever practicable, delegations of representative citizens should call upon Senators and Representatives, either in Washington or when these officials are present in their home communities. More detailed suggestions concerning these various methods are contained in a leaflet entitled *Peace Pressure Primer,* which may be secured upon request from the Women's

International League for Peace and Freedom, 532 17th St., N. W., Washington, D. C.

10. Active participation in local party politics opens the way to effective pressure in behalf of peace legislation. In election years such activity is necessary to secure the nomination and election of suitable candidates.

11. Engage in systematic conversation daily with friends and acquaintances concerning problems of war and peace and seek to awaken their concern and enlist their activity.

12. Teachers, clergymen and other public speakers may wisely select subjects dealing with war and peace, emphasizing especially specific programs of action.

13. Write letters for publication in correspondence columns of newspapers and magazines emphasizing vital aspects of the peace message.

14. Contribute financially to one or more peace societies. The effectiveness of peace education and peace action obviously depends upon funds available. In determining the amount of one's gift, the relative importance of averting war and of other good causes should be kept in mind.

15. Cooperate in presenting anti-war plays and pageants, and in this way appeal to both intellect and emotion.[3]

16. Help to arrange peace parades and other public demonstrations for the purpose of arousing citizens and challenging them to action in behalf of peace.

17. Enlist the cooperation of leaders of orchestras and bands and other musicians in increasing the effectiveness of peace meetings and demonstrations.

18. Display anti-war window cards and billboard posters and in this way challenge the attention of numerous persons who never attend peace meetings.[4]

---

[3] Information concerning plays and pageants may be secured from the National Council for the Prevention of War, 532 17th St., N.W., Washington, D. C.; or from the Women's International League for Peace and Freedom, in the same building.

[4] Information may be secured from World Peaceways, 103 Park Ave., New York City; and from The American Friends Service Committee, 20 South 12th Street, Philadelphia, Penn.

19. Make use of anti-war stickers on window shields of automobiles. Local groups may print their own stickers at small cost, or information may be secured from various national peace agencies.

20. Use illumined maps in schools, churches, libraries, and other institutions to call attention to current events that affect the peace of the world. At a modest cost a map of the world may be equipped with tiny sockets in the principal cities of the various countries. Various colored bulbs (or thumb-tacks) may be used to designate types of events, and ribbons stretched to the margin of the map will call attention to brief typed descriptions or to clippings.

21. Arrange peace exhibits in windows of temporarily vacant stores or in other accessible places. These exhibits may include posters, window cards, stickers, leaflets, pamphlets and books dealing with war and peace. The practice of arranging peace exhibits in connection with conferences and conventions of various organizations is effective.

22. Distribute peace literature, including leaflets and pamphlets. Call attention to significant articles in magazines and to important books on war and peace.

23. Take advantage of anniversaries and special occasions for peace education and peace action.

24. Cooperate in sending youth deputations from colleges and churches to speak on war prevention before various groups in surrounding communities.

25. Encourage student protests against war and cooperate in promoting student peace demonstrations, especially by helping to make effective the annual national student strike against war.

26. Cooperate with the American Friends Service Committee in enrolling students as peace volunteers during the summer. Under this plan carefully selected mature students are trained for two weeks in special institutes and then sent in teams of four to carry on peace education in strategic rural regions throughout the summer.[5]

---

[5] Full information may be secured from Ray Newton, 20 South 12th Street, Philadelphia.

27. Place on record your determination not to approve of or to participate in any future war, or your purpose not to support any war on foreign soil.[6]

28. Cooperate in opening a register in a church, synagogue, college, or other institution, which may be signed by persons desiring to record their determination not to approve of or to participate in any future war, or to declare their purpose not to support a war on foreign soil.

29. Churches, synagogues and other institutions may wisely conduct house-to-house visitations and every-member-canvasses in behalf of world peace. Through conversation and the distribution of literature new recruits for the peace movement may be won.

30. Seek by pacific means to transform competitive capitalism into a cooperative commonwealth; especially by helping to strengthen the labor movement and the consumers' cooperative movement; and by political activity in behalf of a new social order.

31. Be vigilant in safeguarding freedom of speech, assembly and press.

II

Concerning content of American foreign policy, the following courses of action are suggested; through education, evangelism, organization and political procedure:

1. Support the reciprocal trade agreements and other methods of opening channels of international trade. Especially desirable is the lessening of economic tensions in Germany, Italy and Japan by making it easier for them to sell commodities in the United States.[7]

2. Urge the entrance of the United States into the World Court and the signing of the optional clause accepting the compulsory jurisdiction of this tribunal.

3. Advocate the entrance of the United States into the League of Nations on a basis of the Pope Resolution, that is,

[6] See pp. 196 ff.
[7] See pp. 52 ff.

with the reservation that this country is not obligated to use armed force in support of the League's decisions.

4. Endeavor to strengthen the neutrality law, especially through the explicit provision that all trade and all travel by Americans in a war zone must be done at the risk of the trader or the traveler and that the United States assumes no responsibility to use armed action in defense of its citizens abroad; by making mandatory an embargo on materials of war beyond a peacetime quota, with a cash-and-carry provision; and by adopting the Fish amendment making effective in peacetime the embargo against the exportation of munitions and other implements of war.[8]

5. Support the proposal of a nationwide referendum on this question: shall citizens of this country be drafted for war service outside continental United States.[9]

6. Oppose the Hill-Sheppard bill and other forms of conscription through the device of an industrial mobilization plan.[10]

7. Support the Ludlow amendment providing that Congress shall not declare war unless such action is previously approved by a nationwide referendum of American citizens.[11]

8. Urge the adoption of income tax rates which in wartime will absorb all war profits and thus reduce profiteering.

9. Support the plan of nationalizing the munitions industry and thus eliminate the provocative actions of merchants of death.

10. Oppose military training in civilian colleges and high schools, as well as Citizens' Military Training Camps, on the ground that they tend to militarize the minds of American citizens.

11. Hasten the complete independence of the Philippine Islands on terms that safeguard the economic interests of the

---

[8] See p. 157.

[9] Information may be secured from The Women's International League for Peace and Freedom, 532 17th St., N. W., Washington, D. C.; and from other peace societies.

[10] See pp. 141-143.

[11] See pp. 88, 89.

Filipinos; and that relinquish all military and naval bases of American forces in that land.

12. Advocate the placing of Orientals on a quota basis in our immigration law on equality with peoples of other lands.

13. Urge the withdrawal of all American armed forces from China; and adopt officially the permanent policy of refraining from sending American troops beyond our own borders.

14. Support the establishment of a National Peace Department, with a Secretary of Peace and an adequate budget.

15. Urge the Government of the United States to take seriously the obligation imposed by the Kellogg-Briand Treaty "that the settlement or solution of all disputes or conflicts of whatever nature or of whatever origin they may be, which may arise among them, shall never be sought except by pacific means."

16. Advocate drastic reductions in armaments, as a step toward total disarmament and the abandonment of the practice of using armed force as an instrument of policy.

III

Whether or not the United States again goes to war depends on the attitudes and actions of rank and file citizens. *Almost everybody is devoted to peace; and almost everybody insists upon the maintenance of policies which make peace difficult.* To be peaceable is not enough; provocative policies must be changed. Citizens of the favored nations alone can bring about the required changes by pacific means. War is caused not alone by certain actions; but equally so by failure to take certain steps. Passive negation produces war as much as does aggressive action.

The threat of war is so imminent and the consequences of another great conflict would be so calamitous that war prevention is literally the most urgent task before us. What we do about war will determine the future of all those we love and will decide the fate of our civilization. No sensitive and sensible person, therefore, will beg off on the ground that he is too busy to help prevent war.

The challenge to action is made more imperative by reason of the fact that the odds are heavily against success in the endeavor to prevent another world war. Drastic changes must be made quickly; but inertia, illusion, greed, passion and fear block the way. Mountains of obstacles must be removed and the time is short.

No martial trumpet ever sounded a more impelling and urgent call than is now being proclaimed by the peace movement. Patriotic citizens are summoned to give themselves with the same abandon that is demanded in wartime. It is possible to keep the United States out of war and to make a vital contribution to the maintenance of world peace. A million alert and resolute Americans could bring about the required changes. Inaction at this crucial hour is a vote for war.

Let each reader personalize the crisis. If the coming of war depends on ME, will there be war? If MY actions decide the issue, will there be war? If MY INERTIA AND INACTIVITY prove to be determinative, will there be war? Victory depends on ME! If a million American patriots will act resolutely upon this truth, war can be averted. Enroll now as one of that million! [12]

---

[12] See *Creative Pioneers*, by Sherwood Eddy and Kirby Page, Building a New Society Through Adventurous Vocations and Avocations on the Frontiers of the Labor Movement, the Cooperative Movement, Political Action, Racial Justice, and Socialized Religion. Published by Association Press, 347 Madison Avenue, in a 50 cent edition.

Chapter Ten

What Shall We Do About Civil War?

FUNDAMENTAL changes must and will be made. Can the required transformation be wrought by pacific means? Or must we resort to civil war in order to create an equitable society?

In an exploration of these problems, several other questions must be faced: why are basic changes required? what changes must be made? how shall we bring about these necessary changes? is success possible without resorting to civil war? what can we learn from the recent history of Russia, Germany, Italy and Spain? what are the prospects of communism in the United States? what is the likelihood of fascism in this country? what would be the probable outcome of civil war in the United States?

I

The replacement of competitive struggle for private gain by cooperative activity in behalf of the common good would aid substantially in the prevention of war. International war on the present scale cannot be waged without mass support; the rank and file of people must look upon it as justifiable and necessary. In a competitive society the daily experience of citizens produces in them a mentality which may easily be stampeded into support of war. Continuously hammered into consciousness is the idea that self-interest is desirable and necessary, and that a competitive struggle for private gain is beneficent and essential. That a man is entitled to as much money and special privilege as he can obtain is considered axiomatic. The

survival of the fit as a doctrine seems ample justification for
crushing competitors ruthlessly. Callousness is quickly developed by men whose days are spent in seeking gain for themselves by driving their competitors to the wall. Ethical sensitivity is deadened by approving a competitive system in which
the extremes of privilege and privation are considered de-
fensible and unavoidable.

When grown to maturity and magnified on a world scale
the mentality created by the competitive struggle for private
gain produces international war. This mentality readily accepts
as valid the doctrine of national interest. That a nation is entitled to all the privilege and power that it can obtain is an
idea which fits into their scheme of things. Therefore national interest must be pursued zealously even if national policies victimize other peoples. The competitive struggle easily
assumes the form of an international race of armaments.
Ethical sensitivity is still further deadened by acceptance of
planned devastation and organized slaughter as legitimate
means of upholding national interests. There is no mystery
about the ease with which citizens whose minds are saturated
with the ideas and practices of a competitive society may be
herded into international war. Acorns into mighty oaks do
grow.

Excessive concentration of wealth and income increases the
likelihood of war because of the power over foreign policy
wielded by vested interests with most at stake in international
competition, and by intensifying this competition because of
the necessity of disposing of surplus commodities and surplus
capital. To a substantial extent governmental policies are
dominated by the most powerful economic groups; and the more
extreme the concentration of wealth and income, the higher
degree of control thus exercised. If an excessive proportion of
a nation's income flows into the pockets of a small section of
the population, the remainder of the people lack purchasing
power to achieve an adequate standard of living. The result
is not only privation for the masses but industrial stagnation,
because mass production can be continued only if there is mass

consumption. Markets thus become glutted with goods that cannot be sold within the borders of a nation, and the money market likewise becomes glutted with surplus capital that cannot be profitably invested at home. International competition is thus intensified. Under these provocative circumstances, to permit vested interests with a huge stake in foreign affairs to continue exercising dominant power over foreign policy, is merely to invite international war.

II

What changes must be made if the competitive economic order is to be transformed into a cooperative commonwealth? *The fundamental change most urgently needed is the ending of the system of private property in the primary means of production and distribution and the increasing of the volume of private property in users' and consumers' goods.* The key is found in the paradox: more private property through less private property.[1]

No rational solutions of the problems connected with property are possible so long as property is regarded merely as property. The first step must be accurate classification. For purposes of intelligent discussion, various types must be assigned to one of three categories: (1) consumers' or users' property; (2) producers' property in the giant instruments of industry; and (3) miscellaneous property that does not come clearly within the first or the second categories. If a color scheme is used for purposes of illustration, one may refer to the first classification as white, the second as black, and the third as an assortment of grays and browns.

The first category includes food, clothing, modest homes, and countless articles which minister directly to the daily welfare of individuals and families. The second group embraces coal mines, water power sites and other primary sources of electric energy, banks, railroads, telephone and telegraph systems, huge

[1] A portion of this section is printed also in the author's pamphlet, *Property*.

steel mills and titanic manufacturing establishments. And the third classification is composed of border-line types, such as small retail stores, small manufacturing plants, factories which produce non-essentials, and certain kinds of transportation and communication.

The thesis which I desire to set forth is this: *there should be far more private property in the first category, much less private ownership in the second classification, and experimentation in the third group,* including ventures in cooperative ownership and operation through consumers' cooperative societies.

So nearly universal is the conviction in the United States that property in users' commodities should be owned privately that it is futile to seek fundamental changes in the present property system unless a sharp differentiation is made between property for consumption or use and property for production. It is therefore imperative that the social significance of private ownership of the titanic instruments of production be vividly disclosed. The heart of the modern economic problem is found in this second type of property. There is relatively little dispute about the first classification, and decisions concerning the third category are not so urgently demanded. But the action we take with regard to the mass instruments of production and distribution will in large measure determine the future of this nation.

In seeking to evaluate the significance of private ownership of the mass instruments of production, let us consider the effects upon distribution of income and upon utilization of equipment. The struggle for private profit through private ownership of producers' property has undoubtedly resulted in a high degree of industrial efficiency. The best equipped plants in the various industries of this country are marvels of smoothness and their potential productivity far exceeds that of other nations. But a high degree of this efficiency is wasted by failure to achieve an even more significant type of efficiency. It is not enough to secure efficiency in the factory; there must also be efficiency in relationship, efficiency in correlation. Plants must be satisfactorily related to other plants, to sources of raw materials, to supplies of credit, to other industries, and above all to the purchasing power of the consumers.

In several ways private ownership of heavy industry frustrates the effort to achieve high efficiency in correlation. In the first place, this system leads naturally and inevitably to maldistribution of income. It diverts too large a share of the national income into the coffers of owners and investors, with the result that the masses of workers are denied incomes high enough to enable them to buy the goods and services they need. The paradox of too much money in the hands of owners and too little money in the pockets of worker-consumers is inherent in the prevailing property system. Ownership conveys power, and power appropriates privilege. The extent to which ownership is responsible for the chasm between the rich and the poor may easily be demonstrated.

Mr. Robert R. Doane, formerly of the staff of the National Bureau of Economic Research, in his authoritative study, *The Measurement of American Wealth,* cites evidence revealing the percentage of the total national income which is received in the form of wages and salaries, rents, interest, profits, as follows: [2]

Years	Wages	Rents	Interest	Profits
1932............	56.42%	15.53%	14.62%	13.43%
1929............	55.02	15.62	9.63	19.73
1921............	60.36	12.85	10.22	16.57
1917............	47.39	12.04	7.43	33.14
1909............	51.32	9.96	7.04	31.68

From this table it is evident that year after year more than two dollars out of every five of the national income are received from the ownership of property, whereas the vastly greater number of workers receive in the form of wages and salaries combined less than three dollars out of five.

Another significant study of national income was prepared by Dr. Simon Kuznets and other members of the Staff of the National Bureau of Economic Research for the Bureau of

[2] Page 96.

Foreign and Domestic Commerce of the United States and published as a Senate document. The following table is taken from this report.[3]

PERCENTAGE DISTRIBUTION OF NATIONAL INCOME[4]

Years	Salaries and Wages	Dividends	Interest	Rents and Royalties	Profits
1932.......	64.5%	5.3%	11.2%	3.8%	14.4%
1931.......	64.7	6.8	8.9	4.4	14.4
1930.......	64.4	7.7	7.7	4.6	14.8
1929.......	65.1	7.4	7.0	5.1	14.8

According to this classification, property owners received half as much as the total paid out in salaries and wages, although the former group is only a fraction as large as the total number of wage earners.

The significance of these figures stands out more vividly when we examine the proportion of property-income received by individuals who reported an income as high as $5,000 per year. In 1929 the number of incomes as high as $5,000 was just over one million—out of 75 million adults in the United States. Yet this group, constituting in 1929 less than 1½ per cent of the adult population, received the following proportions of the national income.[5]

Years	Wages and Salaries	Dividends	Interest	Rents and Royalties
1932............	6.8%	58.4%	9.7%	8.6%
1932............	8.3	59.9	13.7	11.1
1930............	9.2	64.0	18.2	13.8
1929............	10.0	71.2	22.9	15.8

That is to say, 1½ persons out of every 100 adults in the United States received during 1929 two and one-half times as much in dividends as the other 98½ combined!

In an authoritative study by the Brookings Institution, Harold G. Moulton says: "Out of 15 billion dollars of in-

---

[3] *National Income,* 1929-32, Senate Document No. 124, 73d Congress, 2nd Session, available from The Superintendent of Public Documents, Washington, D. C., at 20c. per copy.

[4] *Ibid,* p. 14.

[5] *Ibid,* p. 40.

dividual savings in 1929, as much as 13 billions were made by 10 per cent of the population. The 2.3 per cent of the families having incomes in excess of $10,000 contributed two-thirds of the entire savings of American families; while the 59 per cent of the families having incomes under $2,000 saved only 1.6 per cent of the total. Sixty thousand families at the top of the income scale, with incomes in excess of $50,000 saved almost as much as 25,000,000 families having incomes less than $5,000. . . . Our capacity to produce consumer goods has been chronically in excess of the amount which consumers are able, or willing, to take off the markets; and this situation is attributable to the increasing proportion of the total income which is diverted to savings channels. The result is a chronic inability—despite such devices as high pressure salesmanship, installment credits, and loans to facilitate foreign purchases— to find market outlets adequate to absorb our full productive capacity." [6]

The disastrous effects of this congestion of income are destined to become more extreme. A far higher ratio of national savings is required in a pioneer land than in a nation which has become industrialized and urbanized. After the growth of population slows down and industrial expansion has reached the point where the national equipment is sufficient to produce all the commodities that can be sold continued saving on the pioneer scale creates social havoc. From now on the percentage of national saving in the United States must diminish and the proportion of spending must increase. But private property in the mass instruments of production blocks the way.

The evidence is cumulatively convincing that plenty for everybody will not be available so long as the present property system is retained. By maldistribution of purchasing power and by inefficiency in correlation, the competitive profit system is inherently unable to provide an adequate physical basis for the good life. Depression has followed boom throughout our history. Extreme instability is a marked characteristic of

[6] Harold G. Moulton, *Income and Economic Progress,* pp. 40, 46.

capitalism. From 1854 to 1930 there were 13 periods of serious depression. In the 36 years from 1890 to 1925 there were 15 years of prosperity, 10 years of depression, and 11 years of decline and recovery.[7] Through excess eagerness to defend the profit system, its upholders maintain that we are certain to pull through the present depression because we have extricated ourselves from many previous bogholes. But what a commentary on the boasted efficiency of capitalism to exult over the fact that it is stuck in the mud only one-third of the time!

Even at the peak of prosperity, however, an appallingly large proportion of the American people were unable to earn enough to provide a decent standard of living. In 1929 only four adults out of a hundred in the United States paid any income tax whatever, in spite of the fact that inhabitants of this country were compelled by law to file an income tax return if, as a single person, an income of $1,500 were received, or $3,500 as head of a family. The number of returns filed was 4,044,327, and due to various exemptions only 2,458,049 paid an income tax. In that year nearly 93 per cent of the total Federal receipts from income tax came from less than 3 per cent of income tax payers, that is from the 102,578 persons who reported incomes as high as $25,000 for the year. In that period the proportion of the tax paid by persons with incomes under $5,000 was less than one-half of one per cent.[8]

In 1929 at the moment when the American people had reached the highest level of living in their history, about 12 million families or more than 42 per cent of the total in the nation, had incomes of less than $1,500 from all sources. This tragic fact is taken from a highly authoritative volume published by the Brookings Institute in Washington, entitled

---

[7] See *Individualism and Socialism*, by Kirby Page, pp. 101-109.
[8] *Ibid*, pp. 74 ff. for further details.

America's Capacity to Consume. Here is the way in which the evidence is summarized by the compilers, Messrs. Maurice Leven, Harold G. Moulton and Clark Warburton.[9]

> "Nearly 6 million families, or more than 21 per cent of the total, had incomes less than $1,000.
>
> "About 12 million families, or more than 42 per cent, had incomes of less than $1,500.
>
> "Nearly 20 million families, or 71 per cent, had incomes less than $2,500.
>
> "Only a little over 2 million families, or 8 per cent, had incomes in excess of $5,000.
>
> "About 600,000 families, or 2.3 per cent, had incomes in excess of $10,000.

"The aggregate incomes of the 6 million families at the bottom of the scale, even when the negative incomes shown by some families are eliminated, amounted to 3.5 billion dollars. In other words, about 21 per cent of the families received only 4.5 per cent of the income. The 11,653,000 families with incomes of less than $1,500 received a total of about 10 billion dollars. At the other extreme, the 36,000 families having incomes in excess of $75,000 possessed an aggregate income of 9.8 billion dollars. Thus it appears that 0.1 per cent of the families at the top received practically as much as 42 per cent of the families at the bottom of the scale. At 1929 prices, a family income of $2,000 may perhaps be regarded as sufficient to supply only basic necessities. However accurate this generalization may be, it is significant to note that *more than 16 million families, or practically 60 per cent of the total number, were below this standard of expenditures.*"

The authors of *America's Capacity to Consume* classify the income groups in the United States in 1929 as follows:[10]

---

[9] pp. 55, 56.
[10] Page 87.

Group	Income Range Families	Unattached Individuals	Number Families	Unattached Individuals	Percentage of Total Population
Wealthy............	$25,000 and over	$15,000 and over	160,000	66,000	0.6
Well-to-do.........	10,000 to 25,000	5,000 to 15,000	471,000	241,000	1.8
Comfortable........	5,000 to 10,000	2,500 to 5,000	1,625,000	632,000	5.9
Moderate Circumstances....	3,000 to 5,000	1,500 to 2,500	3,672,000	1,900,000	13.7
Minimum Comfort..	1,500 to 3,000	750 to 1,500	9,893,000	3,649,000	35.7
Subsistence and Poverty.........	Under 1,500	Under 750	11,653,000	2,500,000	40.6

Let the fact be shouted from the housetops that in the day of greatest prosperity *40 Americans out of every 100 lived on the subsistence-and-poverty level!*

It would be difficult to devise a system of economic production and distribution that would divide mankind into hostile camps more sharply than does the prevailing profit system. The glories of competition have been sounded so eloquently for such a long time that the real significance of the competitive struggle has been obscured. Under pioneer conditions it was possible to move when the conflict became too severe. Sometimes the situation was relieved by the losers moving fifty miles west, and sometimes the stronger and more daring sought new fields of conquest. When communities were small and life was simple the effects of economic competition were less disastrous, especially because of face to face relations. But that type of society has vanished from the United States and will never return. The units of production are becoming vaster and yet vaster. Simplicity and independence have been replaced by complexity and interdependence. Absentee ownership of vast industrial establishments is now the rule, and impersonality is characteristic.

In a complex urbanized, industrialized society economic competition assumes the form of economic warfare. The intensity of the struggle is determined by the life-and-death character of the stakes involved. Business men are pitted against each other, workers must tear at each other's economic throats, organized employers are arrayed against organized workers, and organized citizens fight in the trenches against organized citizens of other lands. Conflict, class war and international war are the red harvest of a competitive profit system. The very idea that competition leads to the survival of the fit is derived from observation of life in the jungle.

That the class struggle becomes more intense as industrialization advances is readily demonstrable. The power of concentrated money in the hands of vast corporations can be resisted only by the collective power of organized labor. Thus the units of conflict become more titanic. In a complex society of delicately adjusted economic relationships, the wreckage of continuous class warfare becomes utterly calamitous. The proposal to minimize this peril by enacting legislation depriving labor of the right to strike, if adopted, would fasten the chains of tyranny tighter around the necks of workers and would certainly be followed by violent revolution.

That modern war among nations is primarily economic in origin is beyond dispute. The doctrines of nationalism transform economic quarrels among merchants, industrialists and financiers of various countries into controversies among their respective governments. These governments in turn are dominated by powerful economic groups which are continuously fanning the flames of nationalism through control of the press, the movies, the radio and other channels of reaching the public mind. So long as the profit system prevails vested interests will seek to enlist governmental armed support for their competitive struggles in other lands. And just this long will international war remain an imminent menace.

In commenting upon this basic problem, Professor Charles A. Beard writes: "One of the hopes for resolving the crisis created by the alleged surpluses and for eliminating the perils to national security created by the outward thrusts of private interests seeking impossible markets for them lies in an *efficient* distribution of wealth within the United States. . . . It is this unbalanced accumulation of capital—overextension of plant capacity and the inefficiency of domestic buying power—which periodically slows down production to a ruinous pace, turns fiercer acquisitive energies into the quest for foreign outlets, sets armament industries in swifter motion, extends the American stake abroad, shifts the center of the nation's gravity from its geographical center toward the borders of the world markets, and makes the economy of the country depend upon the madness of world commercial operations utterly beyond any control on the part of the United States Government. Thus the uncertainty of the domestic market is intensified by the vagaries of foreign markets, fluctuating standards of life, wars, revolutions, political upheavals, tariffs, retaliations, regulations, prohibitions, and naval pressures abroad. So it is here contended that an efficient distribution of wealth within the United States would largely eliminate the unbalance between capital extension and consumption, provide domestic use for a considerable part of the so-called surplus, and reduce the pressures of the outward thrusts—thrusts which engender rivalries abroad, extend the interests of the country beyond the reaches of adequate defense, and lead to armament rivalries and their inevitable outcome—war." [11]

That some form of collectivism must replace unbridled individualism in a complex industrialized society is certain. The choice before us is therefore limited to alternate forms of collectivism. My own answer to this problem may be summarized briefly in this fashion. Private ownership in the following basic industries should without delay be replaced by socialized ownership and operation: banking and credit, the sources of electric energy, minerals and other natural resources, primary means of commercialized transportation, chief means of commercialized communication, and the steel industry. All essential industries remaining in private hands should be subjected to the degree of public regulation required in the public interest.

In my opinion it would be both impossible and undesirable

---

[11] Charles A. Beard, *The Open Door at Home*, pp. 224, 225, 226.

to socialize all property immediately. Even if adequate public support were available, the sheer magnitude of the problem would make undesirable the complete abolition of private property at one time. The resultant chaos and increasing misery would produce a revulsion against socialization and the pendulum would quickly swing toward extreme reaction. Moreover, socialization of the basic industries listed above would be sufficient to secure efficiency through correlation and equalization of purchasing power.

Through social ownership of several basic industries and drastic public regulation of all others it would be possible to diminish both under-privilege and super-privilege. The length to which it would ultimately be wise to go in equalizing income can be determined only by experience, but it is certain that resolute efforts should be made to lift from the bottom and to press down from the top until the margin of difference is not great. Many students of the problem are convinced that *so long as the minimum wage is not higher than $2,000 the maximum income should not exceed $20,000*—and perhaps should be limited to $10,000 or possibly even $5,000. By reducing sharply the excessive flow of income into the coffers of owners and investors and by drastically increasing the proportion going to workers, the effective demand for commodities and services would provide additional employment, which in turn would still further increase effective demand.

Public operation of banking and credit, electric energy, natural resources, the chief means of transportation and communication, and steel would make possible the maintenance of a proper balance between national saving and national spending. The achieving of this result would stabilize industry and regularize income, thus increasing enormously the total productivity of the national equipment.

The system of private property in the primary means of production and distribution is a major cause of international war. In its place must be established a system of common ownership as a necessary condition of the abolition of war.

III

How shall we bring about these necessary changes? *The
minimum requirement includes a triple organization of workers
in labor unions, consumers in cooperative societies, and voters
in a political party that is committed to socialization of the
giant industries.* A prequisite to the transformation of the
property system is the gaining of control of government and
the supporting of government with the economic power of
organized workers and consumers.[12]

Confiscation and purchase are the alternative methods of
transferring private property to public ownership. The former
is advocated by communists and the latter is relied upon by
socialists such as Norman Thomas. The latter is my own point
of view, as a member of the Socialist Party. Confiscation is
possible only as a result of victory in civil war, and therefore
must be ruled out by persons who are resolutely opposed to
armed seizure of power. The first step in utilizing the method
of purchase is to elect to office a government committed to the
policy of buying out specified basic industries. If such a government is wise it will socialize by rapid stages, rather than by
attempting to inaugurate social ownership of all major industries at one time. On the other hand, a policy of gradualism
whereby socialization is stretched out slowly over a long period
is likely to prove fatal, as was demonstrated by the experience
in Germany. Banking, electric energy, natural resources and
chief means of transportation and communication are likely to
come within the first stage. Giant industries such as steel and
automotive works will probably be included in the second stage
of socialization.

Payment for private industries taken over should be made
in government bonds based on the value of the properties purchased, not in gold or other forms of cash. This is a regular
practice under capitalism. When one giant corporation buys
out another huge concern, a usual practice is for stockholders

---

[12] A portion of this section is printed also in the author's *Living
Courageously.*

of the second company to be paid in stock of the purchasing company. This disposes of the question, "Where would the money come from?" Thus the widow who has invested a thousand dollars of insurance money in a coal mine would turn in this stock or bond and receive in return a government bond for one thousand dollars. The two values of her certificate would therefore be conserved: she would be entitled to interest on her investment and she would be privileged to sell the bond and recover her capital.

The method of purchase is less satisfactory in cases of heavy stockholders. Consider the illustration of an individual who has invested ten million dollars in coal mines. Interest at even three per cent on government bonds valued at ten millions amounts to $300,000 per year. Moreover, this rich holder might choose to sell and invest his ten millions elsewhere. It is thus obvious that this method does not bring to an immediate end extreme inequalities of wealth and power. The device of taxation, however, offers a legal means of dealing with this social problem. Through a steeply graduated income-tax supplemented by the removal of all tax-exempt features, all of this $300,000 except a maximum of $100,000 or $10,000 or some other sum decided upon democratically by the citizens of the land could be recovered at once in the form of taxes. By utilizing inheritance-taxes and gift-taxes in the same way, great fortunes could be broken up within a generation, indeed within a short time since most rich men are no longer young.

The statement is frequently made that purchase plus high taxation is equivalent to confiscation and confiscation is unethical. This raises the question as to whether or not democratically-imposed taxes are confiscation. When the government takes 70 per cent of the highest incomes derived from the ownership of private property, is such an act confiscation? Is the taxation of income derived from government bonds more confiscatory than the taxation of incomes received from investments in private property? Taxation in proportion of ability to bear it is one of the most firmly established principles of taxation in the United States and in no sense constitutes confiscation. Moreover, great fortunes are piled up through the cooperation of vast numbers of individuals. To speak of Henry Ford's fortune as being self-made is grossly misleading. His great wealth is due to his own genius, plus the help of tens of thousands of scientists, engineers, and workers; plus the expenditures of millions of consumers, plus the aid of government in maintaining law and order and in preventing armed uprisings by providing public relief on a vast scale; plus the vast market afforded by free trade and the absence of tariff barriers between states on this vast continent; plus innumerable other important factors. An argument may be made that it is unwise to break up the Ford fortune, but surely it would not be immoral for society to take this action.

How should publicly owned industries be operated? Not by Congress, but by boards of control composed of democratically elected representatives of technicians, workers, and consumers. Functional organizations of engineers should be extended and given heavier social responsibilities. That is to say, an engineer should function not only as a voter in a given geographical area, but also as a member of a vocational group. The national society of engineers operating in the coal industry should elect a certain proportion of the membership of the board of control of this industry. Workers also should be organized and given heavier responsibilities. The national union of mine workers should elect a part of the board of control. Consumers of coal should also be organized in consumers' societies and in this capacity should elect members of the board of control. That is to say, the coal industry should be operated by representatives of the groups with most technical ability and with the greatest stake. Coordination of the coal industries with other industries would be provided through a national planning commission, composed of representatives elected by the various boards of control.

This proposal is not as radical as it sounds. At the present time in the United States the great industries are not operated directly by owners, except in rare cases. Giant corporations are owned by tens of thousands of stockholders. Berle and Means point out that in 1929 the largest stockholder of the Pennsylvania Railroad owned less than one-third of one per cent of the total stock, while the combined holdings of the twenty largest holders amounted to less than three per cent of the total. The twenty largest holders of stock in the American Telephone and Telegraph Company owned less than five per cent of the total; while the corresponding figure for the United States Steel Corporation was less than 7 per cent. Many of these richest stockholders played no part whatever in operating the companies. The great corporations are for the most part operated by employees, men and women hired for this purpose. Except in highly infrequent cases, the picture of a frugal, hard-working owner running his own plant is no longer valid so far as the great corporations of the United States are concerned. Under a system of public ownership, substantially the same personnel would operate the railroads as at present. The basic difference would be that they would no longer be controlled by boards of directors primarily concerned about private profit, but would be directed by a board of control, which they helped to elect, chiefly concerned about public service.

Not all socialized industries should be owned nationally. State and municipal ownership are preferable in many instances. Moreover, socialized ownership through voluntary cooperative societies is more desirable in many cases than national ownership through government. Especially in the area of retail distribution, the consumers' cooperative movement has an invaluable contribution to make toward the functioning of genuine democracy. Consumers' cooperatives find it desirable to enter the field of production. Just where the dividing lines should be drawn between national, state, municipal ownership, and voluntary cooperatives cannot be determined with rigidity. Continuous experimentation in this area is imperative! [13]

---

[13] Detailed information about launching and conducting a consumers' cooperative may be secured by writing to the Cooperative League, 167 West 12th Street, New York City. The rapid growth of this movement within recent months constitutes one of the most hopeful signs of the times.

IV

Is success possible without resorting to civil war? Will rich
and powerful industrialists and financiers submit peaceably to
the ending of private property in the giant industries? Is it
true that no ruling class has ever yielded until overcome by
violence? Do recent events in Russia, Germany, Italy and
Spain demonstrate the impotence and futility of pacific means
of social change? How valid for citizens of the United States
are analogies taken from the experience of European countries?

The Russian Revolution

Let us begin with a survey of the forces which overthrew
the czarist regime and established a dictatorship of the proletariat in Soviet Russia.[14]

Just a week after the March revolution had deposed the Czar,
Lenin wrote from Switzerland: "How could such a 'miracle'
happen, that in eight days . . . a monarchy that had maintained itself for centuries, and continued to maintain itself
during three years of tremendous national class conflicts of
1905-1907, could utterly collapse? . . . Let us not harbour
any illusions. The fact that the revolution succeeded so quickly
and, apparently, at the first superficial glance, so 'radically,' is
due to *an unusual historical conjecture* where there combined,
in a strikingly 'favourable' manner, *absolutely* dissimilar movements, *absolutely* different class interest, *absolutely* opposed
political and social tendencies."[15] Two weeks later Lenin
wrote: "We know full well that the proletariat of Russia is
less organized, less prepared, and less class-conscious than the
proletariat of other countries. It is not its special qualities but
rather the *special coincidence of historical circumstances* that
has made the proletariat of Russia for a certain, *perhaps very
short time,* the vanguard of the revolutionary proletariat of the

---

[14] A portion of this section is printed also in the author's pamphlet,
Capitalism and Its Rivals.

[15] *Collected Works of V. I. Lenin,* vol. 20, Book 1, pp. 27, 31. Italics mine.

whole world." [16] After his arrival in Petrograd, on April 27, 1917, Lenin said: "And so, the revolution in its first stage developed in a way that no one had expected. . . . *A most amazingly unique situation.*" [17] So much so that H. N. Brailsford writes: "Lenin, as one of his intimates told me, believed, when he made the November revolution, that he was lighting the beacon for the rising of the German working-class: *his* own experiment would last, he supposed, at the most four months." [18]

Near the end of his classic history, Trotsky writes: "Notwithstanding the number of great social and political crises, a coincidence of all the conditions necessary to a victorious and stable proletarian revolution has so far occurred but once in history: in Russia in October 1917." [19] But once in history! And never in a highly industrialized nation. Never! What combination produced in Russia the "coincidence of all the conditions necessary," "the unusual historical conjecture?" If that coincidence and conjuncture occur in any other land, we may then expect a successful proletarian armed seizure of power. But unless it can be demonstrated that this combination is likely to appear in the United States, arguments based on the Russian analogy are invalid and misleading. It is imperative therefore that we seek the springs of the Russian torrent.

The Bolshevik revolution succeeded because of the following "coincidence and conjecture": *The extent of the revulsion against czarist tyranny, the catastrophic defeat of Russia in war, the appalling degree of economic misery, the absence of a large propertied middle class, the melting away of armed support of the old regime, the lack of experience with democracy, the madness of the Kerensky Government's attempt to continue the World War, the enormous popular support accorded the communists, the limited growth of industrialism and the high degree of economic self-sufficiency of the vast land of Russia,*

[16] *Ibid*, vol. 20, Book 1, pp. 85, 86. Italics mine.
[17] *Ibid*, p. 200. Italics mine.
[18] *The New Clarion*, July 22, 1933, p. 112.
[19] Leon Trotsky, *The History of the Russian Revolution*, vol. 3, p. 175.

the genius and faith of Lenin plus the eloquence and organizing ability of Trotsky.

1. The extent of revulsion against czarist tyranny was a major cause of the Russian revolution. For hundreds of years the people of this vast land had been victimized by almost every conceivable type of despotism. The record is summarized by a recent historian in these words: "The only possible parallel to the sadistic and insensate brutality which became the rule of Russia must be sought in Poland or Turkey. . . . The political despotism of the tsarist regime, which was in many respects absolutely untouched by ideas of progress and humanity from the time of Catherine II to that of Nicholas II . . . could not get on without punitive expeditions into the villages, mass floggings, and banishments to Siberia. . . . Russian history is full of unbridled savagery, excesses, butchery, and terror of every sort." [20] In reply to a question concerning a notorious massacre of workmen, a high official once replied: "As it was in the beginning, is now, and ever shall be!" [21]

A vicious form of serfdom prevailed throughout Russia for four centuries. This type degraded its victims "to a level lower than was ever reached by the serf of western Europe. The western serf was protected by law against personal injury from his lord, but the Russian peasant was absolutely defenceless and had often to endure the most refined cruelties at the hands of his proprietor." [22] Not until 1861 was emancipation secured, and then under such terms as to afford the peasantry no substantial relief. Indeed, in many regions the lot of the former serfs became even more intolerable, since they were compelled to yield a portion of the land formerly cultivated to the nobles and also to pay dues to the state for the remainder. In some areas "force had to be employed to make the peasant comply with the law. . . . In many districts, where the soil was poor, the value of the labor services (required to make the necessary payments) far exceeded the value of the land, and the result

[20] Hans von Eckardt, *Russia*, pp. 82, 97, 173, 174.
[21] *Ibid*, p. 174.
[22] Arthur Birnie, *An Economic History* of Europe, p. 28.

was to saddle many peasants with heavier annual payments than their holdings would bear." [23]

When the victims of despotic cruelty manifested the slightest inclination to rebel, they were ruthlessly suppressed through imprisonment, exile, and execution. In the period of czarism the average yearly number of exiles "rose from about 2,000 at the beginning of last century to about 20,000 toward the end of the century." [24] No wonder, therefore that great agrarian disturbances were "simply never-ending" during the eighteenth and nineteenth centuries. During the period immediately following the emancipation of the serfs "there were no less than two thousand local agrarian revolts, which had to be put down by force of arms." [25] The formidable revolution of 1905 was suppressed with ruthless ferocity. Thus we see that barbarous despotism was the soil in which was nurtured the Bolshevik revolution.

2. The catastrophic defeat of Russia in the World War constituted a major factor in the situation which hurled Lenin and his colleagues into power. The fighting force of no nation in modern times ever collapsed so utterly as did the armies of the czar in 1917. Of the total of about fifteen million Russians who were mobilized, the number of casualties dead, wounded, captured reached the appalling figure of five and a half millions, of whom more than two millions were killed. The woefully backward Russian industrialism and the tragically weak transportation system could not stand the terrific strain of prolonged warfare on this titanic scale.

At the pinnacle of the cruel and corrupt and inefficient Russian government sat a futile and pathetic czar, dominated by a strong-willed but incredibly stupid wife, who in turn was under the hypnotic spell of the most loathsome adventurer of modern times. This trio was surrounded by a court of simpletons, debauches and conspirators. Rasputin could rise to the

---

[23] *Ibid*, p. 30.
[24] Guido de Ruggiero, in *Encyclopaedia of the Social Sciences,* vol. 5, p. 689.
[25] Eckardt, *op. cit.,* pp. 58, 182.

top only in a pool of slime and corruption. "Your Majesty,"
bemoaned the president of the last Duma, Rodzianko, early in
January, 1917, "there is not one reliable or honest man left
around you; all the best men have been removed or have retired.
There remain only those of ill repute." [26]   The worse conditions became, the more frantic were the appeals to the crowned
head from the Czarina: "Be Peter the Great, Ivan the Terrible,
Emperor Paul—crush them all under your feet. . . . Russia
loves to feel the whip." [27]   So little of the handwriting on the
wall was the Czar able to read that only a few hours before the
royal house of the Romanoffs crumpled up like cardboard, he
exclaimed to his Minister of the Court: "Again that fat-bellied
Rodzianko has written me a lot of nonsense, which I won't
even bother to answer." [28]

In spite of the fact that Kerensky was determined to wage
war until victory had been achieved, as I shall point out in a
subsequent section, he was fully aware of the demoralized
condition of the armies at the front.   Here is his testimony:
"As early as January, 1915, a Colonel of the General Staff,
Engelhardt, a conservative member of the Duma, told the
Budget Committee that 'we can oppose the technical perfection
of Germany only by flesh and bones: that is why we have to
fill the trenches to the brim with the corpses of our soldiers.'
'All we know,' said Field Marshal von Hindenburg in his
memoirs concerning the fighting on the Russian front, 'is that
from time to time we had to destroy mountains of enemy
corpses which accumulated in front of our trenches. . . .'" [29]
While the French General Petain said: "The Russian army is
nothing but a façade, it will fall to pieces if it makes a move." [30]
Renewed efforts to move it in 1917 did cause it to fall apart.

3. The appalling degree of economic misery to which the
masses of Russia were subjected proved to be one of the most
powerful dynamics of the Bolshevik revolution.   Although

[26] Trotsky, *op. cit.,* vol. 1, p. 56.
[27] *Ibid,* vol. 1, pp. 64, 59.
[28] *Ibid,* vol. 1, p. 79.
[29] Alexander Kerensky, *The Crucifixion of Liberty,* p. 204.
[30] Trotsky, *op. cit.,* vol. 1, p. 380.

physical suffering by itself never causes a revolutionary explosion, as may be seen in India and China where the level of economic welfare is far beneath that of pre-war Russia, it is the soil out of which revolution springs. This soil in Russia was rich enough to bring forth a hundred fold. Even before the outbreak of the world conflict, the mass of workers and peasants existed in indescribable poverty. In 1914 the national income per capita in the United States was eight to ten times greater than in Russia.[31] The colossal burden imposed by the waging of the war crushed the Russian people deeper into the mire. Hunger, malnutrition and starvation everywhere abounded. Prices sky-rocketed and even the limited supplies available were beyond the purses of the masses, except on a mere subsistence level. Three months after the February revolution and five months prior to the October overthrow, the government was obliged to concede that the condition of the workers "borders for many categories upon chronic starvation." [32] The bread ration in Petrograd and Moscow was cut to half a pound daily, and in some places the ration was two pounds per week.[33]

Industrial strikes and peasant revolts broke out with increasing frequency as the workers in desperation sought to ward off starvation. During the first two months of 1917 more than 575,000 persons went on strike, a large majority of them in the capital.[34] Vermenichev has calculated that between February and October there were 5,278 agrarian conflicts with landlords and peasant bourgeoisie.[35] This evidence was interpreted by Trotsky as firmly establishing "the fact that the peasant movement of 1917 was directed in its social foundations not against capitalism, but against the relics of serfdom. . . . In reality the Russian muzhik was completing a business entered upon many centuries before the Bolsheviks appeared in the world. . . . With revolutionary barbarism he was wiping out the bar-

[31] *Ibid*, vol. 1, p. 9.
[32] *Ibid*, vol. 1, p. 420.
[33] *Ibid*, vol. 2, p. 345.
[34] *Ibid*, vol. 1, p. 43.
[35] *Ibid*, vol. 3, p. 17.

barism of the middle ages. . . . The 17th, 18th, and 19th centuries of Russian history climbed upon the shoulders of the 20th, and bent it to the ground." [36]

4. The absence of a large propertied middle class played an important role in the emergency of the revolutionary situation. The fact that such a small percentage of the total population possessed a substantial stake in the preservation of the status quo turned out to be decisive in the hour of crisis. According to a 1905 land survey,[37] eleven and one-half million peasants held 98 million hectares,[38] an average of eight and one-half hectares per owner; whereas one and one-half million large peasants and capitalists owned 153 million hectares, an average of 100 hectares per owner. That is to say, the holdings of the latter group averaged twelve times as much as the former group. The average of eight and one-half hectares constituted an utterly insufficient quantity of land for the maintenance of a decent standard of living, especially in view of the backward state of Russian agriculture, the tragic shortage of livestock, and the numerous exactions required from them by the state. These millions of peasants were as a consequence barely able to maintain themselves on a subsistence level. The land reforms inaugurated by Stolypin in 1906 were so inadequate and had been in operation for such a short time that they did not dampen the ardor of the masses for radical economic change.

While Russian industry was progressing with great speed in 1917, it nevertheless remained in a retarded condition in comparison with highly industrialized nations. The per capita wealth of various European countries in 1914 has been estimated by Sir Josiah Stamp as follows: United Kingdom, $1,590; France, $1,515; Germany, $1,220; Belgium, $785; Russia, $425.[39] The total number of workers in factories subject to inspection was about two millions.[40] The average size of industrial establishments in Russia, however, was much

---

[36] *Ibid*, vol. 3, pp. 17, 34, 35.
[37] Eckhardt, *op. cit.*, p. 275.
[38] One hectare equals approximately two and one-half acres (2.471 acres).
[39] Arthur Birnie, *An Economic History of Europe*, p. 281.
[40] Trotsky, *op. cit.*, vol. 1, p. 33.

larger than in other countries. Small enterprises with less than 100 workers employed in the United States, in 1914, 35 per cent of the total of industrial workers, but in Russia only 17.8 per cent. Whereas in the giant concerns with 1,000 or more workers, 17.8 per cent of the workers of the United States were employed, as contrasted with 41.4 per cent in Russia. At least 40 per cent of the capital invested in Russian industries in 1914 came from abroad, chiefly from France, England, Belgium and Germany.[41] This high percentage of foreign investment concentrated in large establishments reduced substantially the proportion of holdings in the hands of Russian investors. Due to this combination of factors, the size of the middle class in Russia was much smaller than in the highly industralized countries, especially so in comparison with the United States and England. This fact accelerated the speed toward revolutionary change.

5. The melting away of armed support of the old regime followed as a natural consequence of the ghastly suffering of the masses and the intensity of their resentment. Both in the March revolution and in that of November the transfer of power was practically bloodless. At the former date none of the armed forces remained sufficiently loyal to the czar to be willing to fight in his behalf, while at the latter time the Bolsheviks took power from Kerensky after brief and feeble armed resistance. The significance of this dual fact can scarcely be exaggerated. *In both cases the revolutionaries succeeded precisely because they were confronted with practically no armed resistance.*

The reasons why the military support of the czar faded away are summarized by a contemporary writer in these words: "The support of the majority of the army had enabled the Tsarist Government in 1905 to stamp out the revolutionary movement. Now hardly a single regiment remained loyal to the Tsar and his Government. The populace was resolved on revolution for the purpose of making an end simultaneously of Tsarism and the war. The propertied middle class were also prepared to revolt for an exactly contrary reason. The middle class recognized that the corrupt and incapable Tsarist regime was leading Russia to a catastrophe. . . . Even the reactionary clique surrounding the Tsar gradually came to see that a continuance of the war meant the destruction of all Conservative and traditional authority in Russia.[42]

Concerning the critical period of the February revolution, Trotsky wrote: "One after another, from early morning, the Reserve Guard battalions mutinied before they were led out of the barracks. . . . The military revolt had become epidemic. Only those did not mutiny that day who did not get around to it. Toward evening the Semenovsky regiment joined in, a regiment notorious for its brutal putting down of the Moscow uprising of 1915. . . . The tzarist garrison of the capital, numbering 150,000 soldiers, was dwindling, melting, disappearing. By night it no longer existed. . . . The whole truth is that the fabric of the regime had completely decayed; there was not a live thread left. . . . The dynasty fell by shaking, like rotten fruit, before the revolution even had time to approach its first problem. . . . The country had so radically vomited up the monarchy that it could not crawl down the people's throat again.[43] The forces of the March revolution met with so little opposition in the capital that the total number killed and wounded was only 1,443.[44] On the ruins of an ancient empire, the Provisional Government was established.

6. The lack of experience with democracy proved to be a terrible handicap to the new government. Under the most propitious circumstances such an infant democracy would have been afflicted with excruciating growing-pains. It is not surprising therefore that in an hour of debacle throughout a vast empire, the new regime proved inadequate to cope with the appalling situation.

"Russia's history," writes Chamberlin, "is notably lacking in those elements which placed a bar upon absolutism during the

---

[42] Arthur Rosenberg, *A History of Bolshevism*, p. 81.

[43] Trotsky, *op. cit.*, vol. I, pp. 78, 124, 125, 127, 129, 175.

[44] *Ibid*, vol. I, p. 141.

Middle Ages and paved the way for the ultimate emergency of democracy: powerful, semi-independent feudal lords, free cities, a Church which could face the State on equal or superior ground, a landed yeomanry, free from the shackles of serfdom. Russia has no such traditions as the English barons at Runnymede or John Hampden refusing to pay his ship-money levy on a question of principle or Luther nailing his theses to the door of the Wittenberg church. It knew only the unlimited power of the Tsars, the heavy bureaucratic rule of the Tsarist state machine, occasionally varied by fierce outbursts of anarchy such as the peasant rebellions of Razin and Pugachev." [45]

Prior to 1905 only a tiny fraction of the total population of Russia had any part whatever in determining national policies of government. The so-called constitutional monarchy inaugurated in that year was nothing but "sham constitutionalism." The first two Dumas were dissolved almost immediately after the elections disclosed majorities hostile to the government. Even in the Fundamental Laws of 1906 the czar was specifically designated as autocrat-ruler. While these statutes theoretically guaranteed personal liberty, the secret police continued their deadly activities against persons "politically unreliable." When the fact is recalled that even these elementary beginnings in democracy had been in operation at the outbreak of the war for less than nine years, it will be easy to understand why the sense of civic responsibility and patriotic loyalty were so frail.[46]

7. The madness of the Kerensky Government's attempt to continue participation in the World War in spite of thunderous warnings from every direction proved to be absolutely fatal to its existence. A commander of a corps at the front, Baron Budberg, exclaimed: "Only completely crazy people could dream about an offensive at the present time." [47] The Minister of Supplies, Prokopovich, reported: "I have the follow-

---

[45] W. H. Chamberlin, *Russia's Iron Age*, pp. 263, 264.
[46] See *Encyclopaedia of the Social Sciences*, vol. 7, pp. 65-67.
[47] Trotsky, *op. cit.*, vol. 3, p. 72.

ing telegram from the Northern front: 'The most terrific autocrat—hunger—is menacing the army.' . . . And here is a telegram from General Cheremisov: 'The food situation at the front is catastrophic. Horses are perishing for lack of forage. Bakeries stop working because there is no flour. The last reserves of hardtack are now being consumed.' " [48]

Yet late October General M. V. Alexeev, former Commander-in-Chief, insisted: "An impartial view of the situation will disclose that an immediate peace would be fatal for Russia, leading to her physical disintegration and an inevitable partition of her possessions. . . . It would eliminate Russia from the Great Powers on which depends the solution of all European problems. . . . The masses (of soldiers) have tasted the sweets of insubordination . . . and idleness. They are overwhelmed by the desire for personal safety, which creates longing for a speedy peace. Such an army is a real danger." [49] Concerning the policy of Miliukov, first Minister of Foreign Affairs of the Provisional Government, Kerensky wrote that he "desired at all costs to continue with Sazonov's policy in his dealings with Paris and London. 'The revolution has made no change in our foreign policy,' he repeated day in and day out." [50] Miliukov insisted that Russia must fight on until the war was won so that the terms of the secret treaties could be fulfilled and Constantinople and the Straits annexed.

Kerensky himself was utterly romantic about the war and insisted to the very last moment that it be continued to a victorious end. Listen to these incredible words: ". . . the people immediately recognized the conflict with Germany as its own war; not a government or dynastic adventure, but a war which meant that the destinies of Russia were at stake. The necessity for participating in the defense of the country was therefore recognized by all the parties without exception. . . . 'Russian liberty will be born on the battlefields,' I wrote in the declaration which was read on behalf of the Trudoviks

---

[48] James Bunyan & H. H. Fisher, *The Bolshevik Revolution*, p. 49.
[49] *Ibid*, p. 37.
[50] Kerensky, *op. cit.*, p. 339.

when the Duma was summoned in connection with the declaration of war. . . . Furthermore, the revolution itself, miraculously turning an anarchical explosion into an orderly political movement, was born in an unparalleled burst of patriotic enthusiasm, which entirely precluded separate peace. . . . We had wanted a revolution before the war, but during the war we tried to avoid it.   When it came, in the flame and thunder of the sudden collapse of Russian monarchy, it came unwanted by anyone." [51]   Believe it or not!   These are words from the most influential member of the Provisional Government!

8. The enormous popular support accorded the communists was due to the despair and resentment of the masses against all other alternatives and to the glowing promises made by Lenin, Trotsky and their colleagues.   To the soldiers they promised immediate peace, to the peasants they held out the immediate expectation of receiving land, to the proletarians they offered control of industry and domination of government, and to non-Russian citizens of the empire, they offered freedom and self-determination.

So overwhelming was the public desire for peace and bread and land, and so universal and complete was the loss of confidence in the old regime and in the Provisional Government, and so effective the educational campaign, that the Bolsheviks carried everything before them to such a degree that the October Revolution in Petrograd, the capital city, was almost bloodless.[52]   "The unique thing about the October revolution," wrote Trotsky, "a thing never before observed in so complete a form, was that, thanks to a happy combination of circumstances, the proletarian vanguard had won over the garrison of the capital before the moment of open insurrection.   It had not only won them over, but had fortified this conquest through the organization of the Garrison Conference." [53]   The strategic Petrograd fortress of Peter and Paul, and the Kronverksky arsenal containing 100,000 rifles, were captured from the in-

[51] *Ibid,* pp. 235, 196, 295, 159.
[52] See Trotsky, vol. 1, p. 460.
[53] *Ibid,* vol. 3, pp. 181, 182.

side without the firing of a shot. The central telegraph office
of the capital city was taken over by two armed revolutionaries,
while the Nikolaevsky railway station was occupied within 15
minutes by a company of the sapper battalion, without resistance.[54] The staff headquarters offered no resistance and was
occupied by a small detachment of Red Guards.

Rather than being a highly dramatic affair, the assumption
of power by the Bolsheviks was accomplished with amazing
ease. Here is the account as presented in a recent history:
". . . it was not until after nightfall that the Bolshevik
forces actually began to close in on the defenders of the government. About 7:30, without meeting opposition, they occupied the headquarters of the military district and arrested
General Bagratuni. The forces guarding the palace began to
melt away. By a ruse the cadet artillery was led out of the
palace yard and disarmed and the Women's Battalion of Death
marched out and surrendered. About 8:30 Antonov sent his
ultimatum to Kishkin. The ministers refused to surrender and
the Peter and Paul and the 'Aurora' (previously occupied without fighting by the Bolsheviks) were ordered to open fire. The
firing lasted for an hour, and made a great deal of noise but
did very little damage. . . . The news of the arrest of the
Provisional Government reached the City Duma at about
3:00 A.M " [55]

In an official Bolshevik publication we read: "Hardly any
one can now be found to argue that the Revolution was organized artificially. It was an irresistible and elemental movement." [56] "The masses were in a state of ecstasy," reported a
member of a vast audience which was addressed by Trotsky
at a critical hour. ". . . ready to join in a religious hymn.
. . . I could see the eyes of men and women burning with
enthusiasm. Was it the fever of spiritual exaltation? Or,
perhaps, they caught a glimpse of the promised land?"[57] In
the *Encyclopaedia of the Social Sciences* we read: "In taking

[54] *Ibid,* vol. 3, pp. 222, 224.
[55] Bunyan and Fisher, *op. cit.,* pp. 106, 118.
[56] Quoted by Rosenberg, *op. cit.,* p. 111.
[57] Quoted by Bunyan and Fisher, *op. cit.,* p. 83.

over the government of the former Russian Empire Lenin was supported by the good will of all numerically important elements of the population—the soldiers, the peasants, the workers and the non-Russian nationalities." [58]

"It was not necessary to employ force," wrote Trotsky, who was chief director of the October revolution, "for there was no resistance. The insurrectionary masses lifted their elbows and pushed out the lords of yesterday." [59] "The bourgeois classes had expected barricades, flaming conflagrations, looting, rivers of blood. In reality a silence reigned more terrible than all the thunders of the world."

In Moscow insurrection required eight days before all opposition was crushed, although the revolutionaries outnumbered their opponents by ten to one, according to Maralov, one of the chief leaders of the Moscow insurrection.[60] The fact is now indelibly recorded in history that the Petrograd insurrection required just 24 hours and was practically bloodless, and that the Moscow insurrection took just eight days, with a relatively small loss of life.

9. The limited growth of industrialism and the high degree of economic self-sufficiency of the vast land of Russia enabled the Bolsheviks to hold power more easily than would have been the case in any other Western country. The dislocation produced by revolution is far less catastrophic in a predominantly agricultural country than in a highly industrialized and urbanized nation. From the beginning of the communist regime, city workers have exploited the peasants. Control of the machinery of government, coupled with the fact that there are four residents in rural communities for every dweller in a Russian city, made it possible for the proletarians to survive and therefore to preserve the revolution. If half of the population of Russia had lived in urbanized areas when production fell to 15 per cent of the low pre-war level, as it did in 1921 just before

---

[58] *Encyclopaedia of the Social Sciences,* vol. 13, p. 482.

[59] See Trotsky, vol. 3, p. 225.

[60] See *Ibid,* vol. 3, p. 300.

the New Economic Policy was inaugurated, the continuance
of the Bolshevik administration would probably have proved
to be utterly impossible.   Wholesale starvation would have
produced indescribable anarchy and chaos.   Likewise, the high
degree of Russia's economic self-sufficiency enabled the Bolsheviks to withstand armed intervention, diplomatic and economic
opposition from the outside world.   So vast is Russian territory, so varied and abundant are the essential resources, that
the communists were able to continue building a new society
within the walls erected by hostile nations.

10. The genius and faith of Lenin plus the eloquence and
organizing ability of Trotsky played a crucial role in the
achievement of success.   What if the Kaiser's government had
refused to permit Lenin and his companions to cross Germany
at a highly critical moment?   What difference would it have
made if Kerensky had succeeded in arresting Lenin during the
111 days he was in hiding from July 6, 1917, to October 25?
What if Trotsky had been detained by the Canadian government until after the Armistice?   What would have been the
consequences if on the eve of the revolution the Smolny had
been seized and the inner group of Bolshevik leaders arrested
and executed?

The various letters and official minutes of crucial meetings
of the Bolsheviks which have now been published reveal clearly
the heavy odds against Lenin as he sought furiously to spur his
comrades on to the seizure of power.   In a letter to the members of the Central Committee on the very eve of "the" day,
Lenin wrote: "With all my power I wish to persuade the comrades that now everything hangs on a hair. . . ." [61]   Concerning
the controversy between Lenin and his comrades Kamenev and
Zinoviev, during which Lenin demanded their expulsion from
the party, Trotsky wrote: "It is hardly necessary to explain
that the truth in this dramatic dialogue was wholly on Lenin's
side. A revolutionary situation cannot be preserved at will.
If the Bolsheviks had not seized the power in October and

[61] Lenin, *op. cit.*, vol. 21, Book 2, p. 122.

November, in all probability they would not have seized it at all." [62]

Just how much difference the removal of Lenin and Trotsky from the scene would have made can never be known. But one fact at least is incontestable. *"Notwithstanding the number of great social and political crises, a coincidence of all the conditions necessary to a victorious and stable proletarian revolution has so far occurred but once in history: in Russia in October 1917."* [63] Not in France or Germany or Italy or England or the United States; only in Russia!

With the utmost emphasis let me point out that, in relation to the American scene, arguments based on the Russian revolutionary situation are absolutely invalid unless evidence is produced to show that this nation is likely to be confronted with a combination of factors similar to those which made possible the success of the Bolsheviks. In estimating the prospects of communism in the United States, vigorous emphasis should be placed upon the fact that *in no highly industrialized and urbanized country have the workers ever succeeded in overthrowing capitalism by armed might.* Over against the contention that a just society cannot be achieved without violent revolution must be set the unassailable fact that under modern conditions the workers have never succeeded through armed violence in establishing a proletarian government; not even in Russia, where the Bolsheviks succeeded precisely because they were able to gain power without armed warfare. Advocates of pacific revolution, therefore, are able to draw as much support from history as are defenders of civil war.

The Rise of Fascism in Germany

One frequently hears the assertion that the impotence of the Social Democrats in Germany and the consequent emergence to power of Hitler demonstrates the futility of relying upon pacific means of social change. Hindsight does reveal glaring

---

[62] Trotsky, *op. cit.*, vol. 3, p. 154.
[63] *Ibid*, vol. 3, p. 175.

weaknesses in the tactics of leadership on the part of the Social
Democrats, but these mistakes of judgment were not primarily
responsible for the rise of fascism in Germany. Five other
factors in combination played an even more important role:
Passionate resentment against the tyranny imposed by the
Treaty of Versailles and consequent resentment against the
political parties that accepted and sought to administer this
obnoxious instrument; appalling and prolonged economic misery; lack of majority vote by the Social Democrats; inexperience with and aversion to parliamentary democracy on the part
of a huge section of the German people; skillful and continuous
propaganda by the Nazis in playing upon the hatred and misery
and despair so nearly universal throughout the land.

There is no need to cite further evidence of the bitter enmity
of the German people to the Treaty of Versailles, or the utter
degradation into which they had fallen as a result of the war,
the treaty, inflation, and the world-wide economic depression.[64]

In periods of acute suffering peoples always tend to blame
the existing government for their troubles. Political parties
dread nothing so much as the coming of "hard times." Under
the circumstances which prevailed in Germany during the
decade following the armistice, no political party could possibly
have retained popularity; for the reason that it was compelled
to assume responsibility without having power. The Social
Democrats labored under two fatal handicaps: they lacked
power to control national policies because of the strangle-hold
maintained by France and the other Allies; and at no time did
they possess a majority of votes in parliament or throughout
the country.

It is a waste of time to contend that the Social Democrats
should have broken the power of reactionary forces within Germany and should have liquidated opponents of complete socialization of the primary means of production and distribution.
They lacked votes to accomplish radical changes by peaceable
means and they lacked both the will and the power to achieve
this result by violent confiscation. The repudiation of repara-

[64] See pp. 20, 129-134.

tions and the confiscation of private property would have brought about the armed occupation of all Germany by France and the other Allies. With less provocation, the Ruhr was later seized. At this distance it is impossible to realize the depth of fear of bolshevism which prevailed in most capitals of Europe. That the French would have acquiesced in the establishment of a red dictatorship in Germany is unthinkable.

This fear of bolshevism was equally prevalent throughout vast sections of the German people, the idea of a dictatorship of the proletariat being utterly abhorrent to farmers, peasants and the middle class, as well as to industrialists and financiers. The essential condition of success was lacking: advocates of armed seizure of power and proletarian dictatorship did not have the support of a majority of the people of the land. It was Lenin who said: "The party of the proletariat cannot by any means make its aim to introduce Socialism in a country of small peasantry as long as the overwhelming majority of the population has not realized the necessity of a Socialist revolution. . . . To become a power, the class-conscious workers must win the majority over to their side. . . . We are not Blanquists, we are not for the seizure of power by a minority." [65] The fact that at no time did the Social Democrats command a majority is illustrated in the accompanying chart. The further fact must be remembered that within the ranks of the Social Democrats were powerful elements of conservative trade unions members who were utterly opposed to armed seizure of power and confiscation. There is therefore no realism whatever in the post-mortem assertion that the Social Democrats should have established a dictatorship of the proletariat.

Moreover, the failure of the Social Democrats was due in considerable part to lack of experience with and aversion to parliamentary democracy on the part of a huge section of the German people. The fact that Woodrow Wilson announced that he would deal only with a democratic government proved to be a boomerang, as subsequently the argument was used powerfully that democracy had been forced upon Germany

[65] Lenin, *op. cit.*, vol. 20, part 1, pp. 144, 117.

by the Allies. In commenting upon the political background of the German people, Professor Zurcher writes: "Throughout its history, Prussia, the largest section of the Reich, has been the world's foremost exponent of an efficient, bureaucratic, military state. The tradition of such a government, deeply ingrained in Prussian thought, dies slowly, if indeed it is to die at all. It has a latent reservoir of protagonists in the old feudal and official aristocracy, in the old army and among large numbers of the bourgeoisie who attribute much of their material prosperity and social preferment to the existence of such an order. Moreover, much of German political philosophy, from Hegel onward, has been deeply authoritarian. . . . A shibboleth of the nineteenth century, democracy was already somewhat tarnished when it came into the saddle in 1919 and its welcome was hardly enthusiastic. . . . With large numbers of its sponsors not sure of their loyalty, the republic might have had a difficult enough time even if the seas had been smooth. But those seas have hardly been smooth; they have been rougher by far than those which came so perilously close to engulfing the Third French Republic. At the moment of its birth, Germany's republic had to assume responsibility for signing the 'shame of Versailles.' Thereafter it was logically committed to the policy of 'fulfilment,' the payment of reparations, the acceptance of the territorial and military settlement, and a European concert of powers with France in the key position. . . . With such a record in its wake, whether morally responsible or not, the 'Weimar System' became discredited with large numbers of the German people." [66]

Professor Marriott, a British authority on parliamentary government, calls attention to the fatal weakness in German democracy: "To suppose that Parliamentary Democracy is a form of polity to be suddenly conferred upon or adopted by peoples who have not submitted to the discipline of a prolonged apprenticeship seems, then, in the highest degree, fantastic. The break-down of premature experiments in Greece, in Italy,

[66] Arnold John Zurcher, *The Experiment with Democracy in Central Europe,* pp. 275, 276.

PERCENTAGE OF TOTAL VOTE BY VARIOUS GERMAN PARTIES *
* Taken from chart published in *Die Tat*, September, 1932; revised and reprinted in *New Governments in Europe*, Raymond Leslie Buell, Editor, p. 161.

and elsewhere should, accordingly, excite no surprise, still less contempt. . . . In the Weimar Constitution German democracy reached its high-water mark. Nor, on paper, could anything better have been devised. Nevertheless it functioned indifferently. Proportional representation resulted in the return of no fewer than ten parties. A strong Executive, indispensable to national recovery, was thus made impossible. In eleven years (1918-29) there were nineteen changes of ministry. But the chief among other reasons for the failure of the Weimar Constitution was the lack of the 'political sense' among the German people, and the inadequacy of their apprenticeship to the difficult craft of self-government. Apart, however, from this, the parliamentary experiment was tried under circumstances inimical to success. The grotesque figure at which reparation payments were fixed, the currency chaos due to inflation, the French occupation of the Ruhr, alternate threats to the Republic from Communists and Nationalists, the murder of good citizens like Matthias Erzberger and Walter Rathenau—these things would have strangled, at the birth, any infant Constitution." [67]

Any infant constitution would have been strangled! Especially if it were the victim of Nazi propaganda which played upon the hatred and misery and despair of vast sections of the German people. "There were three principal causes for the tremendous Nazi increase," writes Mildred S. Wertheimer. "In the first place, the deepening depression had already thrown three million people out of work by September 1930. Second, the inner political difficulties in the Reich created an increasing distrust and antipathy for the Republic and parliamentary government. The Reichstag, with its multiplicity of parties, seemed incapable of coping with the complex economic and financial problems confronting the country, while the situation of the German people grew progressively worse. Both of these factors contributed to the third cause of Nazi growth—the success of the untiring agitation of the Hitlerites themselves. Between the autumn of 1929 and September 1930, the National

[67] John A. R. Marriott, *Dictatorship and Democracy*, pp. 9, 208, 209.

Socialists staged meeting after meeting; during the fortnight before the September elections, the *Völkische Beobachter,* official organ of the party, listed some 3,300 meetings; many of these were held in small out-of-the-way villages, where few if any political gatherings had been held before. Hitler's stalwarts, clad in their brown uniforms, toured the countryside in trucks, unceasingly addressing the peasants and farm workers. In many small villages these meetings, well advertised beforehand, were much like a traveling circus to the inhabitants. The stage management of all Nazi gatherings has been dramatic in the extreme. Flags, bands, the marching of uniformed men appealed to a people which react *en masse* to the spectacular, especially in a Republic singularly devoid of colorful ceremonies which had succeeded an Empire with all its pomp and circumstance of kings, princes, courts and army." [68]

Arguments against the possibility of pacific change in the United States which are based upon the German analogy possess little weight unless evidence is presented to demonstrate the probability that parallel conditions will be confronted in this country.

The Rise of Fascism in Italy

When Mussolini marched to Rome in a railway sleeping compartment, did he demonstrate the futility of attempting by pacific means to bring about a transformation of the property system in the United States? The economic, political and emotional soil of postwar Italy was admirably adapted to blackshirt seed. Prices were soaring, war-profits were no longer enriching industrialists, wages were being sliced, and the government deficit was mounting. Cabinet after cabinet was overturned by the tidal wave of discontent and distress. While Italy technically won the war, and recovered certain "lost provinces," her people bitterly resented the "betrayal" of her allies in not fulfilling war-time treaties. National frustration and humiliation prepared the way for revolution. All this appeared as the ful-

---

[68] Raymond Leslie Buell, *New Governments in Europe,* "The Nazi Revolution in Germany," by Mildred S. Wertheimer, pp. 138, 139.

filment of radical prophecy and was interpreted as the signal for the violent seizure of power.

The seizure of factories began at Dalmino, near Milan, in May, 1919, where the workers took possession of an engineering works, to the applause of the still-radical Mussolini.[69] Other factories were taken over in Milan, Lombardy, Piedmont, and elsewhere. The insurrectionists "kidnapped owners and managers and tried to force them to run the works exclusively for the workers; armed 'Red Guards' were organized, revolutionary tribunals set up and persons approaching the factories were shot at." [70] It was absolutely inevitable that, under such circumstances, the revolutionaries should prove unable to keep the factories running. Confiscation is certain to be fatal except as part of a revolutionary seizure of governmental power, and it was nothing short of stupidity for the Italian workers to adopt this half-way measure.

The radicals failed to press forward and capture control of the government for the simple reason that they lacked power. Revolution cannot be achieved at will. The situation must be ripe. Italy is predominantly an agricultural country and the industrial working class is therefore in the minority. The Socialist vote reached its high peak in the elections of 1919, with 156 seats out of 535 in the Chamber of Deputies.[71] The army and police forces, in contrast to the revolutionary situation in Russia, were vigorously opposed to a workers' government, and the entire country was swarming with demobilized soldiers who were embittered by the "antipatriotic" attitude of the Socialists. The owning class, unlike the ruling regime in pre-revolutionary Russia, still retained enormous power and was prepared to use it ruthlessly, so alarmed were its members by threats of expropriation. Moreover, the middle class was much more strongly bulwarked than was the case in Russia, while the proportion of landowners among the peasants was incomparably greater. Furthermore, the influence of the Cath-

[69] Jerome Davis, *Contemporary Social Movements*, p. 435.
[70] *Encyclopaedia Britannica*, vol. 12, p. 820.
[71] Jerome Davis, *Contemporary Social Movements*, p. 440.

olic Church over the masses of Italian people was immeasurable and strongly hostile to socialism and communism. Damning Italian Socialists is a favorite indoor sport among radicals of other countries, but the fact remains that they had no chance whatever to seize the reins of government. Only heretical Blanquists can maintain otherwise, for the evidence is incontrovertible that, even before the Communists split off, the Socialists constituted only a minority, and were confronted with hostile and armed forces overwhelmingly more powerful. The most serious blunder of the Socialists was their willingness to use violence at all. Another vital factor was the inexperience of the masses with genuine democracy, universal suffrage having been introduced in Italy as late as 1913.

It was under these circumstances that Mussolini, the former Socialist, now turned chauvinistic nationalist and opportunist, gathered a band of ex-soldiers and matched clubs and shots with radicals. Eloquent and utterly courageous, he attracted a wider and wider following composed of amazingly heterogeneous elements. "The industrial and commercial middle classes," writes Prezzonlini, "and the landowners, during the reign of these Bolshevik tendencies, were only too obviously seized with panic. They saw themselves dethroned. . . . Thus it came about that in all the big towns where *Fasci di combattimento* had been formed by the ex-service men, the sons of the industrial and commercial classes, young men of the middle classes, students, clerks, professional men, flocked to swell their ranks. In the country districts the *Fasci* enrolled the sons of the landowners, administrators, farmers and farm laborers—that is to say, all who recognized in Socialism the enemy of their rights and privileges." [72]

In August, 1922, the Fascists succeeded in breaking a crucial strike and thereafter their forces were augmented still more rapidly. At this moment Mussolini shrewdly championed the monarchy, thus securing the backing of the army and strengthening his position with conservative financiers and landowners. Mussolini now made plans for the seizure of power, but the

[72] Davis, *op. cit.*, pp. 433, 434.

October revolution proved to be bloodless because "Italy had capitulated even before the Fascist march on Rome." The King was terror-stricken and invited Mussolini to head the government. Mussolini responded by climbing into a sleeping car and riding comfortably to dictatorship.[73] This revolutionary seizure of power was made possible by the winning of support from a large majority of the population, and especially by cooperation of the army. Indeed, in the march on Rome, a regular army general was placed at the head of each of the five divisions of black shirts.[74]

In interpreting the reasons for the weakness of Italian democracy, Professor Marriott writes: ". . . the War left Italy terribly exhausted, and the terms she obtained at the Peace Conference bitterly disappointed nationalist expectations. . . . The disappointments of the Peace combined with the suffering and sacrifices of the War to prepare the ground for Fascism; and other things contributed to the same end. Most of the belligerent countries were threatened after the War, with revolution. Italy did not escape the common fate. But Italy was peculiar in this: the hostility of large sections of the city populations was directed, with paradoxical impartiality, against the 'profiteers' who had grown fat on the War, and the soldiers who had endured its hardships. To wear war medals was, in some towns, to invite assault. . . . Unity was finally achieved only in 1871. But Cavour, who, more than any other man, was responsible for its creation, was responsible also for imposing on it a form of government alien to its traditions, and painfully unsuited to its circumstances. . . . Such democracy as it had known had been the direct democracy of the City-State. Those States had known Dictators also; but the idea of representative democracy was entirely alien to the Italian temper and tradition." [75]

Americans who are deliberating concerning ways and means of bringing about fundamental social changes are not warranted

---

[73] See Raymond Gram Swing, *Forerunners of American Fascism*, p. 21.
[74] See *The Yale Review*, Winter, 1935, p. 304.
[75] Marriott, *op. cit.*, pp. 182-185.

in basing their conclusions upon the recent course of events in Russia, Germany and Italy. But what about Spain? Does not the failure of the moderate elements there demonstrate the futility of pacific means of social change?

The Spanish Civil War

The prevailing conflict in Spain is not civil war so much as it is international war. The rebels would not have constituted a serious threat if they had not received early, substantial and continuous support from Italy, Germany and Portugal; whereas the properly elected government has been sustained only by powerful assistance from Soviet Russia and France. In a later section I take account of the Spanish situation in an evaluation of the validity of religious pacifism. But in discussing the possibilities of pacific change in the United States, analogies taken from the Spanish scene deserve consideration only if they present evidence that our territory will be the battleground of international armies.

V

The situations in Russia, Germany and Italy have been considered in some detail because of the frequency with which the contention is made that pacific change is not possible in view of what has happened in these countries. Is communism the only way out for the people of the United States? How much likelihood is there that communism can succeed in this land? Is America doomed to fascism? Must there be another civil war in this country? Let us now examine some of the evidence.

Of the factors which produced proletarian dictatorship in Soviet Russia, how many of them are now present or are likely to be reproduced in the United States? That there are ominous possibilities of widespread armed conflict in the industrial arena will be denied only by the deaf and the blind. But the realization that economic strife may burst forth into flames of civil war does not necessarily commit us to the conclusion that com-

munism is bound to succeed.   On the contrary, the outcome is
far more likely to be fascism than communism.

The success of communism in the United States appears
extremely doubtful because of the following combination of
factors : *the presence of a large and powerful middle class; the
absence of experience of despotism and barbarous tyranny; the
depth of commitment to individual liberty and emotional attach-
ment to democracy; the ability of owners through high productivity of modern industry to make substantial concessions to
insurgents; the improbability that this nation will meet crushing
defeat in war; the likelihood of fascist dictatorship if America
becomes involved in international warfare or in the event of
the utter collapse of capitalism; the high degree of industrialization and urbanization; the suicidal nature of civil war with
modern weapons of destruction in a highly complex and interdependent society.*

1. Twenty million families in the United States have something to lose besides their chains.   In many of these cases the
stake in the existing order is small but the psychological effects
of ownership are powerful nonetheless.   A primary cause of
the success of the revolutionaries in Russia was furnished by
the extremely small percentage of the total population that possessed property.   The fact is generally recognized that persons
with a stake in the preservation of the status quo are unlikely
to resort to civil war in behalf of a proletarian dictatorship.
The size of this company in the United States is indicated by
the following figures :

> 10,500,000 owner-occupied homes, with an average value of $4,788.[76]
> 22,565,000 registered automobiles, exclusive of trucks.[77]
> 41,315,000 depositors in savings accounts.[78]
> 22,652,000,000 dollars deposited in savings accounts.[79]
> 117,370,000 insurance policies in force.[80]
> 100,730,000,000 dollars insurance provided by policies in force.[80]

---

[76] *Fortune,* June, 1935, p. 172.
[77] *Statistical Abstract of the United States,* 1936, p. 363.
[78] and [79]. *Ibid,* p. 253.
[80] *Ibid,* p. 282

If we divide the occupations of the American people into those that constitute fertile soil for revolution and those that incline toward preservation of the status quo, the result appears as follows:

More Fertile Soil
Mining.. 984,000
Manufacturing and Mechanical Industries....... 14,111,000
Transportation and Communication............. 3,843,000
Farm Wage Workers........................... 2,733,000
Unpromising Revolutionary Soil
Agriculture (Exclusive of Wage Workers)........ 7,739,000
Trade.. 6,081,000
Domestic and Personal Service................. 4,952,000
Clerical Occupations......................... 4,025,000
Professional Service......................... 3,254,000
Public Service............................... 856,000

It is thus apparent that the first division embraces about 22 million workers, as compared with some 25 millions in the second classification. It would be absurd to maintain that no revolutionaries will come from the ranks of trade, clerical occupations or professional services, but Communists would be the first to admit that in the United States these classes offer little hope so far as the violent seizure of power is concerned. Even more significant results are yielded by an analysis of the composition of the first grouping. In this country skilled and semi-skilled workers more often than otherwise are merged indistinguishably with the other members of the middle class, in ideology and status. It is natural therefore that the organized labor movement should be predominantly conservative and cautious. Its members as a rule have too substantial a stake in the existing order to make self-sacrificing revolutionaries, as is revealed in the policies of the American Federation of Labor. The history of the labor movement in Great Britain and Germany sheds light upon this aspect of the American scene. Trade union leaders have usually been more conservative in their policies than political leaders of Socialist parties, and thus far it has been impossible to secure vigorous and sustained efforts on the part of powerful unions to abolish capitalism without delay. The trade union movement in the United States is, of course, far more reactionary than in Europe, and the probability of enlisting the big unions as allies of revolutionary forces bent upon the overthrow of capitalism is even more remote than on the Continent.

The evidence is inescapable that this nation is overwhelmingly middle-class or bourgeois in composition. Genuine proletarians do not constitute more than one-third of the population, while the entire body of completely disinherited—those who have only their chains to lose—probably does not exceed 20 per cent. While it is utterly disgraceful that, in a rich and luxurious nation, millions should be condemned to privation and hunger, we should not be blind to the fact that most Americans do receive rewards from capitalism on a sufficiently extensive scale to make them extremely reluctant to destroy the present system.

2. While the masses of people in the United States have never been as free as they have imagined themselves to be, nevertheless they have enjoyed a high degree of individual liberty. Moreover, they have been nurtured on the doctrines of democracy and equality. Under pioneer conditions a high level of liberty and fraternity was reached. This heritage makes it extremely unlikely that the American people will acquiesce in the establishment of a proletarian dictatorship or long endure the consequent prohibitions of dissent. Sentimental eulogies of communism should not blind us to the realities of dictatorship.

Mr. Wm. Z. Foster, communist candidate for President of the United States in 1932, in his volume *Toward Soviet America* has included a chapter on "The United Soviet States of America," in which he describes the proposed communist regime. Here are vivid words: "The American Soviet government will be organized along the broad lines of the Russian Soviets. . . . The American Soviet government will be the dictatorship of the proletariat. . . . Under the dictatorship all the capitalist parties—Republican, Democratic, Progressive, Socialist, etc.—will be liquidated, the Communist party functioning alone as the Party of the toiling masses. Likewise, will be dissolved all other organizations that are political props of the bourgeois rule, including chambers of commerce, employers' associations, rotary clubs, American Legion, Y.M.C.A., and such fraternal orders as the Masons, Odd Fellows, Elks, Knights of Columbus, etc. . . . the right of self-determination will apply to Negroes in the American Soviet system. In the so-called Black Belt of the South, where the Negroes are in the majority, they will have the fullest right to govern themselves and also such white minorities as may live in this section."

To establish and maintain such a dictatorship would require prolonged warfare and the application of mass terror with a savagery that would make the Russian civil war appear as a pleasant pink-tea affair. And the full significance of this statement cannot be understood unless one is familiar with ruthless liquidation of all opponents of the Bolshevik regime—socialists, pacifists, priests, clergymen, engineers, successful farmers, etc.

Persons who hanker for proletarian dictatorship in the United States would do well to read and reflect upon the evidence presented by William H. Chamberlin in *Russia's Iron Age*. Mr. Chamberlin was for a decade Russian correspondent of the *Christian Science Monitor* and during much of this period was known as a sympathetic interpreter of Russian communism. Further evidence may be found in his former volume *Soviet Russia*. From *Russia's Iron Age* the following words are taken: "There has been a huge 'liquidation' of the more well-to-do and incorrigibly individualistic peasants, loosely and conveniently dubbed 'kulaks.' They have been packed in freight cars and shipped off in hundreds of thousands, if not in millions, for forced labor in timber camps, on canals, in new construction enterprises. . . . The measure was often executed with great brutality, men, women and children being driven out in the bitter cold of the Russian winter; and its toll of death, especially among young children and old men, was very great. It was quite in the spirit of the Iron Age; it showed that the Communist leaders would spare no weapon of ruthlessness in breaking the recalcitrant peasantry to their will . . . the total number of Soviet citizens who, during the

Iron Age, have been deprived of liberty without anything that could plausibly be called 'due process of law' can scarcely be less than two million. . . . No single organization in the world, it is safe to say, bears the responsibility for cutting short so many human lives as the Gay-Pay-Oo, which is simply the old Cheka, dreaded instrument of Red Terror during the civil war, under another name."

3. Modern technology has placed at the disposal of the owning class a degree of productivity which enables its members to make progressive concessions to the workers and still retain luxuries and powers for themselves. Capitalism stands nakedly revealed as abhorrent because of the cancer of hunger in the midst of plenty, but the fact remains that in spite of grave maladjustments and cruel exploitation, it is actually affording American workers better living conditions than are to be found elsewhere on earth. Even if the marvelous machines placed in our hands by modern science are used so inefficiently that we are now able to reap only one-third or one-quarter of the potential harvest of food and commodities and services, nevertheless, the flow of comforts and privileges is nowhere else equalled. It is probably true that under communism or socialism the standard of living for American workers could be increased several fold, but as yet there is no living demonstration of this conviction.

Many radical critics of the present economic order are gravely underestimating the vitality of American capitalism, and are laboring under the illusion that the decaying corpse will shortly be ready for burial. A more realistic interpretation seems to me to be found in the recognition that capitalism is utterly unsatisfactory, coupled with the admission that for a long time to come it will probably continue to dole out just enough rewards to the workers to keep their minds off the serious business of revolution. The mechanical energy at the disposal of this generation of Americans approximates a billion horsepower. . . . The power of human muscles is about 2,000 kilogram calories per day; but A.D. 1775 man's capacity had been doubled by the utilization of waterwheels, windmills and other simple devices;

while in the United States today "the energy consumed by virtue of coal, oil, natural gas and waterpower alone, is the equivalent of 154,000 kilogram calories per capita per day! . . . some forty times the energy limit of our earlier cultures. The machine age has stepped up our capacity to perform work fortyfold. . . .[81] During the past century the energy resources from coal, oil, natural gas, and water power consumed in this country has grown from 75 trillion to 27,000 trillion British Thermal Units.[82] No wonder Stuart Chase raves about our billion wild horses! The equivalent of the human labor of over five times the present total world population! The more we emphasize the potential productivity of modern industry and agriculture, the more damning becomes the indictment of capitalism, and the heavier the responsibility resting upon us to replace it with a system of socialized production and distribution. But it is sheer stupidity to overlook the possibility or probability that the marvelous technological equipment now in the hands of the capitalists will enable them, in spite of inefficiency and exploitation, to hand out the minimum of comfort and privilege required to deaden the revolutionary spirit among large masses of workers, and thus prolong the life of the profit system. After some ten years of residence in Russia, William Henry Chamberlin found himself in the United States during the weeks prior to the complete suspension of the banks, in March, 1933. In a penetrating analysis in the *Atlantic Monthly* he draws a series of contrasts between the general situation in the two lands. "What is regarded as acute want in America might easily pass as a satisfactory standard of living in the Soviet Union," he writes. "The food allotments which our unemployed receive in cities like Milwaukee, where relief work is well organized, are about equal to the normal ration of many employed workers in Russia. . . . Nothing could be more paradoxical than the causes underlying the crisis in the two countries. In America, supply is far in excess of effective demand; in Russia, demand is much greater than available supply."

[81] Stuart Chase, *Technocracy*, p. 20.
[82] *Ibid*, p. 23.

4. That this nation will meet crushing defeat in international warfare is nothing more than a remote possibility, and therefore a situation analogous to the debacle of the Russian imperial army is not likely to occur. If this government staggers into another big war, the clamping down upon us of a patriotic and conservative dictatorship is almost certain, with the result that communist activity would be suppressed as savagely as counter-revolution is now being liquidated in Soviet Russia.

VI

Is pacific transformation of the property system in the United States probable? Will the effort to achieve this result incite vested interests to overthrow parliamentary government and establish a fascist dictatorship?

In laying foundations strong enough to sustain arguments in favor of peaceable methods of revolution it is not necessary to prove that success is inevitable or even highly probable. It is sufficient to demonstrate the *relative* advantages of this strategy in contrast to revolution through civil war. The fact that the odds are heavily against victory in the effort to transform capitalism through non-warlike means does not invalidate this procedure, since the barriers to triumph through violent seizure of power are far higher. To struggle only when the tides are running in one's favor means that a just society will never be created. Epoch-making social changes have usually been brought about in the face of titanic obstacles. Pacifists should therefore refuse to be discouraged by assertions that in no country has non-warlike revolution ever abolished capitalism. It is equally true that *in no highly industrialized and urbanized nation with conditions at all comparable to those existing in the United States has victory been achieved through violent means.* Indeed, the fact must be emphasized that even in Russia, success was made possible both in March and in November precisely because the revolutionists were not compelled to seize power through armed violence, as I pointed out in an earlier section. It is sheer nonsense to maintain that the Bolsheviks overthrew czarist tyranny. Lenin, Trotsky and a large proportion of other Bolshevik leaders were living in exile and did not return to Russia until after the collapse of czardom. Persons seeking pacific revolution in the United States have more valid reasons for hope than have their opponents who rely upon civil war.

Advocacy of pacific revolution is preferable to reliance upon armed seizure of power for three primary reasons: it is more likely to succeed in the United States; its processes are accompanied by less destruction of human values; and, on grounds of religion, its means are more consistent with the ends sought.

Revolution by any strategy is dependent upon winning the active support or friendly acquiescence of an outright majority of the population, and in the United States there is a far higher possibility of enlisting the required support in behalf of pacific processes than of gaining a sufficient number of adherents in the ranks of armed revolutionists. Lenin was emphatic in repeated assertions that the winning of a majority is a condition of successful revolution, and this is still the orthodox position of the Communist Party. The notion that a small company of revolutionists through a *coup d'etat* can inaugurate a revolutionary regime is sheer sentimentalism.

To win a majority in this country means gaining the support of a substantial proportion of skilled workers, white-collar employees, professional men, women and farmers. There are not enough genuine proletarians in the United States to seize power, even if the prevailing lethargy and impotence of a large section of this group could be overcome. It is easy to point out obstacles in the way of winning a majority of the population for any strategy of revolution, but surely the evidence is beyond dispute that the task of enlisting sufficient adherents in the ranks of armed revolutionists is far more formidable than the winning of a majority for pacific processes of revolution.

An examination of the accompanying chart reveals the high proportion of poor revolutionary timber among the people of the United States:

PERCENTAGE OF "GAINFULLY EMPLOYED" BY
OCCUPATION [83]

	1870	1880	1890	1900	1910	1920	1930
Farmers (incl. family workers)	41	38	33.5	29.5	24	20	16
Farm laborers..............	13	10	8	7.5	7.5	6	5.5
Businessmen...............	6	6	6	6.5	7	7	8
Professional workers (incl. teachers)................	3	4	4.5	4.5	5	5.5	7
White-collar workers........	3	4	6.5	8.5	11	14.5	17
Government employees (not elsewhere classified).......	.5	.5	1	1	1	1.5	1.5
Service trades..............	2.5	2.5	3	3	4.5	4	5
Servants..................	7.5	7	7	7	5.5	4.5	5.5
Industrial workers..........	23.5	28	30.5	32.5	34.5	37	34.5
	100	100	100	100	100	100	100

While the road to a cooperative commonwealth is blocked by high barriers, it is by no means impassable. The foundations of individualism are rapidly being undermined by the ceaseless pull of swift economic current. The passing of the frontier, the growth of urban communities, the development of mass production and mass distribution, the marvelous advances of technology, the extreme concentration of industrial and financial power, the increasing impotence of the individual, the hunger for security, the deepening conviction that poverty in this land is unnecessary and that plenty for everybody could quickly be made available if our resources were used efficiently —all these are combining to make certain the doom of anarchistic individualism, with its devastating competitive struggle. There is a fair chance that its successor may be inaugurated by peaceful means, rather than by civil war and mass terror.

In discussing the disintegration of individualism it is almost impossible to exaggerate the significance of modern technology. The cost of equipping giant industries with the up-to-date machinery required in the competitive arena, and the necessity of maintaining output at high speed in order to cover overhead expense and leave a margin for profit have destroyed the possibility of continuing individual ownership of huge concerns.

[83] Alfred M. Bingham, *Insurgent America*, p. 233.

Corporations are rapidly supplanting private concerns and partnerships. Henry and Edsel Ford are the last of the Mohicans! As the scale of production becomes magnified, the percentage owned by single individuals grows less. Large corporations are now controlled by boards of directors whose combined ownership constitutes only a fraction of the total assets of the company. In the case of the American Telephone and Telegraph, the most gigantic of American corporations, the largest holding is less than one per cent, while the 20 most substantial holdings combined approximate only four per cent of the total. The 20 largest holders of stock in the United States Steel Corporation own a mere five per cent of the total. Berle and Means, in their monumental study, *The Modern Corporation and Private Property,* show that more than one-third of the entire business wealth of the nation is owned by 200 giant corporations, controlled by 2,000 directors. Only six per cent of the total capital of these huge aggregations of wealth is controlled by persons owning a majority of the stock. The size of manufacturing establishments had reached the point in 1929 where 69 per cent of the value of the products represented the output of companies each with capital of a million dollars or more.

All this means that collectivism is rapidly replacing individualism. Unrestrained competition among huge corporations is absolutely ruinous, whereas combination on the part of such titanic institutions magnifies opportunity for exploitation. The point that is highly relevant to this discussion is that millions of Americans are swiftly being taught the meaning of the dilemma which confronts them. Under private ownership of mass industries, the suffering public is impaled upon one horn or the other: ruinous competition or exploiting monopoly. There is reason to be hopeful that a majority of the American people would choose pacific socialization of the basic industries, in preference to monopolistic collectivism of private capital or to dictatorships black and red—if the alternatives could be presented vividly.

At this point it is desirable to emphasize the peril of assuming that the only alternatives to capitalism are fascism and communism. By an interesting coincidence extreme right and extreme left alike are endeavoring to drive home this contention. Many conservatives are lumping together as "reds" all liberal and radical individuals who are opposed to capitalism, whereas communists classify liberals and socialists as social-fascist allies of capitalism. The reason for this double tendency is apparent. Conservatives endeavor to gain support for capitalism by holding aloft the communist bogey, and at the same time communists seek to strengthen their cause by maintaining that there is no other alternative to the horrors of capitalist dictatorship. Morning, noon and night we must hammer home the truth that another possibility is at hand in the form of pacific socialization of industry.

But the objection is raised that control of the organs of public opinion by the owning class makes impossible the vivid presentation of pacific methods of building a cooperative commonwealth. The magnitude of the difficulties of securing a hearing for a radical point of view in the daily press, over the radio, through the movies, and in schools and colleges will not be slurred over by anyone who has had wide experience. On the other hand, it is sheer stupidity to say that the task is utterly impossible. The pressure of economic events may prove to be a sufficiently powerful leverage. Indeed, there are numerous indications that the influence of the press over the public mind has been exaggerated. Time and again in political campaigns huge votes have been polled by candidates who faced almost solid opposition from the press. Upton Sinclair secured more than 800,000 votes in California in spite of unrestrained vilification in daily newspapers and over the radio. Economic interest weakens the tendency to accept contrary arguments as valid. The British Labor Party has never possessed more than a feeble press. British voters have been affected by economic frustration, by innumerable meetings in parks and labor halls, by a vast circulation of leaflets and pamphlets, and by conversation on the part of millions of trade unionists and other adherents of the labor cause. While this relatively feeble effort would be washed away by the torrent of propaganda in favor of the status quo except for the powerful educative value of frustration, insecurity, and suffering, there is reason to believe that the ceaseless activities of intelligent and determined minorities may turn the tide.

The responsibilities of the churches in this connection are tremendous. Millions of individuals are powerfully affected by the message proclaimed from pulpit and class room of religious education. If even a substantial minority of ministers and other religious educators would throw themselves vigorously into the crusade for a cooperative commonwealth, their influence would prove to be of incalculable value. That this very thing is happening constitutes one of the hopeful signs of the times. It is probably true to say that the minds of religious leaders concerning economic questions have been changed more drastically during the past six years than in the preceding century. The 1934 questionnaire, which was responded to by nearly 21,000 clergymen and rabbis, showed that 18,324 of these ministers favor a cooperative commonwealth, as contrasted with 1,035 supporting rugged individualism. Moreover, 87 per cent of those replying were willing to have their answers made public. Approximately 6,000 expressed themselves as favoring socialism, and nearly 11,000 as supporting drastically reformed capitalism.

The speed with which the public mind is being changed with regard to economic questions stands out vividly when viewed from the perspective of history. The degree of regulation to which railways and other public utilities are now subjected was simply unthinkable a generation ago and would have then been regarded as rankest radicalism. The heresy of rate regulation was so obnoxious that even the *Nation* raved against it as "confiscation, or, if another phrase be more agreeable, the change of railroads from pieces of private property, owned and managed for the benefit of those who have invested their money in them, into eleemosynary or charitable corporations, managed for the benefit of a particular class of applicants for outdoor relief—the farmers." So far has public opinion moved that today no sane man objects to governmental regulation of railway rates.

The operation of a public parcels post no longer creates a ripple of opposition, but for decades its establishment was successfully resisted by vested interests with such arguments as these: "The tremendous losses entailed by revolutionizing the existing mode of distribution would spell disaster to hosts of wholesalers and manufacturers . . . an 11-pound limit will put two-thirds of the retail merchants in all lines out of business . . . the institution of the parcels post would mean the destruction of thousands of hamlets, the lessening of activities of innumerable towns, and cessation of growth in many flourishing cities."

During the banking crisis of 1933, the postal savings banks were the only section of our national banking system that withstood the storm. But forty years of advocacy preceded the adoption of this institution, including recommendations of eight postmasters-general and the introduction of a hundred bills in Congress. So powerful is public support of drastic rates in the upper brackets of income and inheritance taxes that the 1935 Congress boosted the limit to 75 per cent. Contrast this with the reception received by the 1894 income tax! In that year Congress levied a tax of 2 per cent on all incomes above $4,000. This law was passed by "wildmen" from the West, only five votes being cast in its favor in the House by representatives from New England, Pennsylvania and New York combined. Two per cent! Complete exemption below $4,000! In his successful argument against the income tax law before the Supreme Court of the United States, Joseph H. Choate exclaimed: "This is a doctrine worthy of a Jacobin Club . . . it is worthy of a 'Czar of Russia proposing to reign with undisputed and absolute power. . . ."

The fact that radical changes in public opinion have occurred within a generation does not, of course, prove that the shift required to transform competitive capitalism into a cooperative commonwealth will take place in time to prevent civil war and dictatorship. But the impressive record of history should warn against dogmatic assertions that prevailing economic attitudes will be maintained indefinitely in the future. Especially so in view of the fact that as minorities favoring new ideas grow stronger they have wider and wider access to the press, the radio, the movies. They are also able to entrench themselves more firmly in educational institutions.

Undeniably there is a possibility that vested interests may read the handwriting on the wall and attempt to forestall pacific revolution by clamping down a ruthless dictatorship that suppresses freedom of speech and freedom of organization. But, and let the fact be reiterated endlessly, the likelihood of fascist dictatorship is increased, not diminished, by threats of proletarian dictatorship. Whereas many liberals are inclined to minimize the peril of fascism in the United States, many radicals fall over backward in predicting the inevitability of reactionary dictatorship if vested interests are seriously threatened by the approach of pacific revolution.

An attempt to combine the strategy of pacific revolution and that of violent seizure of power will prove disastrous to the cause of non-warlike social change. A radical political party that says to the citizens of the United States, "We prefer to secure power by ballots, but if necessary we will use bullets," has no chance whatever of success at the polls. A regime inaugurated by violence can maintain itself only by ruthless dictatorship. To appeal to the voters of this country to furnish a mandate for radical dictatorship is to engage in a fantastic procedure. Conceivably a conservative coalition might establish dictatorship through popular support at the polls, but a radical party has no chance of success whatever by this means. It is therefore apparent that the threat of proletarian dictatorship, if seriously presented by a political party, would utterly destroy any possibility of winning support from a majority of voters. When due consideration is given to the heritage and prevailing convictions of most citizens of the United States, the evidence becomes clear that we must choose: ballots or bullets, democracy or dictatorship. To combine these strategies is equivalent to throwing one's influence in favor of bullets and dictatorship.

VII

To abandon hope of pacific transformation of the property system is to embrace despair, because this generation of Americans has no chance whatever of building a decent society through resorting to civil war. The armed seizure and maintenance of power is far more difficult of achievement in a highly industrialized and densely urbanized country than was the founding a communist regime in Russia. The capture of two or three strategic centers would by no means insure success for revolutionaries. Seizure must take place simultaneously in numerous regions throughout this vast continent. Moreover, holding power would probably prove to be more difficult than seizure. During a period of civil war the feeding of metropolitan populations would present titanic difficulties. Yet failure at this point would provoke starving people to counter-revolution and thereby destroy any possibility of enduring success. The magnitude of the problem is indicated by these figures: 20 million persons reside in 13 cities each with upward of half a million inhabitants, 36 millions dwell in 103 cities above the 100,000 level, whereas 69 millions live in urban communities. Simultaneously to wage civil war and to feed these multitudes would prove to be impossible in the face of powerful armed resistance, especially so if a substantial proportion of farmers were lined up against the revolution.

The attempt to establish a just society in the United States through civil war against the owning class would almost certainly result in appalling misery and indescribable chaos. Nothing is more stupid than to imagine that success could be achieved by a *coup d'etat* and brief fighting at the barricades. It is imperative that two facts be vividly emphasized. First, if support for the old regime is so weak that it can be toppled over without prolonged fighting, then it could be pushed aside by economic pressure and other non-warlike procedures. Second, if the owning class cannot be overthrown quickly and easily, then success for armed revolutionaries cannot be achieved unless the latter are equipped with weapons of modern battle. This means preparedness for civil war on a vast scale with aeroplanes, poison gas, machine guns, tanks, and other forms of modern military equipment. The notion that a capitalist government would permit communists to assemble these weapons of war is nothing less than a pipe-dream of romantic radicals. Such a threat would quite certainly be met with fascist dictatorship and massacre of revolutionaries.

Even if half the army mutinied and went over to the insurgents, prolonged fighting would follow. Every war is abhorrent, but civil war is the most ghastly of all. And nowhere would the devastating effects of fratricidal conflict be more annihilating than in a highly industrialized and urbanized country like the United States. Months of war between somewhat equal fighting forces would create a holocaust throughout the nation never surpassed in all history. Supplied with numberless airplanes and vast quantities of poison gas, the red terror and the white terror would alternately scourge the land. Production and distribution would be thrown into utter chaos. Central power houses could easily be crippled alike by revolutionaries and counter-revolutionaries. Continental pipe lines of oil and natural gas could be wrecked by a few blows on strategic valves. Railway tracks could be torn up within a few hours and transportation stopped at important terminals. The food supply of vast metropolitan communities could be shut off and entire populations would quickly face starvation. Under such circumstances, writes Stuart Chase, "lethal epidemics, those great scourges which medical science has steadily been forcing back for a hundred years, will break their fetters overnight, and fall like avenging demons on a population weak with hunger and with thirst. . . . Violent revolutions are bitter medicine, but medicine, in handicraft societies ground down by feudalism. In societies pledged to the machine, they are a lethal poison, swift and terrible."[84] No wonder, therefore, that an outstanding radical writes: "If violence can be justified at all, its terror must have the tempo of a surgeon's skill and healing must follow quickly upon its wounds."[85] And to lay down this condition when speaking of economic change in the United States is equivalent to saying that resort to armed violence is wholly unjustifiable.

[84] *The New Deal*, pp. 159, 160.
[85] Reinhold Niebuhr, *Moral Man and Immoral Society*, p. 220.

INDEX

275

276   INDEX

INDEX